TABLOID TELEVISION

Fires, floods, accidents, celebrity lifestyles, heroic acts of humble people, communities in crisis, reversals of fortune and the weather. Television's non-news about non-events takes up an increasingly large part of contemporary broadcast journalism, but is regularly dismissed by television pundits as having no place on our screens. To its critics, this unworthy news distracts our attention with trivialities and entertainment values, and undermines journalism's relationship with the workings of democracy. Yet, in spite of these protests, this type of reportage remains as entrenched and as popular as ever.

In *Tabloid Television*, John Langer argues that television's 'other news' must be recognized as equally important as 'hard news' in the building of a genuinely comprehensive study of broadcast journalism. Using narrative analysis, theories of ideology, concepts from genre studies and detailed textual readings, this 'other news' is explored as a cultural discourse connected with story-telling, gossip, social memory, the horror film, national identity and the cult of fame. Langer's study also examines the political role played by an allegedly non-political news and explores the links between this type of news and recent broadcasting trends towards 'reality television'.

Tabloid Television: Popular Journalism and the 'Other News' provides an eclectic and intriguing look at one of the most maligned areas of television news. By offering an extended and thoroughly grounded analysis of actual news stories, John Langer locates the question of representational power as one of the central concerns of the media studies agenda and offers some interesting speculation about where television news may be heading.

John Langer is Senior Lecturer teaching media studies in the Department of Communication and Language Studies at Victoria University, Melbourne, Australia.

COMMUNICATION AND SOCIETY
General Editor: James Curran

TABLOID TELEVISION

Popular journalism and the 'other news'

John Langer

London and New York

First published 1998
by Routledge
11 New Fetter Lane, London EC4P 4EE .

Simultaneously published in the USA and Canada
by Routledge
29 West 35th Street, New York, NY 10001

Typeset in Garamond and Bembo by
RefineCatch Limited, Bungay, Suffolk
Printed and bound in Great Britain by
T.J. International Ltd, Padstow, Cornwall

British Library Cataloguing in Publication Data
A catalogue record for this book is available from the British Library

Library of Congress Cataloguing in Publication Data
Langer, John
Tabloid television: popular journalism and
the "other news" / John Langer
p.   cm.—(Communication and society)
Includes bibliographical references (p.   ) and index.
1. Television broadcasting of news.   2. Sensationalism in television
I. Title.   II. Series: Communication and society (Routledge (Firm))
PN4784.T4L29   1997
070.1'95—dc21
97–12734

ISBN 0–415–06636–0 (hbk)
ISBN 0–415–06637–9 (pbk)

For Beryl, Zev and Sam

CONTENTS

1

THE LAMENT, CRITICAL PROJECT AND THE 'BAD' NEWS ON TELEVISION

The following conversation between a seasoned veteran of television journalism and a fledgling reporter is recounted by Edwin Diamond in his discussion of the connection between television news and politics:

> I'm going to tell you a story and after I tell it, you will know all there is to know about television news . . . The executives of this station [in New York] were watching all three news shows one night. There had been a fire in a Roman Catholic orphanage on Staten Island. One executive complained that a rival station had better film coverage. 'Their flames are higher than ours', he said. But another executive countered: 'Yes, but our nun is crying harder than theirs.'
>
> (1975: xi)

Such apocryphal stories circulate with enough regularity to make them notable as more than a passing shot at broadcast journalism. They function as provocatively succinct commentaries which resonate with assumptions not just about what television news is, but by implication, what it ought to be. Presented less anecdotally, a series of propositions might be unravelled:

- Television news is primarily a commodity enterprise run by market-oriented managers who place outflanking the 'competition' above journalistic responsibility and integrity.
- Television news is in the business of entertainment, like any other television product, attempting to pull audiences for commercial not journalistic reasons.
- Television news has set aside the values of professional journalism in order to indulge in the presentation of gratuitous spectacles.
- Television news is overly dependent on filmed images which create superficiality and lack information content.
- Television news traffics in trivialities and deals in dubious emotionalism.
- Television news is exploitative.

The list could go on, but essentially the assumptions embedded in such a story seem to lead to what might be generally designated as the 'lament' for television journalism. Diamond's book is in fact one version of this lament but there are many others (Shulman 1973; Littlejohn 1975; Conrad 1982; Esslin 1982; Diamond 1982; Postman 1985; Bennett 1988; Altheide and Snow 1991; Postman and Powers 1992). One variant from Australia (where this study was done) is provided by Clements (1986) writing about the way television news suffers from a pronounced inability 'to adequately inform':

> The familiar newscasts, strategically placed at the on-set of prime time, cram a large number of stories into thirty minutes, each averaging about ninety seconds. The problem of deciding on how wide or how narrow a context to set each item is hardly faced here, time is so short. Unfortunately, the most important stories of the day, mainly political or economic, receive the same narrow focus as the latest . . . robbery.
>
> (Clements 1986: 5)

According to Clements, we are 'lulled by the entertainment values which often replace news values' and 'are left contentedly confused'.

The various manifestations of the lament for television news spring from what is held to be a fundamental relationship which must exist between journalism and the successful workings of a liberal democracy. Liberal democracy, the argument goes, needs an informed citizenry who can make rational decisions on the basis of the kinds of information available, especially in the realm of politics. That information is often complex, untidy or even held back; the task of the journalist is to overcome these obstacles, to shed light in dark corners, to act as the nation's watchdog, to present information on the events of the day with impartiality and objectivity. Diamond's version of the lament is certainly grounded in these precepts. Before the anecdote about television news he places this observation by Walter Lippman:

> All that the sharpest critics of democracy have alleged is true, if there is no steady supply of trustworthy and relevant news. Incompetence and aimlessness, corruption and disloyalty, panic and ultimate disaster, must come to any people which is denied an assured access to the facts. No one can manage to live on pap. Neither can a people.
>
> (Lippman in Diamond 1975: xi)

It is this contention which provides the foundation for much of the lament. Television news has systematically undermined the crucial arrangement which is meant to operate between a working democracy and its citizens. At its most reprehensible, television news actively turns away from the 'most important stories' completely.

Too often television has been content to take the easier path of irrelevant coverage: sports, weather, traffic accidents and smoky fires. Too

2

often 'access to facts' has been translated to mean higher flames and more tearful nuns.

(Diamond 1975: xiv)

Moreover, it is argued, the inclusion of such 'irrelevant coverage' actually changes the character of the 'serious' news. The preoccupations and strategies used to produce 'irrelevant' news begin to interfere with, to shape and finally overwhelm the 'relevant', 'important', 'consequential' news. For Conrad (1982: 132–3), the restless search for images which accompanies the reporting of what he terms 'non-events' ultimately compromises the coverage of important political developments, so that 'significance' is determined solely by the extraction of 'visual highlights'. Bennett (1988) detects a further wayward tendency in contemporary journalism, arising out of an unwarranted 'preoccupation with drama', a unfortunate spill-over from the conventions of news reportage used principally for stories which the lament would categorize as irrelevant coverage. Like Diamond, he draws on a troubling tale to make his point. An American journalist recalling his early days as a reporter explains how he used to marvel at the ease with which a senior staffer could write 'accounts of routine catastrophe' (Lapham in Bennett 1988: 37). After several months on the job the novice discovers the veteran's secret:

> In the drawer, with a bottle of bourbon and the manuscript of the epic poem he had been writing for twenty years, he kept a loose-leaf notebook filled with stock versions of maybe fifty or sixty common newspaper texts. These were arranged in alphabetical order (fires, homicides, ship collisions, etc.) and then further divided into sub-categories (fires – one-, two-, and three-alarm; warehouse; apartment building; etc.). The reporter had left blank spaces for the relevant names, deaths, numbers, and street addresses. As follows: 'A _____ alarm fire swept through _____ at _____ St yesterday afternoon, killing _____ people and causing _____ in property damage.
>
> (Lapham in Bennett 1988: 37)

For Bennett, the formulaic use of a 'dramatic script' is especially evident in television news where pressure to win ratings has resulted in the distinctions between news and entertainment becoming worryingly blurred. Postman and Powers (1992) are even more scathing, suggesting an analogy between television news and the carnival sideshow, each using 'temptations' to obtain an 'immediate, largely emotional reaction' in order to get and keep audiences in the (electronic) tent.

Whichever manifestation of the lament one encounters, there seems to be a consistent tendency, in the first instance, to link what Littlejohn (1975: 64) describes as the 'simplification and popular reductivism' of broadcast journalism to particular *types* of news stories. At one point it was thought that

3

television news could be redeemed by 'cleaning it up', expelling the disreputable elements and relegating them to the dustbin of journalistic history.

> crimes, accidents, beauty contests, royal weddings and sports . . . rarely have relevance as such to the life of the audience or to intellectual activation . . . the use of such materials attracts the interest of the audience away from more important issues to trivialities. Therefore, there is reason to exclude such items from news broadcasts.
>
> (Nordenstreng 1972: 404–5)

More recently however the path to reformation, according to some, has become permanently blocked. And again, particular kinds of stories prove to be the most stubborn obstacles in the way.

> If you are expecting to hear the most important news . . . on any given day, you will often be disappointed. Never forget that the producer of the program is trying to grab you before you zap away to another news show. Therefore, chances are you will hear a story such as Zsa Zsa's run in with the law, Rob Lowe's home videos, Royal Family happenings, or news of Michael Jackson on tour. Those stories have glitter and glamour in today's journalism. And if glitter and glamour won't do the job, gore will.
>
> (Postman and Powers 1992: 38)

The voices that make up the lament have been wide ranging and insistent, yet broadcasters, it seems, have not been sufficiently remorseful to change their practices, nor apparently have audiences felt enough shame to avert their eyes or demand alternatives; and if Australian television news is anything to judge by, this type of news is estimated not only to be solidly in place in the bulletin but actually to be on the increase (Gerdes 1980; Bell, Boehringer and Crofts 1982; Gerdes and Charlier 1985). To make matters worse, those 'items' which 'rarely have relevance' appear to have propagated more elaborate versions of themselves, growing into what broadcasters like to call 'reality programming' and critics prefer to label 'tabloid tv'. *Rescue 911*, *Australia's Most Wanted*, *Emergency 000*, *Cops*, *Hard Copy*, *Lifestyles of the Rich and Famous*, *Police, Camera, Action* are just a few of the many available examples where smoky fires, accidents, home videos, royal family happenings, pop music tours, beauty contests and tearful nuns have all become key ingredients for an entire television genre. Perhaps these are the kinds of developments Altheide and Snow (1991: 51) had in mind when announcing that, as it pertains to television, 'organized journalism is dead'.

One of the difficulties with the lament is that in its disapproval and its concern to reform certain assumptions about television news are left only partially examined. Although the lament offers a sustained commentary on broadcast journalism the basis of its arguments seems to rest on the notion that, given the right conditions and circumstances, news on television has the

4

capacity to act as a transparent and neutral vehicle for relaying information. Altheide and Snow (1991: 51), for instance, talk about 'the journalism enterprise, especially TV news' treating events through its own 'frames of reference, rather than attempting to understand the events in their own terms' and Bennett (1988: xiii) refers to news as a 'broadly shared window on reality'. This point of view seems to implicitly subscribe to the idea that news can apprehend the world impartially and factually – recently it has been looking out at the wrong things but this is a problem which could be corrected by adjustments in orientation and content, providing access to different facts or substituting the 'serious' for the 'trivialities'. However, such strategies may have little overall effect on some of the more fundamental ways in which television news works. Events, whether they are defined as inconsequential or important, cannot be treated outside specific presentational practices.

> For television news is a cultural artefact; it is a sequence of socially manufactured messages which carry many of the culturally dominant assumptions of our society. From the accents of the newscasters to the vocabulary of camera angles; from who gets on and what questions they are asked, via selection of stories to presentation of bulletins, the news is a highly mediated product.
>
> (Glasgow University Media Group 1976: 1)

Another difficulty with the lament's position comes from its desire to define news and the institutional workings of journalism as primarily about the transmission of information which can be used by a citizenry to accumulate knowledge and engage in responsible judgements. Yet, relying on the 'informational model' to explain television news and its unworthy tendencies may fail to recognize that in the daily recurrence and recognizable features of such programming viewer linkages to the news and the larger world it represents may be more ritualistic, symbolic and possibly mythic than informational, and in this sense television news might better be conceptualized as a 'form of cultural discourse' (Dahlgren 1988: 289). The intransigence of broadcast journalists to remove such insignificant reportage from their bulletins may have its motivation in news values based on commercial considerations which promote drama, sensation and visual impact in order to create and build an audience. But if Dahlgren is correct in posing television news as a cultural discourse, a different and perhaps more broadly based explanation still needs to be found for why such news remains 'popular'.

If there are limitations to the ways in which the lament conceptualizes news, the general importance of its preoccupations has to be acknowledged as well. A considerable time before contemporary communication research and cultural studies definitively focused on the 'entertainment' and non-political components of news with their analytical gaze (Curran and Sparks 1991), the lament had these features in its sights, arguing that these were a doggedly persistent, albeit problematic part of news which had to be confronted. The impulse of the lament however has been primarily corrective, attempting to imbue journalism with a more 'responsible' attitude. The best solution for some was simply to dump the disreputable elements altogether, but if this was not entirely possible, at least to get journalists to adopt a set of 'critical guidelines' (Bennett 1988: 187) in order to reflect on their practices. More recently, with the realization that neither of these strategies has been remotely workable, the lament has taken to addressing the audience directly with practical 'recommendations' for 'adjusting [its] relation to TV news shows, or in helping others to do so' (Postman and Powers 1992: 159).

This study begins where the lament in a sense ends. It argues that this purportedly insignificant news has to be approached and understood in exactly the opposite way, and precisely for the reasons the lament would wish it to go – its longevity, its palpable and influential presence, its use of a logic based less on models of information transfer than on structures of sentiment and sensation, its commitment to story-telling, its formulaic qualities as well as its search for visual impact are all key features which provide the grounds for assessing this disreputable news from an analytical perspective rather than through mere prescription. More critically perhaps, it will be suggested that the significance of the insignificant news resides in the way it needs to be theorized around the question of what the Glasgow University Media Group refer to as broadcast journalism's 'communicative power'. To study news on television, they contend, it is necessary to be engaged in an investigation of 'the right to define and demarcate situations . . . to typify, transmit and define the normal, to set agendas . . . to reproduce highly selected events . . . to do . . . judgmental work for society' (Glasgow University Media Group 1976: 13–14). Whereas the lament leads to a focus on journalistic practice as a 'problem' requiring prescriptive interventions, a critical project can conceptualize this same practice as a site from which certain 'ideological work' can be accomplished (Hall 1977: 340).

A formulation offered by Thompson (1990) might provide the initial parameters of such an approach.

> the concept of ideology can be used to refer to the ways in which meaning serves, in particular circumstances, to establish and sustain relations of power which are systematically asymmetrical – what I shall call 'relations of domination'. Ideology, broadly speaking, is *meaning in the service of power*. Hence the study of ideology requires us to investigate the ways in which meaning is constructed and conveyed in symbolic forms . . . [and] to ask whether, and if so how, the meaning mobilized by symbolic forms serves, in specific contexts, to establish and sustain relations of domination.
>
> (Thompson 1990: 7; italics in the original)

There has, of course, been a large volume of research work done which attempts to uncover and scrutinize meaning in the service of power as this manifests itself in the institution of journalism and the practices of news production. However, the 'angle of vision' has overwhelmingly tended to focus on that news which, at first glance, seemed to fit most overtly with what could be described as the 'purer' forms of political culture, where the relations and structures of power, control and legitimation appeared to be most explicitly represented. Industrial disputation, law and order, political dissent, race relations, institutional politics, forms of deviance, drug use, unemployment and terrorism, and environmentalism were just some of the problems, events and issues which have commanded most research attention in terms of news coverage.[1] A serious discussion of the news assumed an investigation into what was apparently most 'serious' in the news, perceived to be most politically salient or most troubling for the maintenance or otherwise of the relations of domination, consensus and legitimacy while news which was presumed not to fit this context tended to get a cursory mention – sometimes as the 'lighter items' (Glasgow University Media Group 1976) or 'soft stories' (Hartley 1982). This contrasts markedly with the lament which *has* actively drawn attention to the 'lighter items' but without providing much sustained analysis.

More recently, perhaps because of the burgeoning and apparent wide-spread success of tabloid journalism, more scholarly effort has been made to track down and account for the 'trivialities'.[2] Although the results of these investigative incursions into popular journalism are an encouraging sign that news analysis is according 'irrelevant' reportage some degree of critical importance, the tendency of much of the work in this area has been largely on print media, still leaving broadcast news, especially what television networks like to call their major news bulletins of the day, relatively unexamined. This remains a particularly notable omission for two reasons. In television programming terms, the day's main bulletin – typically, the early evening news broadcast – is 'high profile' in content. In the 'flow' of television, on most network channels, it remains the programme which is generally given 'flagship' status. Provided with very generous budgets and resource allocation, even in times of recession, broadcast 'news services' are often the type of programme around which a station makes its bid for seriousness and consequentiality. The time and effort spent searching for, and the subsequent promotion of 'authoritative' newsreaders attests to this valuation. Typically, at least in Australia, it is also the programme which leads into the rest of the evening's viewing, so its premier status is attached to audience market share considerations as well. Perhaps more importantly, in the context of this study, is the fact that the lament sounds most forlorn and baleful when it casts its eyes (and ears) over this particular format for news – where claims to important journalistic standards are given frequent rhetorical emphasis by broadcasters ('eye-witness news', 'live to air', 'on the spot report', 'the day's most comprehensive news round-up', 'that's the way it is' and so on) but where, upon closer scrutiny, the profession of journalism is found to be disturbingly flawed, especially when it is reported that so many people are ready to accord these news broadcasts a high degree of trustworthiness and reliability (Philo 1990; Bennett 1988; Western and Hughes 1983). Tabloid journalism may be popular, but from the point of view of the lament its status as 'real' journalism is questionable, so it can be marginalized and then disqualified; but not the major television news bulletins, where the lament's expectations are high and disappointments profound. According to Altheide and Snow (1991: 51–60), for example, it is television news, overwhelmingly oriented around a 'media logic' of entertainment values which has led inexorably and fatally to the 'postjournalism era' where in news terms a 'kind of entertainment programming' is always given precedence over 'doing deeper, more complete and accurate reports'. For them, the flaws of broadcast news actually become a harbinger for the ultimate degradation of the potential of television itself as a 'source of public information', once 'looked to with hope by those who felt that more detailed information could reduce the great misunderstandings that had for so long widened cultural and territorial gaps between peoples' (Altheide and Snow 1991: 57).

This book begins then, around the subject of everyday broadcast news, specifically at the point where the discourse of the lament and a critical project might be drawn productively together. From here the premise being advanced is relatively straightforward: in order to provide a more developed and comprehensive analysis of television news, it will be argued that the 'disreputable news', which the lament finds so damaging and unacceptable as journalism, needs to be given a central place within any critical undertaking in the study of news. Crucially, rather than locating these types of stories as merely tangential to questions of communicative power due to their ostensible non-political or non-serious inflection, it will be maintained that it is precisely these characteristics which render such stories so 'political', investing them with a particular, even unique, capacity to do ideological work, perhaps in ways which are unavailable to the more conventionally defined serious, significant news.

That residual category, the types of news stories that have been consistently left out of the kind of analysis which a critical project has provided, and which seem least connected with questions of 'meaning in the service of power', I propose to call, for the sake of convenience, the 'other news'. The 'other' news is what in a sense has been left over after critical scholarship has scanned the news horizon and selected the coverage in which it intended to invest its not inconsiderable analytic energies. To use an awkward analogy, it is almost like the use of the category 'other' which might appear on a hypothetical news coding sheet where, after the more obvious political, economic, or social issues-oriented stories have been classified out, the rest are placed, when no specific category is there to hold them. The 'other news' can be thought of as 'remaindered' news, recognized in passing, but left aside in order to focus full attention on what was perceived as more serious and more pressing news matters. This category of 'other news' gains its contours, in the first instance, from its close correspondence with what the lament has identified as television's least responsible form of journalism. It should be noted, however, that for the purposes of this study the 'other news' is not merely an alternative designation for what sometimes get called 'human interest' stories (Hughes 1968; Curran, Douglas and Whannel 1980) or for what journalists describe as 'soft news' (Tuchman 1973). Rather, as a descriptive – classificatory formulation, the 'other news' will include human interest or soft news items as well as coverage of fires, accidents, natural, social and personal 'disasters' and the like, all of which are events likely to qualify as 'hard news' (Tuchman 1973).

This book has several threads of analysis which run through it starting with the proposition that a comprehensive understanding of television news will occur only when broadcast journalism's 'trivialities' are given the same level of attention and theorization as news about 'more important issues'. To ignore the former, as the sample of stories used for this study will show, may be to overlook up to a third of all major news bulletins on any one day. It will also be argued that the apparently least political of news stories need to be scrutinized in terms of a special kind of 'politics' which serves to maintain 'asymmetrical relations of power', made all the more resonant because of the way this type of news as a 'symbolic form' draws upon the domain of common sense and lived experience. In this context, the 'other news' has to be situated and examined as it traverses the terrain of ideology. Referring to some of the work done on hegemony, the winning of consent and ideological effectivity (Hall 1977; Goldman and Rajagopal 1991) these themes will serve to frame the enquiry and will be taken up especially in Chapters 2 and 8. An investigation of its ideological trajectory, however, requires that the 'other news' also be interrogated in terms of how it makes the world to which it refers intelligible, how it produces its 'sense' and meaning. Here the lament's concern for the dramatic and formulaic qualities of unworthy news will be taken seriously in order to arrive at some understanding of how such news retains its 'staying power' and popular appeal. A range of concepts derived from work done on the newspaper gossip column (Smith 1975), on 'symbolic leaders' as victims and fools (Klapp 1964), on 'sympathy' and identification (Frye 1957) and on models of narrative and story-telling (Propp 1968; Todorov 1970, 1977) is used to provide a series of broadly-based textual readings of the stories which inhabit the 'other news'. These will make up the substance of Chapters 4, 5 and 6.

The textual readings provide the basis for and lead into another of the propositions which this book puts forward. Despite giving the appearance of a rather disparate array of stories, it will be argued that the 'other news' emerges out of two underlying paradigmatic 'systems' which are capable of generating particular structures of meaning and linkages across a wide range of television news reports. One of these operates a little like a philosophical meditation on temporality and causality and the other connects journalistic practices as they are embedded in the non-serious news to a particular realm of the ideological. The metaphysical system and the ideological system of the 'other news' are examined in Chapters 7 and 8. At the same time that the ideological system is engaged in the production, meaning in the service of power, it is also showing signs of contradictions and instabilities, opening the way for counter-ideological complications. These tendencies are also looked at in Chapter 8. In a final section in the book, at the end of Chapter 8, a number of these propositions will be drawn together in order to address recent developments taking place in broadcast journalism in the form of new actuality genres like 'reality programming' and 'tabloid tv' and to demonstrate how these new formats might be considered the programming descendants of the 'other news'.

2

OF PARADIGMS, PENDULUMS
AND MEDIA POWER

'EFFECTS': THE EARLY YEARS

But why communicative power, why ideology when this kind of approach seems to have all but dropped out of the media studies lexicon in what have been the expansive days of reception theory and active audiences, when as Corner (1991: 267) observes, so much 'effort has been centred on audiences' interpretive activity that even the preliminary theorization of influence has become *awkward*' (original emphasis). Attempting to provide some brief and tentative answers to this question could be a way of locating the analytical priorities which inform this study of television news. A rather inelegant, albeit useful metaphor will be pressed into service as a starting point: it might be said that in terms of one of its most long-standing interests, the question of 'effects', at least three pendulum 'swings' have occurred in the study of media communication (McQuail 1977; Curran, Gurevitch and Woollacott 1982; Hall 1982), and with the recent focus on and promotion of audience studies over the past few years a fourth 'oscillation' may be currently underway.

From the beginning of the century up until the end of the 1930s, researchers and commentators attributed to the media a powerful and pervasive influence. The creation of mass audiences, the belief that the members of these audiences were 'atomized' and isolated from community affiliations leaving them highly susceptible to the messages of the media, the seemingly successful deployment of propaganda during the First World War and rise of the advertising industries made for a model of effects which suggested that the media were an extremely potent force in contemporary social life. Variously known as the hypodermic needle model, the transmission belt theory, the bullet theory or the stimulus–response perspective, the equation was simple but convincing: on the one side were the invasive commanding media forces, on the other the vulnerable, dislocated mass audience (De Fleur 1970). The content of the media, whatever its form – film, radio, print, popular literature – could actively mould behaviour on a large scale, even to the extent of imposing a particular political system onto entire

11

nations. It was in this theoretical climate that Walter Lippmann sounded his warning about nations distracted by 'pap' being led away from democracy by the power of the media.

With the growth of mass communication research, particularly in America, a reassessment of the alleged power of the media and the 'mass society thesis' took place (Bramson 1961). A succession of social survey and laboratory-based studies (De Fleur 1970) on 'persuasive communication' and opinion change as these related to political campaigns, consumer decision-making, the diffusion of information and group dynamics sought to identify the critical 'variables' in the successful use of communication for effecting alterations in attitudes and behaviour. These studies taken together seemed to provide systematic evidence for refuting earlier assumptions about the power of the mass media and the breakdown of community. Instead of individuals reacting as isolated 'atoms' in a mass society, it appeared that factors such as group membership and selective attention were important mediating factors in shaping the reception process. Assumptions about the power of the media were called into question by an approach which postulated a limited media influence view: 'People, it was argued, manipulated – rather than were manipulated by – the mass media' (Curran, Gurevitch and Woollacott 1982: 12). As a result, research shifted ground: now issues were posed not in terms of what the media did to individuals, but rather what individuals did with the media. The 'uses and gratifications' approach, as it came to be known, (McQuail 1969: 71) viewed the media as much more benign, more servant than master. The media provided a wide variety of message 'outputs' for diverse, heterogeneous audiences who then selected the content and the message source which met a plurality of individual needs and dispositions. News, in this context, had an 'information function', operating to allow audience members to selectively 'participate . . . in the great events of the day' (Mendelsohn 1964: 244), or served as part of the ritual process of daily life (Nordenstreng 1972: 391).

ENTER THE 'CRITICAL PARADIGM'

By the middle of the 1970s, a third pendulum 'arc' of theorizing about the mass media had commenced, defining its worth partly through a direct challenge to the assumptions, methodologies and model of society of the limited influence perspective (Curran, Gurevitch and Woollacott 1982: 12–13). Conducted on several fronts and manifesting itself through a variety of local and regional 'interventions', this reassessment had a particularly vigorous and sustained moment in the news research carried out in the United Kingdom. The emergence of an 'alternative critical paradigm', according to Hall (1982: 56), had to be seen as not simply methodological or procedural, but in terms of a specific kind of 'political calculation' which might begin with an examination of the media but would end with an analysis of 'social formations' and the relations of domination and subordination.

It was noted that the evidence for the 'negligible effect' view had been frequently based on the results of experiments or surveys designed to measure only short term changes in attitudes and opinions and that these were often not of central importance to the individual anyway (McQuail 1977: 73–4). The persuasive impact of the mass media was being investigated at the expense of charting its 'cognitive effects' (Gurevitch and Blumler 1977: 271). This type of research might be able to tell how people were influenced by an advertising campaign in the media but it could not explain what part the media might play in winning allegiance to the conditions of consumerism in the first place.

> The media are conveying much more than a single message on who to vote for, or which brand of product to buy. Messages are situated within political and cultural assumptions about what is normal and . acceptable within society. In news production, these include beliefs about hierarchies of access, about who has the right to speak, what are the key political institutions, and what is 'acceptable' behavior. On an everyday level, the television, press and radio also provide information about specific events, which tacitly relate to these unspoken assumptions.
>
> (Philo 1990: 5)

A pluralistic, individuated focus on decision-making also tended to regard audiences like customers in *laissez-faire* economics, able to choose freely and rationally in the 'free-market' of media messages those that they wanted or needed. Questions about the social determination of such needs, even by the media itself or about how needs and media usage were independently estimated were never raised (Bonney and Wilson 1983: 19–20). On one level this approach did appear to offer a conception of audiences as more active, but ultimately, it was seen as a way by which media producers could argue to keep things as they were, claiming that they were satisfying all needs and simply giving people what they wanted. More importantly, there was the strong sense that the issue of media effectivity was not being addressed in all its social and cultural complexity. It was argued that the reduction of communicative power to occasional or relatively defuse forms of 'influence' had to be rethought in terms more appropriate to understanding a type of social formation, ostensibly:

> democratic in its formal organization, [but] committed at the same time by the concentration of economic capital and political power to the massively unequal distribution of wealth and authority [which would have] much to gain from the continuous production of popular

consent to its existing structure, to the values which supported and underwrote it, and to its continuity of existence.

(Hall 1982: 63)

The mass media, it was held, had to be situated as a privileged sphere around which the securing of popular consent could be enacted. To begin with, it was becoming increasingly clear that the mass media, particularly in the paradigmatic case of television, was becoming a major institutional force in the production of 'social knowledge', in the codification of problematic events and in the provision of 'explanatory contexts' which made sense of such events and of the world more generally. An investigation of communicative power, according to the critical paradigm, had to explore the ways that the media could be in a position to win a kind of generalized validity and legitimacy for accounts of the world which were in fact partial and particular, and then to be able to ground these particular constructions in what Hall (1982: 65) termed 'the taken-for-grantedness of "the real"'. Representing vested interests as natural and inevitable, and conveying these as 'the order of things', it was argued, were crucial operations in the realm of 'the ideological'.

Once the issue of media effects was posed in these terms, it was necessary to offer explanations about what 'the ideological' might look like and how it worked. Despite the tendency to talk about 'the media' in general, it was actually the news which initially provided a central focus from which these theorizations about 'ideological effects' and cultural power were first worked out. Some initial formulations returned to the base/superstructure metaphor in Marxist theory, arguing that media power had to be firmly located in an economic process and in the structures of media ownership and production. As an agency of the superstructure the media engage in concealing the fundamental nature of social relations in capitalism. Misrepresenting these relations, especially as they are constituted through the asymmetrical and antagonistic structures of class, the media's role is to manufacture legitimacy, through the production of 'false consciousness', in relation to the interests of the economically powerful groups who also include those who own and control the media. This was a version of the classic passage from Marx and Engels: 'the ideas of the ruling class are in every epoch the ruling ideas'. Both the formal properties and the content of television news could be explained by the fact that much of mainstream broadcasting, as part of a commercial market system, is interested primarily in selling audiences to advertisers as commodities who pay to have their products displayed. Accordingly, the pressure to maximize audiences and revenues results in the commercial media systematically avoiding 'the unpopular and tendentious', and instead drawing on values and assumptions most familiar and most legitimized 'which almost inevitably means those which flow authoritatively downwards through the social structure' (Murdock and Golding 1977: 37).

Despite placing the issue of media power firmly back on the research agenda and furthering the theoretical oscillation away from the minimal influence tradition, what came to be known as the political economy account of ideology was seen by some to be conceptually problematic. One difficulty was that not enough autonomy was granted either to the workings of ideology through the media nor to the professional practices of media personnel (Curran, Gurevitch and Woollacott 1982; Hall 1982; Bonney and Wilson 1983). This view, it was felt, relied too heavily on some notion of the media 'belonging' to the ruling groups and purposefully 'distorting' reality for their entrenched interests. Television news for example would be 'a kind of megaphone' amplifying the ideas of the economically and politically powerful across all sectors of the social formation (Connell 1979: 87). If this were the case broadcast journalism would lose its authority, and simply be relegated to the domain of propaganda. News practitioners do not see themselves as in the business of taking orders from the dominant power bloc and despite economic ties with these ruling groups, media professionals are fiercely protective of their 'independence'.

The search for another version of the ideological began in order to counter the problematic tendencies implied in the notion of a 'biased' media distorting reality for the benefit of ruling groups and, in the case of news, to take account of the professional practices and beliefs of journalists as more than 'a polite fiction'. Underpinning these considerations was the sense that whatever formulation was adopted, it had to explain how ideology was connected to legitimacy in terms of the non-coercive elements of power typical of liberal capitalist social formations. It was Gramsci's work on hegemony that proved a useful point of departure (Hall 1977, 1982; Gitlin 1980; Goldman and Rajagopal 1991). In broad outline, Gramsci argued that in the liberal-capitalist state the ruling groups, those dominant economic and political forces, cannot simply produce the ruling ideas and impose them on the subordinate groups and classes. Rather, the exercise of power in the interests of those who rule, and who benefit from it, is achieved not by 'ideological compulsion' or by coercion (although this is always at the ready) but through 'cultural leadership' (Hall 1982: 85), by routinely winning the active consent of those subordinate classes or groups to 'the way things are' which systematically favours the dominant group's interests. Most crucially, hegemony does not operate in the economic or productive sphere alone, but must be organized at the level of 'everyday consciousness' (Gitlin 1980: 2) – it is on the terrain of the ideological that hegemony is won. This means that a whole range of practices, perceptions and expectations – 'definitions of reality' – favourable to the dominant social groupings and class fractions and institutionalized in the spheres of civic and social life come to constitute a primary 'lived reality' for most people (Williams in Goldman and Rajagopal 1991: 4; Hall 1977). This operates, as Hall (1977: 342–3) explains, 'not because the dominant classes can prescribe and proscribe, in detail, the mental content of the lives of subordinate classes . . . but because they strive

15

and to a degree succeed in framing all competing definitions of reality within their range ... '. This does not imply, however, as some critics of this position have suggested (Windschuttle 1984) that ideology functions merely as a monolithic univocal discourse, which finally and irrevocably subsumes and overwhelms all competing definitions and maps of meaning from above. The notion of hegemony refers to a 'field of relations structured by power and difference' in which positions of dominance and subordination are always in play, especially around questions of ideology. This, according to Hall (1989: 51), 'is an altogether different notion from that of "ruling ideology", which comes from outside, descends on passive subjects, blankets their ordinary discursive understanding of the world, and simply superimposes its own highly homogeneous perspectives ... '.

Gramsci also makes the point that the operation of existing ideologies always has to be understood as a 'complex field' traversed by the pushes and pulls of potentially contradictory articulations within the ideological system. Bonney and Wilson (1983: 176–7) provide a useful explanatory footnote to this tendency in an Australian context citing the case of mass market advertising which is able to utilize the ideology of rugged individualism to sell cigarettes and beer while at the same time mobilizing a sense of collectivism to whip up nationalistic feeling around spectator sport. Nor is it simply a matter of those in dominant positions automatically winning the consent of the subordinate groups. For Gramsci hegemonic control is not just given and permanent, but has to be actively struggled for and won; this means it can also be lost. Winning consent and legitimacy is in a 'continuous process of formation', a succession of 'unstable equilibria' between the interests of the dominant and subordinate groups where the dominant group interests tend to prevail 'but only up to a certain point' (Gramsci, quoted in Hall 1977: 334). The agencies of the superstructure – the family, education, the church, cultural institutions and the media – are where hegemony is secured.

To explain how news might win consent, journalism has to be taken seriously in its claims of 'independence'. Legitimacy crucially depends on not being seen to be taking directives from the powerful or consciously bending accounts of the world to square with vested interests or dominant definitions (Hall 1982: 87). The professional self-image of 'the watchdog of democracy' depends on journalism's relative autonomy. News accomplishes its work of winning consent not by being biased, as this has been defined by the political economy thesis, but by scrupulously adhering to editorial policies of 'balance', 'impartiality', 'neutrality' and 'objectivity'. Where lapses occur, they are the exception rather than the rule. From here it becomes easier to see how broadcasters can so unselfconsciously proclaim that television news is simply a 'mirror held up to reality' (Epstein 1973) reflecting events out-there-in-the-world, without moulding or shaping them in the process of communication. The Walter Cronkitism – 'that's the way it is' – lays bare the essential features of the assumptions about neutrality and transparency. 'Eye-witness news', 'live satellite report', 'direct broadcast' is the rhetoric which is used to advertise and frame this position – television news is the relay of 'impartial' information for a viewing citizenry which contributes to its understanding and knowledge of the world. When television news is assumed to be analogous to a mirror, or sometimes a window, transmitting whatever appears before it in a relatively unplanned fashion, questions concerning selection and construction become less important, possibly irrelevant. Television news needs no explanation, it just happens: random reactions to random events (Murdock 1973: 163). Such a position provides the news with the degree of immunity it needs to counter accusations of bias and hence gain credibility and authority for its 'way of doing things'.

When 'actuality' does become news however, it must be processed by communicational devices which allow it intelligibility as 'the real'. Raw 'events' have to be represented in 'message form' and as Hall (1982: 64) emphasizes 'representation is a very different notion from that of reflection. . . . It implies the active work of selecting and presenting, of structuring and shaping: not merely the transmitting of an already-existing meaning, but the more active labour of making things mean'. Along with all the other output of the mass media, news had to be understood as a 'signifying practice', and uncovering how the process of 'meaning making' works to produce discourses which can establish and sustain relations of dominance, shut down enquiry into these relations, and secure the consent of those made subordinate through the structural organization of these relations became one of the central strategies employed by the critical paradigm to demonstrate the ways that journalism, despite its commitment to fairness and 'due impartiality', was implicated in the sphere of the ideological.

CENTRING THE MESSAGE

In the light of the minimal influence orientation, it was argued that the focus of analytical attention ought to turn away from attempts to measure effects, or lack of them, in relation to audience response to the media's messages and concentrate instead on the messages themselves. The second stage of media research, it was felt, had either oversimplified the 'content' of these messages or had defined it merely as a way to approach audience reactions and predispositions: 'conceptually, the media message, as a symbolic sign vehicle or structured discourse, with its own internal structure and complexity, remained theoretically wholly undeveloped' (Hall 1982: 61). The distinguishing feature of the mass media as an organized institution of production, unlike other productive institutions, was that it engaged specifically in generating 'symbolic goods', messages articulated within complex discourses, the rules and meanings of which were taken-for-granted and which could be beneficially connected with discussions about ideology and power. The question of media effectivity, at least in the first instance, could be promisingly

17

addressed through what McQuail (1983: 65) describes as 'message centred theory'. The discursive aspects of the message, it was argued, had a privileged place in media communicational exchanges, acting as a 'determinate moment' (Hall 1980). So while seemingly concerned with only one element of mass communication, this approach could lead to knowledge about the assumptions and categories upon which the culture depends and could direct attention to the ways in which messages structure the production of meaning for audiences from particular ideological vantage points. As a result of this reformulation news became a 'text' from which could be 'read' a complex series of interdependent organizational, technical, professional and symbolizing practices that would show 'meaning in the service of power'.

How then might the production of meaning in news texts operate to do ideological 'work' through various processes of signification? News research based around some of the tenets of the critical paradigm consistently found clusters of sedimented, taken-for-granted enunciative logics involved in the representation of reportable events, and although these have been given different designations – the Glasgow University Media Group (1976) calls them 'standard interpretive frameworks', Gitlin (1980) and Rachlin (1988) use the term 'media frames', Hartley (1982) describes them as 'mapping processes', Goldman and Rajagopal (1991) refer to 'framing practices' – their underlying importance was demonstrated to reside in the way that everyday journalistic routines produce socially constituted knowledge, oriented within a framework of communicative power. These enunciative logics came to be discussed around a number of recognizable and seemingly permanent features of news, including television news.

Preferred meanings

News-making routines operate to render events intelligible through a whole array of structuring and processing operations. Although news 'signs' – visual and aural – are sites of a plurality of potential meanings, the use of specific presentational codes work to override 'multi-accentuality' by offering a 'preferred meaning'. Attempts at 'closure', however, as Hartley (1982: 24) points out, need to be read as evaluative, and hence ideological, but in terms of journalistic values, which emphasize clarity and unambiguity such preferential sense-making can be unproblematically grounded in a credo which claims to be dealing with just 'the facts' of the matter. This is one way in which television news wins consent, not to a particular point of view, but to the legitimacy of the range or limits within which it operates. The determinacy of the 'encoding' process which operates in a number of meaning-producing registers simultaneously (pictures, sounds, speech, editing, graphics), all to do with the 'message form', becomes *naturally* the way television news does things (Goldman and Rajagopal 1991: 115). The 'necessary' form of appearance tends to make the event 'mean' all by itself:

'sense making in television news so often seems to flow smoothly from the event itself, having nothing to do with the way it is told' (Hartley 1982: 63). With the help of visualization, and the conventional wisdom which insists that the (news) camera never lies (Western and Hughes 1983), broadcast news can 'tell-it-like-it-is'.

Consensus

'Making things mean' involves the presentation of events to an assumed audience. In order for 'events' to be identified and assigned to a context meaningful to these audiences the signifying practices of journalism need to make use of 'cultural maps' of the social world already in place (Hall *et al.* 1978: 54). The unusual, unexpected or unpredictable occurrences which constitute 'news' can only make sense if they are referred implicitly to the background assumptions already underpinning cultural knowledge. One strategy which tends to be used to underscore journalism's definition of news is the calling out of a 'consensual model' of what is taken to be the realm of immediate experience and social process, frequently expressed in notions of unity – our nation, our society, our economy. If 'my' values happen to be discrepant to 'yours', the assumption is that 'we' all still have enough mutuality of interests 'to keep a level head' and to use the proper channels to reconcile 'our' differences. Those who act to the contrary, taking their grievances 'to the street' can be conveniently mapped as out of bounds, deviant, beyond the pale or worse. As Hartley (1982: 83) explains: 'The bread and butter of news is conflict, violence, rivalry and disagreement. But for all these negatives to be newsworthy, a prior assumption of the "underlying" consensus to which they are a threat must be at work'.

Structures of access

The desire to appear impartial and objective means a heavy reliance on what journalists call 'accredited sources' who provide 'authoritative' information. In matters deemed to be important for public disclosure, news makers tend to favour those from high ranking groups who are assumed to have a better 'overview' and be more 'credible' on such matters than those lower down. Who gets to speak, to present a point of view on current issues is embedded in a 'hierarchy of credibility' (Becker 1967) which tends to be skewed in favour of perspectives provided by the already powerful. As a result controversy can be dominated by 'primary definers' whose privileged points of view as 'sources' come to frame subsequent debate. The organizational problem of producing stories on a regular scheduled basis also tends to orient coverage around the already powerful. As journalists position themselves close to institutions which can generate a useful volume of reportable activity at regular intervals, e.g. parliament, the courts, the agencies of law enforcement, professional associations, employer groups, the stock exchange, and trade union councils, the voices of dominant groups are routinely given prominence. Hence, the structures of access – between television news and its influential sources – suggest how it is possible that broadcast news can be both relatively autonomous and still hegemonic in its signifying practices. Strict adherence to editorial criteria – here the professional imperative for impartiality – leads journalism to operate 'free of compulsion', a necessary condition for gaining legitimacy, yet in the same moment to be 'freely articulat[ing] ... definitions of the situation which favour the hegemony of the powerful' (Hall 1982: 86).

Common sense

Access alone is a necessary but not sufficient explanation to account for the symbolic reproduction of frameworks of power. Television news has to address *someone* and events and opinions have to be made meaningful in terms of who that is thought to be. A workable 'mode of address' has to be developed which expresses not only the content of events but also an orientation towards the viewer. One solution to this problem is a conception of viewers 'as a mass of ordinary people of "ordinary common sense", men and women with their feet on the ground who take the world as it is' (Westergaard 1977: 108). As issues unfold and events are scrutinized broadcasters probe 'on our behalf', their questions are of a kind 'anybody might ask if they had the chance' (Hartley 1982: 89–90; Connell 1978: 83; Kumar 1977: 247) and explanations are cast using a language, a set of images and a common stock of knowledge which it is assumed will be reciprocally shared with the audience/'reader' (Hall *et al.* 1978: 61). The appeal to common sense, however, is not a neutral procedure. When television news is to a large measure governed by a structure of access which allows the powerful special privileges in defining and delimiting situations, the use of common sense as a mode of address can act to translate these very specific orientations into a more generalizable 'public idiom'. The apparent spontaneity, instant recognizability and timeless quality which makes common sense feel like 'sedimented bedrock wisdom' can imbue dominant perspectives and the interests they represent with a type of 'popular force', contributing to their continuance and irrefutability because they end up sounding 'so familiar', 'so natural', so much a part of our own 'vocabulary'.

Conventionalism

The construction of news works through what Chibnall (1977: 33) calls the 'operation of conventionalism, the situating of emergent phenomena in existent structures of meaning'. Instead of promoting historically grounded procedures for the interpretation of events, news relies on a circumscribed stock of already available explanations and contextualizing devices to deal with 'problematic realities' and make them intelligible. In this sense 'news' is actually 'olds' (Galtung and Ruge 1973): the current manifestation of industrial disputation becomes one more strike to endure; 'Watergate' resurfaces as 'Irangate'. According to Murdock (1973: 165) the news process 'establishes its own links between situations, links not at the level of underlying structures and processes, but at the level of immediate forms and images'. In this way news rewrites history for immediate popular consumption. When news is considered as a type of television programme, conventionalism operates in relation to formats, permitted story length, strategies of presentation and a 'repertoire of communicative roles' (Connell 1979; Langer 1983; Altheide and Snow 1991). At the level of form Rock (1973) suggests that news is a 'series of cycles', endlessly resurfacing motifs and story structures which are familiar and well understood. Such recurring patterns are 'routinised and sedimented over time ... [and] contain their own 'logic-in-use' which serves as a set of loose generative rules' governing the way events get explained as news and the mode of presentation of such events (Hall 1973a; Hartley 1982).

Good television

Securing consent also has to be located in terms of the specificity of news *on television*. Since broadcast journalism traffics in discourses directed at large publics, its aim will be to extend its explanatory reach as 'effective televisual communication'. In this sense television news not only has to be perceived as worthy journalism but also as 'good television' (Hall 1976). Consent is won in this case not only by insisting on the professional imperatives of journalism, but also by employing the whole repertoire of encodings specific to what is accepted as exemplary practice for the *'institution* television' (McArthur 1978): visualization, actuality, transparency, flow, smoothness, narrativity, performance, seamlessness and consequently, how news is organized to produce meaning comes to have much in common with the fictional programmes which surround it (Sperry 1976; Fiske and Hartley 1978; Bazelgette and Paterson 1980/81).

NEITHER FIXED NOR FINAL

One last but crucial point needs to be raised, which returns us to Gramsci's observation that hegemony is never 'given and permanent' but always in a process of formation. In order to be understood in all its potential complexity hegemony has to be located in relation to its 'dialectical character' (Goldman and Rajagopal 1991: 4). Despite the communicative power associated with news-making practices, it cannot be assumed that these representational logics and modes of address straightforwardly evince a type of ideological 'capture'. Hall (1977: 333) reminds us that 'even under hegemonic conditions, there can be no total incorporation or absorption'. Questions of domination and legitimation in this context are always posed in terms of struggle, negotiation and resistance: winning consent is never automatic or spontaneously delivered; and even when it is won, it can also be lost. Hegemonic tendencies always involve 'the on-going rearticulation of the relations between and the identity and position of the ruling bloc and the subordinate fractions within the larger social formation' (Grossberg 1992: 245). This opens the way for counter-hegemonic possibilities and a politics of contestation which has been located at two levels with regard to mass media output. The first concerns the reception of media texts – the degree of correspondence between the preferred meanings of, say, a television programme and the subsequent 'decodings' which might be done by various 'interpretive communities'. In order to account for differential readings or 'aberrant' decodings (Eco in Fiske 1987: 65), but mindful of not wanting to slip back into the more individualistic explanations based on a 'uses and gratifications' approach, the critical paradigm proposed a model of reading which would link together issues of ideological inflection and 'real readers' by locating reception around three 'ideal-type' moments of decoding (Hall 1980). In the 'dominant-hegemonic position' decoding takes place in close alignment with the ideological agendas embedded in the preferred meaning; a 'negotiated' interpretation contests specific truth claims or framing presumptions in a particular programme or news story, but retains acceptance of the overall encoding rules and grammars; and an oppositional stance questions fundamentally the content and the formal properties of a text, substituting an alternative set of practices and interpretations. Using what came to be known as the encoding – decoding model, research by Morley (1980) on television current affairs viewers, was one of the first empirical reception studies emerging from the critical paradigm which attempted to demonstrate that winning consent could not be posed as automatic or inevitable.[1]

The second level of contestation was located in media texts themselves. Some initial work done on Hollywood cinema and popular television drama observed the way in which a text's ideological trajectory could be crisscrossed with contradictions and discontinuities – between theme and 'style', character and performance, or technical codes and narrative – leaving gaps, openings and points of tension which worked against a 'perfect transmission'. In these instances the ideological inflections and relays coded into the text could be opposed or undermined by certain other textual inflections and operations. For example, television soap operas offering traditional representations of women and, at the same time, 'strong' women in the role of powerful villainesses who essentially control the narrative (Modleski 1979), or Hollywood melodramas of the 1950s pursuing and subverting the 'ideal'

22

of family life and femininity (Nowell-Smith 1977). A recognition of the negotiated terrain around which ideology has to work – through reader/text relations and through ideological tensions in media texts themselves – was used as a corrective to the notion of a 'dominant' set of representational practices and demonstrated that in order to offer a full account for the capacity of the media to win consent these instabilities and countervailing tendencies would need to be addressed and placed in any theory of communicative power.

BACK TO THE FUTURE, OR THE RE-RETURN OF THE NEARLY REPRESSED

Primarily it has been developments around these countervailing tendencies where we might ascribe the latest pendulum swing in theorizations about the power of the media, especially as these have been emphasized in the emergence of what is sometimes labelled the 'new' audience research. In some ways this most recent paradigm 'arc' signals something of a revamp, albeit with a more elaborated conceptual toolbox, of a perspective not unlike the one which characterized the period of uses and gratification studies. Specifically, this 'new paradigm' has tended to turn away from accounts of ideology, legitimation and the media's place in the constitution of public knowledge, sentiment and value (Corner 1991: 267) to focus instead on the 'moment' of reception and decoding. In the context of television, it was argued 'that a radical reassessment of viewer practices is warranted . . . [and] . . . would-be critics of the media industries need to recognize that television audiences hold far greater power over the medium than is generally acknowledged' (Seaman 1992: 306). A call went out to attend to the 'openness' of the television text, the plurality of possible readings on offer, and the multitude of ways that audiences engage in 'making over' such texts for their own purposes and pleasures, evading/resisting/subverting the ideological trajectories inscribed in the medium's output. Fiske's exposition (1987: 64) on 'active audiences' was one example which seemed to signal this position most exuberantly: analysis had to redirect attention away from the textual strategies exerting ideological influence to 'the reader as a site of meaning'. Some like Curran (1990) however, in attempting to document and contextualize the re-emerging tendencies towards reception models of communication began to sound a warning – the 'new revisionist' imputations of a relatively negotiable media influence may be exaggerating the degree to which 'there are no dominant discourses, merely a semiotic democracy of pluralist voices'. Still others, like Murdock (1989), exceedingly sceptical of the theoretical progress claimed by the 'active audience' perspective, drew uncomfortable parallels between the notion of the active audience and the celebration of consumer sovereignty promoted by the 'commercial populism' of a rising new conservatism. While these assessments did not discount a view that argued that users of the mass media are diversely creative and the makers of meaning, nor did they consider the 'reinstatement of the pre-audience text' (Brunsdon 1989: 125) to be a serious option, cautionary notes like these have been heard with a degree of regularity, especially in the writing of various media analysts who see their work as having some continuity with the legacy of the critical paradigm; and indeed in some quarters these 'notes' have been building into an intensity of orchestrated proportions. Even Morley (1992), whose work on current affairs television audiences has been frequently used as a kind of touchstone for the analytic progression from the encoded text to the decoding reader, has raised concerns about the 'affirmative model' and its tendency to overlook issues connected with the economic, political and ideological forces acting on both the construction of texts and the active reader. The move from 'bad' texts to 'good' audiences (Brunsdon 1989: 125), it has been observed, is a slippage which perhaps is overly optimistic in its claims about the autonomy of reception and the concomitant notion of audience empowerment, and which, in its more celebratory forms, may be inadvertently delegating to 'the people' and their pleasures a kind of romanticized independence which they simply do not have.[2] Perhaps the most sobering comments have come from those who see the paradigm 'turn' to the notion audience power as a path which leads to 'complacent relativism' (Corner 1991: 281) and the final bracketing out of that certain 'political calculation' so important in the initial theorizing done by the critical paradigm.

Heath (1990: 274) locates the retreat from 'the transforming dialectic of appraisal and critique' in a misplaced and depoliticized valorization of 'the everyday', which in terms of current scholarly approaches to television and popular culture increasingly gets expressed through the search for a 'plurality of positions of reception' that ultimately 'just leaves television intact, unthought . . . ' including its fundamental role in cultivating those positions within 'the governing terms of plurality' in the first place. For Heath (1990: 297) the task at hand is to 'make the critical distance that television itself continually erodes in its extension, its availability, its proximity'. However, and this is important for Heath's argument, to produce critical distance is not necessarily to reduce television solely to the operations of the ideological.

Much of television, our experience of it, is *also* not ideological, not to be brought down to the production-reproduction of oppressive social relations and their validation . . . we watch and react in different ways to a multitude of things, and the extent of those things . . . goes beyond any possibility of its being read off according to some single functionalization of it as ideological transmitter. . . . Simply, we have to take the 'also' seriously.

(Heath 1990: 297; original emphasis)

Indeed, a sizeable portion of the analysis in this current study of television's 'other news' is based precisely on taking the 'also' seriously, in that the news stories discussed in what follows are examined for their sense-making properties in relation to a 'multitude of things' – story-telling, gossip, the manufacture of fame, ritual, social memory, pleasure as well as ideology. That is, the signifying logics of the 'other news', like all of television, are heterogeneous and working at a number of levels at the same time, all of which need to be accounted for as textual operations and as ways of addressing the audience. Yet, it *also* needs to be remembered, as Heath (1990: 297) emphasizes, that 'television is always at the same time bound up in our societies in the work of ideology'.

In order to accomplish the task of examining this 'work of ideology', as it is done in television news, the redeployment of one of the central conceptual categories used by the critical paradigm will be an important requirement. Studies of the media which invoke the concept of class as an explanatory framework have fallen on distinctly hard times. As a dimension of analysis the issue of class may get acknowledged along the way but its power of determination is often seen as operating mostly 'in the last instance', if at all. Other types of 'subjectivities' and 'discursive formations' have been allocated explanatory priority – gender, ethnicity, race, nation and subculture to name a few. Of course, to resuscitate a class-inflected analysis as a way of finally making critical sense of media output generally and broadcast news texts specifically may seem, at least to some, a retrograde step, running the risk, as Miliband (1991: v) puts it, 'of instant dismissal, [the work of] an unreconstructed fundamentalist, obstinately blind to the vast changes which have occurred' which render the 'old notions' of class irrelevant. Yet despite its substantially reduced analytic status in media studies and its replacement by other non-class 'subject positions', in different areas of critical work the apprehension of class as an explanatory framework has not been totally discounted. Marshall *et al.*'s investigation (1988) in Britain, for instance, demonstrates quite explicitly the way class is a central category for the articulation of 'social identity', and even in a recent Australian study which takes issue with the claims put forward by Marshall *et al.* about the primacy of the 'identity of class' in determining social identity, it is acknowledged that while class may be less significant alongside other sources of identity, such as nation or family, 'it may be that these disparate identities are themselves "class identities" of a sort, in that they may be partially class determined' (Baxter, Emmison and Western 1991: 302).

The analytical authority of the concept of class is used here cautiously and knowingly. As Heath (1990: 290) has suggested, if ideology 'has to be brought back into an understanding of television, recredited as it were . . . this is not to be done in a single way'. This study is clearly not an attempt to reprioritize class around an assumption that it is 'the only structure of

25

importance, the "basic" one in a logical sense' (Connell and Irving 1992: 20). However, the approach taken does stand as an attempt to re-inscribe class in terms of a need to acknowledge it as a central feature of social life and lived experience, a 'discursive organizing principle' (Baxter, Emmison and Western 1991: 302) around which ideological operations as they are manifest in media texts can be seen to work. Thinking conceptually about the notion of class does not preclude different discursive elaborations and subjectivities, nor does it necessarily make class the controlling, determinative social moment but it does offer a kind of 'intellectual accent', energizing certain areas of investigation, prompting 'certain kinds of questions into the heuristic foreground' (Dimock and Gilmore 1994).

In 1982, Hall published an essay in which his aim was to document the central importance of the hitherto mostly neglected area of ideological analysis for the study of media influence. He referred to this intervention on behalf of 'the ideological' as the return of the repressed. He also pointed out in this same essay that the conceptual categories by which the ideological gets examined were by no means fully developed, so that extensive work would still be required to demonstrate the adequacy of explanatory terms as well as to refine and build up further insights (Hall 1982: 88). But these have become 'new times', when the lure of the fashionable, the up-to-date, the next super-cessionary fragment can sometimes overwhelm these more prosaic kinds of requirements, leaving worthy theoretical projects, to use Goodwin and Whannel's colourful description (1990: 5), 'abandoned by the analytical road-side, like clapped out old cars'. One of the side effects of the proliferation of cultural theory during the past decade or so, according to Goodwin and Whannel (1990: 5) has been the tendency to latch enthusiastically onto new ideas only to be critiquing and prematurely casting them aside a short while later, before their full potential for critical enquiry can be developed. Perhaps at least one 'phase' of this recent pendulum swing needs to be directed to recapitulation and consolidation, to encourage, following Hall's metaphor, the re-return of what appears at the moment to be the nearly re-repressed, making discussion of media power less 'awkward' than it seems to have become.

In a plea to reinstate the 'profoundly political impulse' which motivated the field of cultural studies in the first place McRobbie (1991) argues broadly that 'new times' do not mean jettisoning 'founding categories' like power, class and ideology, rather using and adapting them, but 'without guarantees'.

> since Marx was if nothing else the most sophisticated critic of capital, and since capital is simultaneously in crisis and globally dominant, the abandonment of what Marxist cultural theory has taught us about, for example, the meaning and the modalities of the mass media, would be nonsensical. In so far as the urgency which fuelled the establishment of

culture as a field of political inquiry has come from a concern to understand the dynamics of social and cultural inequality and the ways in which these are lived in and through a variety of social categories and ideological identifications, some of which are mobilizing, others of which might be seen as immobilizing, then the very rationale for cultural studies disappears when this critical and analytical imperative is lifted. The question might be, why bother?

(McRobbie 1991: 14)

3

SITUATING THE 'OTHER NEWS'

In addressing the issue of 'the ideological' in news, the critical paradigm has primarily been occupied with an inventory of reportage which could be used to demonstrate most explicitly the connections between journalism and communicative power. In practice, this turned out to be an investigation of that news which appeared to have the most direct relationship to questions about the exercise of social control, the construction of legitimacy, and efforts to forge consensus and maintain hegemonic leadership; in short, to questions related to various historical and institutional manifestations of political culture. There were some notable exceptions. Brunsdon and Morley's textual analysis of *Nationwide* (1978), a British current affairs programme specializing in human interest and non-political topics; historical work by Curran, Douglas and Whannel (1980) on the 'political role' of the 'apolitical human interest content' in the popular press; and Curran and Sparks's account (1991) of the 'essentially conservative "common sense" views' lodged within the 'dimensions of entertainment' in the tabloid newspaper. Within the critical paradigm however, attempts to examine the non-consequential news, especially as this occurs in television, have been marginal to its main research agenda. Disregard for what Fiske and Hartley (1978: 189) describe as television news reporting's 'great preoccupation ... [with] disasters, accidents and human interest stories' becomes a notable omission in an Australian context given the evidence which suggests that the amount of this type of news may actually be increasing during the major daily news bulletins on television (Gerdes and Charlier 1985).

Concentration on the politically salient news and setting aside most of the rest tends to assume that the former category is more illustrative – more 'symptomatic' perhaps – of the processes involved in journalistic practices as these might relate to issues of communicative power. This separation however may be inadvertently ignoring an important observation about all news: that it is a cultural product, a socially constructed symbolic discourse. As Hall (1973c: 86–7) has argued, the process of news production has its own structure and internal validity and the role of the news journalist is to mediate by identifying and recording news from a landscape of potential events. News does not merely reflect a world of facts pre-existing 'out there'. Rather, journalistic practice creates the conditions for the selection and interpretation of events which end up constituting 'the news' for any one day. Certain procedures are followed to gather news as well as process it in an acceptable form. Tuchman (1976: 93) points out that 'reports of news events are stories – no more no less'. Reporters learn story forms which are used as professional equipment and can be applied as operational rules to transform and give meaning to encountered events as news. This process of transformation is governed by the operation of presentational codes which make the correspondence between 'event-as-it-happens' and 'story' less than direct, despite broadcasters claims to the contrary. In the case of television news, the process at work may have as much to do with what we think of as the conventions of fiction as it does with 'presenting the facts'. The now fabled memorandum from an executive producer of the American National Broadcasting Company's news service explains:

> Every news story should . . . display the attributes of fiction or drama. It should have structure and conflict, problem and denouement, rising action and falling action, a beginning, a middle and an end. These are not only the essentials of drama; they are the essentials of narrative.
>
> (Reuven Frank in Epstein 1973: 4–5)

Hartley (1982: 33) puts this another way: 'for news, what makes it meaningful is not the world it reports but the sign system in which it is encoded'. This is not to contend that there is no world 'out there' but that the 'institution television as constructor of reality . . . is distinct from the social world inhabited both by broadcasters and audiences and . . . is subject to its own principles of construction that have to do primarily with the institution television rather than with the ostensible topics' it chooses to examine (McArthur 1978: 14). If television news 'does things its own way', having a degree of relative autonomy as a cultural form, it may be unsustainable to select *some* news stories as more analytically representative or significant in relation to the workings of the ideological, and therefore more worthy of research attention. Journalistic practice makes 'its own kind of sense', regardless of the topic or event at hand; therefore all news stories operated on by its codes – not just those which appear most directly implicated in structures of domination and subordination – become important for understanding the place of news as a 'symbolic form' where meaning can be mobilized in the service of power. In fact, it might be argued that the very non-political nature of the trivial, non-serious news, is precisely the feature which renders it *so* 'political'.

The terrain of common sense may be important here. If ideology is inflected through the classifications, interpretations and language of common sense understanding, it may be those 'other news' stories – items about fires, floods, accidents, civic rituals, twists of fate, heroic acts of humble people, victims – so dependent upon, yet at times so disruptive of ordinary life where the discourse of common sense has most efficacy and as a result where ideology resides in one of its most 'available' forms. In these instances, the common sense stance, the public idiom, is not translating the opinions of the powerful 'down', but depicting the world of 'everyday people' in all their trials, tribulations and triumphs. Even when élites and celebrities make an appearance, in the context of the 'other news', as they frequently do, they are revealed in terms of their ordinariness, their 'like us' qualities. It will be argued that the stories constituting the 'other news' operate, not as a set of randomly selected 'lighter items' scattered through the news broadcast merely for the purposes of pacing, sensationalism, relief, exoticism or happy endings, but form the basis of a particular ideological 'field' which is constituted as an organized structure of 'associated meaning'. This structure forms a type of sub-system in the news broadcast, having its own internal coherence and order of relevance and offering a series of important nodal points for recognition and identification through which consent is potentially secured.

One view of ideology suggests that it works by and through 'interpellation', that is, a process whereby the individual is 'hailed' or addressed as a subject (Althusser 1971: 160). There are a number of ways that interpellation might be at work in television news. The direct address of the newsreader who speaks to 'us' is the most obvious. The 'other news' can be seen to be accomplishing something similar. This type of news seems to be constructed out of a consistent reference to 'the ordinary'. The mundane, the world of everyday life is the baseline from which 'other news' occurrences gain newsworthiness: the fire occurs in an ordinary house; the flood submerges an ordinary suburb; the explosion happens in an ordinary hospital; the star has ordinary doubts about his abilities. Located in the everyday world ourselves, this kind of emphasis 'calls us out' as subjects in a relation of equivalence which asserts that 'we' all share more or less the same fundamental conditions of existence, a mutuality of 'being' in the world.[1] If there is a sense that the television news is exclusively about the opinions and actions of the powerful, there is another in which it can be seen to 'make room' for 'us' via our proxies in the 'other news'. This space which opens up interpellates us into the news so that, even if most coverage seems remote or irrelevant, there is still an assurance granted: despite our ordinariness, 'we' have a position in the unfolding scheme of things. Rather than distracting audiences away from 'more important' issues, as Nordenstreng (1972) contends, the 'other news' paves a way into the news discourse where those important issues reside, functioning not to trivialize the serious news, but instead to act as an identificatory wedge into it.

PROFILING THE 'OTHER NEWS'

To start with, it was important to firmly establish the range and consistency of the 'other news' across television news bulletins. A sample of news programmes was assembled from broadcast material simultaneously recorded off-air from the four major Melbourne television channels over a total of four different time periods – Week I: 29 May – 2 June 1978; Week II: 14 – 18 May 1979; Week III: 12 – 16 November 1979 and Week IV: 3 – 6 July 1990.[2] The first three weeks of news were used as the major data for the analysis and the fourth week served primarily as comparative material. It was decided to include only the early evening news service as this is the one most regularly watched by the largest number of people (Windschuttle 1984; Tiffen 1989). This bulletin also tends to draw substantial resources and funding as it is frequently defined by station programmers as a way to draw an audience for the rest of the night's viewing (Sperry 1976). Weekday bulletins were chosen as the focus since they contain more news and feature the channel's regular, identifiable newsreader 'personality', whereas bulletins at the weekend tend to carry more sport oriented reports and are 'anchored' by irregular presenters. Three channels had a half hour news bulletin, Channels 7 and 9 between 6.30p.m. and 7p.m. and Channel 2 between 7p.m. and 7.30p.m., the Channel 0 broadcast ran for one hour between 6p.m. and 7p.m. Channels 7, 9 and 0 are part of commercial networks, while Channel 2 is a federally funded and operated public broadcaster similar to the BBC.

The time period of this off-air material may seem a little puzzling; the sample, some might say, should have more immediacy, especially given that the subject of the study is the news. Eagleton (1983) however reminds us that:

> it is not a matter of starting from certain theoretical or methodological problems: it is a matter of starting from what we want to *do*, and then seeing which methods and theories will best help us to achieve these ends. . . . What we choose and reject . . . depends upon what you are practically trying to do . . .
>
> (Eagleton 1983: 210–11; original emphasis)

Given that this study of television's 'other news' is starting from the forlorn prognostications of what has been called the lament for broadcast news and that these have been heard for some years, a sample of broadcasts with less recency may actually be advantageous in confronting the historical *embeddedness* of this type of news, something which Curran and Sparks (1991: 215) acknowledge has always been difficult to achieve with news research customarily preoccupied by 'overtly political content'. The sheer volume of disreputable news in the sample will show that this type of news could be ignored only through a particular kind of 'astigmatic perspective' (Curran and Sparks 1991: 215). It might also be suggested that although the material may seem a little creaky at first glance, in television news terms it is not. The

31

orientations of broadcast journalism have both changed and not changed at all: there may be more current affairs shows, more reality television programmes, more docu-dramas and a relative increase in global reporting, but the early evening news, at least in the Australian context, has remained remarkably unaltered. Graphics are restylized, pacing and editing quickened, more commercial breaks inserted, but in terms of format structure, story selection, conditions of narrativity, use of visuals and mode of address, the shape of coverage and its preoccupations are recognizable and familiar from then to now. (One channel still retains the same newsreader.) The lesson seems to be that if the major bulletin is altered too much its ability to speak authoritatively about the events of the day is also altered. Conventionalism in broadcast news is steadfast and durable. The requisite continuity governed by conventionalism also provides the opportunity to examine the way that the 'other news' may be connected to what are being described as new 'reality' forms of broadcast journalism. For example, as one recent manifestation 'tabloid television' is often unproblematically regarded as a direct descendent of the tabloid newspaper (Knight 1989; Lumby and O'Neill 1994) and clearly there is a linkage at work here. But if Gitlin (1985) is correct in describing television as primarily a 'recombinant discourse' motivated by production values and signifying practices which seek to reproduce themselves by way of models already pre-tested and proven in the field, it could also be argued that much of the coverage which qualifies as 'other news', an already constituted and historically regenerating part of the regular and ongoing concerns of television journalism, provides a comparably solid basis from which to produce 'new news' programming genres (Sternberg 1995: 43). Using a sample which is somewhat removed from the immediate present may provide a special opportunity to assess these connections.

Locating and classifying 'other news' stories for detailed analysis required a second step – the 'disaggregation' (Brunsdon and Morley 1978: 39) of each bulletin into individual reports in order to select out the 'main news' items. Although the broadcast as a whole is described as 'news', a good proportion of time is actually taken up by items which would not conventionally be defined as news stories. A thirty-minute news bulletin on a commercial station in Australia can contain as little as seventeen minutes worth of news (Bonney and Wilson 1983: 289). When title sequences, headlines, teasers ('coming up after the break . . . '), advertisements, sport, weather, sign offs, end credits and feature current affairs stories with longer running times were excluded, in the sample of seventy broadcasts there was a total of 994 news stories. These were sorted in order to select out all items which could qualify as 'other news'. Initially this was done on the basis of a story's manifest content with a view to include all the types of news stories which the lament would regard as unworthy journalism. Items about fires, accidents, beauty contests, celebrities, peculiar occupations and hobbies, those 'trivialities' which take audiences away from 'intellectual activation', were all considered to be part of the 'other news'. Stories were also selected if they had correspondence to what Hughes (1968: 184–216), in her work on the human interest story, describes as the 'perennials', relatively self-contained news narratives with little in the way of 'quickening urgency' but noteworthy for certain recurrent themes: 'curiosities and mysteries', 'life's little ironies', 'changes of fortune', 'lost children' and 'romantic adventure'. Further story inclusions were made on the basis of Barthes' account (1977a) of a type of news item in the French press known as the *fait-divers* (sometimes translated as 'filler', or perhaps in the vocabulary of the lament, 'trivialities'). Similar to the human interest story the *fait-divers* exists as a form of 'total news' where everything required for sense-making is provided in the moment of telling. This closed structure, requiring no reference to 'an extensive situation outside itself, previous to and around it' is unlike conventional news according to Barthes (1977a: 190–2), and constitutes the *fait-divers* as a kind of 'literature', especially adept at presenting tales of discontinuity shaped by surprise, coincidence and illogicality: 'A train is derailed in Alaska: a stag tripped the switch'; 'the same diamond brooch is stolen three times'; 'Iceland fishermen net a cow'. In its usage here as a conceptual category however, the 'other news' does not just reiterate the parameters of the human interest story or the *fait-divers* but includes coverage which journalistically would be defined as 'hard news' (Tuchman 1973). For example, the story of a fire in a small Australian country town which takes the lives of five of a seven-member family may have human interest on the level of 'changes of fortune', but it also makes its appearance as the major news report of the day, coming first in the evening's line-up on all four channels. Such prominence would qualify this story as 'big news' (Hughes 1968: 67–8). From the point of view of the lament, however, this attention is just the kind of wayward prioritizing which leads broadcast journalism down the road to ruin.

Certain exclusions were also applied in the selection process, starting with the lament and what it might define as 'important' news. This meant not only disregarding coverage of events related to party politics, governmental action, industrial relations, international affairs but also stories which could be situated in the context of social problems – unemployment, race relations, illegal drug use, the environment. A very small number of exceptions were made where the 'angle' of the story appeared to be in the direction of human interest. Thus, an item about the Premier of New South Wales was not omitted even though it was a report which focused on a key figure in Australian state politics, since its major (indeed only) emphasis was his unexpected involvement in an airplane 'mishap'. Crime news was also excluded from the pool of 'other news' even though these types of stories are generally cited as one of the major contributions to the degradation of television journalism. This decision was made primarily because news about crime and law and order issues had been dealt with thoroughly in several different research contexts,[3] but where a story's manifest content was framed primarily in terms

33

of human interest – 'the toll of human suffering' – rather than the crime itself it was categorized as part of the 'other news'. Mostly, this meant excluding stories concerned with occurrences like murders and robberies. Had crime news been included, the proportion of time occupied by the 'other news' would have increased dramatically, especially on the commercial channels.

Out of a total of 994 news items in the sample broadcasts, 341 were classified as 'other news' (34.3 per cent of all news stories). When the time taken up in the sample bulletins by 'other news' stories was calculated as a proportion of the time given over to all news items, nearly one third (30.6 per cent) of early evening news time on all channels, on average, was taken up with the 'other news' (see Appendix, Table 1). The highest proportion of news time taken by the 'other news' occurred on Channel 9 with 42.8 per cent, Channel 0 followed with an average 32.8 per cent while Channel 7 had 30.5 per cent. The bulletins on the commercial channels (7, 9, 0) appear to have more than double (35.3 per cent) the amount of time allocated to this type of news compared to the public channel (16.2 per cent; see Appendix, Table 1). On some days the proportion of time allocated to the 'other news' was strikingly high, even without the inclusion of crime news. From Table 3 (see Appendix) it can be seen that in Week I, on day 5, Channel 9 had 61.1 per cent of its news time devoted to the 'other news', and in Week II, on day 5, 63.6 per cent. In Week II Channel 7, on day 3, had 54.5 per cent of news time allocated to 'other news' items. Between 1979 and 1990 the amount of time given over to the 'other news' stayed remarkably constant.

STORY-TYPES

In her discussion of the 'perennial' quality of the human interest story Hughes (1968) observes: 'topics that made "good ones" are just the topics that have made "good ones" in the past and have become traditional'. To appreciate this process however requires that news stories be acknowledged as 'represent[ing] types and that, while every day's news is fresh, there are essential likenesses and repetitions' (Hughes 1968: 209). Over time the operation of the 'type' becomes progressively paradigmatic and autonomous with its own internal logic, thematic predispositions and syntax. A final classificatory procedure involved grouping the selected 'other news' items into more generalized categories based on the notion of a story-type. The operation of the type might be accorded a similar kind of status to that identified in discussions of film genre. In relation to popular cinema, Alloway (1971: 60) explains:

> It is always the schematic parts, the symmetrical plots, the characters known beforehand and their geometrical relationships that characterize the movies. . . . A convention is always dominant, the extent to which

movies as mass art accords with the accepted manner, model or tradition is the extent to which it will reach its audience.

Like a film genre, news story-types characteristically utilize patterns/forms/ styles/structures which transcend individual reports and supervise both their construction and their 'reading' by the audience (Ryall 1975). Knowledge of the generic elements of perennial stories enables television journalists to produce accounts of occurrences as news for various audiences – editors, viewers, sources – as well as to produce copy and images rapidly within accepted codes of presentation. Conversely, organizing journalistic production along generic lines ensures that audience expectations are met and the means by which to 'read' a story are provided routinely and systematically. To facilitate the aggregation of stories into types reference was also made to an item's 'dominant form of thematisation' (Brunsdon and Morley 1978: 39) which was a way of proceeding beyond manifest content – what the story was about – to account for the presence or absence of certain 'propositions' or assumptions of a more abstract or 'latent' kind.

Assigning the 'other news' to a range of story-types was a way to establish a 'basic structure of discourse' (Brunsdon and Morley 1978: 40) which could run across the reporting of numerous, seemingly disparate, events over time. From these selection and classification procedures emerged the major story-types around which the textual formation of 'other news' is built.

1 *The especially remarkable*:   This story-type included news items specifically concerned with scrutinizing or providing 'up-dates' on the comings and goings, the doings, sayings and way of life of institutional and celebrity élites or, with presenting the 'triumphs' and achievements of ordinary people.

2 *Victims*:   The central focus of this story-type was on individuals caught up in untoward and often uncontrollable circumstances which bring radical dislocation to the procedures and routines of everyday life. The emphasis in such stories was regularly narrated through a focus on relatively well defined 'characters' and often inflected through some reference to 'personal tragedy'.

3 *Community at risk*:   This story-type was based on reports where the forms of disruption and disorder were played out at a collective rather than individual level. Impact is swift, preparedness is minimal and the results produce unanticipated, often inexplicable, turmoil.

4 *Ritual, tradition and the past*:   This story-type gained its contours from items focused on community-based observances or commemorations, and more generally, on notions of social memory manifested in the remembrance of past deeds and historical moments.

FINDING A METHOD

In order to account for the generic patterns and modes of thematization in particular story-types and how these may be connected to certain ideological domains, it was important to go further than a conventional content analysis might allow, in order to attend to the 'message form [as] a determinate moment' (Hall 1980) in the organization of meaning in the 'other news'. Proceeding from a methodology interested in examining stylistics and 'rhetorics' of representation, news stories were approached semiotically as cultural 'texts: literary and visual constructs employing symbolic means, shaped by rules, conventions and traditions intrinsic to the use of language in its widest sense' (Hall 1975: 17). In addition to preserving some of the complexity of meaning and providing a sensitivity towards unnoticed, perhaps unconscious processes of news-making, both of which are often lost in content analysis, interrogation of 'other news' stories in these terms offered a way to emphasize how 'the ideological', through specific journalistic practices, comes to have material existence (Curran, Gurevitch and Woollacott 1982: 24). As Belsey (1980: 5) explains, ideology 'is inscribed in discourse in the sense that it is literally written or spoken in it: it is not a separate element which exists independently in some free-floating realm of "ideas" and is subsequently embodied in words, but a way of thinking, speaking, experiencing'.

Subscribing to 'literary–critical linguistic and stylistic methods of analysis' does not, however, negate the search for 'recurrence' as an indicator of significance. It is still important for the analyst 'to "hear" the same underlying appeals, the same "notes", being sounded . . . in different passages and contexts . . . taken as pointers to latent meanings from which inferences as to the source can be drawn' (Hall 1975: 15). Given the large amount of material being handled an investigative focus on recurrent patterns of textual organization, both visual and aural, seemed to be a practical place to start. Yet recurrence cannot be taken as the only clue to significance. Important textual features may not be the ones continually reappearing but those which stand out as the exception in the general pattern by way of position, placement, tone, intensification or imagery (Hall 1975: 15). To 'examine the conditions of textual meaning' (Goldman and Rajagopal 1991: 33) the news stories under consideration were approached by way of four signifying registers – image, language usage, narrative modes, and textual address.

News film

Among the pre-eminent signs of television news are its photographed images of events 'in the real world'. These visual signs operate with a good deal of iconicity, that is, the visual image appears to resemble its subject matter in a rather close way. The image of the picketer with the placard seems to 'resemble' a person engaged in standing outside the gate of the closed plant. Barthes (1977b: 36) describes photography as a 'message without a code'. The image seems to select itself and be capable of communication without mediation. As Hall (1973b: 188) explains, the image offers itself, especially in news discourse which makes claims for objectivity and neutrality, as the 'witness to the *actuality* of the event' and carries an implicit inscription that 'this event really happened and this photo is the proof of it'. When a report can include participants observed in the event, the image draws on what Brunsdon and Morley (1978: 87) call its 'being-thereness', which additionally encourages the notion of 'direct perception'. However, the 'choice of *this* moment of the event as against that, of *this* person rather than that, of *this* angle rather than any other, indeed, the selection of this photographed incident to represent a whole complex chain of events and meanings, is a highly ideological procedure, (Hall 1973b: 188; original emphasis).

In this context a semiotic approach sees 'the real' as it is constituted in news as the effect of a set of signifying practices: 'The natural and social world does not consist of objects, forces or events which exist ... in a state where their identity and characteristics are intrinsic to their nature and self-evident' (Hartley 1982: 12). Meaning is not simply caught and relayed by the 'technical' capacity to produce the image, but constructed by it. Now a whole range of codes of constructedness are revealed to be at work: framing, composition, lighting, focus, angle, camera movement and proximity (see Monaco 1977: 142–80). Investigation of the television news image requires a model which can point to its 'orders of signification' (Fiske 1982: 90) – a denotative level where the sign–image appears simply to designate that to which it refers; a connotative level where 'additional implied meanings' are derived from the repertoire of representational strategies which circulate as a cultural stock of knowledge at hand (Hall 1973b: 184); and a mythic level in which the sign–image begins to order and classify the world into conceptual categories (Hartley 1982: 28). It is the mythic 'order of meaning' of the photographic sign–image, especially, which can be used to investigate the discursive elaborations of ideology (Hall 1973b).

Television news, of course, does not rely on single photographs but on combinations of moving images produced in sequences. These 'news film' sequences, according to the Glasgow University Media Group (1976: 29), are typically composed of shots which 'do not directly relate to one another in the ways we are used to from the feature cinema'. In these instances news film might be said to work something like the 'descriptive syntagm', a term used by Metz (1974: 127) to designate a filmic sequence where relatively unconnected images are pulled together in a visual ensemble in order to offer some generalized sense of an event. While the determinations of news images and their sequentialization can be governed by a non-cinematic visual logic, it is important not to overstate the case. Certainly, as the Glasgow University Media Group (1980: 333) claim, the matched cut is rare but other filmically inspired devices seem to be in use which do create a visual continuity of action, coherent spacial arrangements and a sense of chronology – the shot/reverse shot in interview sequences, establishing wide shots during on-location reports, and the use of light to create atmosphere are just some examples (see Bordwell and Thompson 1979). Television news film may not have the 'seamless' quality of the classic Hollywood cinema but it does contain several other of its characteristics.

The argument about the non-cinematic use of images in television news frequently rests on the assumption that the performative capacity of news speech and commentary, oriented to a 'journalistic logic', always overwhelms the image, binding it to the verbal register as 'the dominant carrier of meaning' (Glasgow University Media Group 1980: 347). 'News talk' is seen as the privileged signifying site which anchors images to a preferred reading. Barthes (1977b: 26) suggests, however, that photographic images under certain circumstances can also manage to produce meaning on their own so that if there is an accompanying linguistic text, it becomes 'only a kind of secondary vibration, almost without consequence'. The relative autonomy of news images to produce meaning might be explained through the notion of the 'condensation symbol' (Graber 1976; Edelman 1964). Journalism's perceived need to facilitate audience understanding by framing new occurrences in terms of familiar and already constituted sense-making strategies and the sheer pressure of time (see Schlesinger 1978) results in the utilization of recurring sets of 'stable images' (Epstein 1973: 5). These crystallize and become self-perpetuating so that selected and rehearsed visual signs from past stories control the patterns of visual representation in subsequent reports, a process somewhat similar to the use of the iconographical codes in Hollywood film genres. With the capacity to be evocative and supply shorthand categorizations the condensation symbol operates as a highly economical form of visual communication which can codify events without complete reliance on language – precisely what television journalists need to have available in order to produce a steady, routinized, intelligible flow of news in a hurry. Situating and commenting on such condensation symbols will be important for a discussion of the generic properties of the story-types which make up the 'other news'.

News talk

Like news film, news talk is the result of sets of choices and combinations through which events are made meaningful and can also be implicated in various orders of signification. News talk does not simply reflect or express the world, but is active in its reconstitution. Eagleton (1983: 60) explains that 'it is not as though we have meanings, or experiences, which we then proceed to cloak with words; we can only have these meanings and experiences in the first place because we have a language to have them in'. The codes that govern the production of news talk provide 'contexts of interpretation' (Bell, Boehringer and Crofts 1982: 6) where the ideological is played out. Kress and Hodge (1979) explain this very succinctly:

> a reporter may witness an event and then be faced with the choice of calling it a 'demonstration' (or a 'demo'), a 'riot', a 'street battle', 'war on the streets', a 'confrontation', or so on. As he writes his report in whole sentences he needs to make the further selections of verbs (representing the actions) and other attendant circumstances (other people involved, effect of the actions, place where it happened). So the reporter might choose 'demonstrators confront police' or 'police confront demonstrators' . . . ; 'police disperse rioters' or 'riot disperses'. . . . These initial selections are crucial, for they set the limits within which any ensuing debate or thinking of reworking of 'reality' takes place.
>
> (Kress and Hodge 1979: 15)

What are seen to be issues of technical journalistic competence to write news copy about occurrences defined as newsworthy – sedimented, habitual and taken-for-granted – are on another level ways by which news talk codifies the real in particular ways.

The language that television news utilizes to discuss and describe occurrences is a specialized and ritualized form of speech. Compressed and foreshortened (Tuchman 1978), it is also characterized by the narrow range of words, phrases and descriptions which make up the 'vocabulary' used in particular types of stories. The Glasgow University Media Group (1980: 166,170), for example, demonstrate that the usage of 'key words' in the coverage of industrial disputes is severely restricted and despite broadcasters claims to neutrality, language tends to be aligned with a particular managerial perspective. The regular appearance of such key words might be regarded as a linguistic version of the condensation symbol. Instantly recognizable and evocative, offering immediate classifications and evaluations, eminently suitable for journalists searching for a shorthand way to provide intelligible reports quickly on a routine basis, key words – and indeed phrases and descriptions – are clearly an important part of the way that television news conveys meaning about events.

News as story

Approaching news as a 'cultural discourse' means being attentive to the claim by journalists that what they do is search for 'good stories'. Although it has been increasingly recognized that both print and broadcast journalists are engaged, to a greater or lesser extent, in the production of news as stories (see Bird and Dardenne 1988) there has actually been little in the way of examining at close range what these stories are – their 'story-ness', to use an awkward term – or how they might be organized and structured.

Darnton (1975) observes that becoming a journalist is not just a process of learning about institutional structures, work routines or peer group and editorial expectations, but requires learning to write in a particular way and according to specified narrative possibilities. Story forms themselves are as much an organizational socializing agent as any on the job training in the workplace. If news is produced by situating emergent occurrences in already pre-established structures of intelligibility, Darnton argues that pre-existing story-making structures are crucial for this process and need to be examined in their own right. In this context the lament is correct – broadcast news *is* formulaic; but rather than dismissing such formulae as symptomatic of a corrupted and wayward journalism it might pay to examine these story forms in order to better understand their appeal and survival as news. Adapting the analysis done by Propp (1968) on the morphology of the folk tale and the syntactic model of narrative proposed by Todorov (1970, 1977) the 'other news' will be examined in order to demonstrate how narrative construction can bind together certain patterned thematic pre-occupations which occur in specific story-types, and to show the way that the 'other news' as a form of story-telling might produce positions of identification and pleasure.

Positioning

It has been argued that media texts 'situate' us as spectators/subjects through a variety of operations, 'offering us positions from which we are invited to see experience in particular ways' (Masterman 1985: 229). In the case of television news, for example, Connell (1979) suggests that the audience is alternately positioned in relation to 'the mode of vision' – the direct address and gaze of newsreader and reporter and the indirect line of vision of the interviewee–protagonists bracketed 'into' the news item creates the possibility of involvement and detachment in relation to reported events. The 'public idiom' used by the language of news to 'translate' the opinions of the powerful positions to us as 'people of ordinary common sense'. The linking and framing 'metalanguage' of the presenter in current affairs programmes, delivered in direct address, positions us to use this metalanguage as the point of 'truth' from which all other appropriated, external realities and voices are compared (Brunsdon and Morley 1978: 61). For some theorists of representation it is important to recognize that the spaces we are invited to occupy are linked to the operations of ideology which 'as it were, "calls us" to itself, presents us with its picture and invites us to recognize ourselves in this picture as if the picture were in fact a mirror' (Burgin in Bourne 1981: 50). The mechanics of ideology at this level are crucial for the winning of consent.

Typically, the issue of positioning as it pertains to television news is discussed in terms of broad textual features and formal structures. It might also prove useful to have an approach which could take account of possible diversity and specificity in story 'contents' and story 'forms' recognizing that on certain levels not all news stories operate to position the subject in exactly the same manner. Compared with what the lament would define as serious news, the 'other news' seems to have an important distinguishing feature: a massive investment in the everyday, the notional, the taken-for-granted. Trafficking in the small change of the everyday world, the 'other news' positions us with an invitation to recognize our likeness in its stories. When ordinary routines are reported destroyed or the everyday world is shown turned on its head, literally and figuratively, we are 'hailed' by these stories partly because of the newsworthiness of the event, but perhaps more significantly because we *do* recognize the routine, the everyday, the community, the family, the children, the suburb, the bedroom, the school notebook and so on. These stories, in this sense, address us with a 'what if . . . ' proposition, into which we can readily insert ourselves 'there'. It may be particularly important then to be examining the devices, strategies and tactics used to produce 'the everyday' which allows for the construction of these equivalences, recognitions and identifications.

THE ACT OF READING CRITICALLY WITH ONE'S OWN EYES (AND EARS)

An investigation of television news as an ideological 'apparatus' using critical reading as the privileged moment of analysis inevitably raises questions about the adequacy of such a method and the analytical status of the 'object' under scrutiny. Although it can be claimed that the 'encoded' message form is a particularly important point from which to begin investigation, media research more recently has stressed the conditions of reception and the act of 'decoding' as the primary site of meaning production. Hartley (1982: 148) reminds us that simply because the 'same' news is televised it does not follow that the same meaning and understanding is taken from the message. Viewers' readerly competencies and cultural capital are differentiated by such factors as class, gender, ethnicity, race, age, subculture and nationality so that the conditions of 'social subjectivity' brought to the text may not correspond to the constructed subjectivity 'inscribed' in and offered by the text. This discrepancy, according to some, points the way for recognizing the ability of the reader to evade or renegotiate the 'semiotic power' of the television text (Fiske 1987). From here, the notion of the autonomy of the audience is sometimes extended even further into claims about the 'polysemic' quality of media texts and the corollary – that the meanings derived from such texts are ones that viewers are able to produce themselves. Ironically, it has been this latter view, perhaps more than any other, which has been instrumental in a

41

reassessment of critical reading as a valid and necessary procedure. Recent work on the process of decoding has shown that to rely exclusively on a text-based analysis is to offer a truncated version of how meaning is culturally produced and received. Yet it is also important to avoid the overly optimistic assumption that texts are completely open, like 'an imaginary shopping mall in which audience members [can] wander at will, selecting whatever suits them' (Murdock in Morley 1992: 31). If it is taken as a contemporary given that the 'mass media are not only one of the major sources of information about society but also one of the key sources for interpretive frameworks, too' (Curran and Sparks 1991: 227), detailed attention to the textual production of meaning in the service of power seems an indispensable methodological requirement.[4] However, 'message oriented' analysis is clearly only one of a number of possible research directions that could be followed regarding the 'other news'. In the best of all possible analytical worlds, the conditions of production, representation, circulation and reception would be included in order to facilitate a comprehensive investigation; however, as this book is attempting to situate relatively untried ways of looking at a relatively under-scrutinized type of news, a text-based methodology might potentially serve as the first step for further non-textual investigative excursions.

There are no claims being made here that a critical reading is the key to unlock the intentions of news makers as 'author'. The capacity to locate these is a notoriously slippery affair especially if the cultural artefact is collectively produced. As Hartley (1982: 83) explains, when journalists are accused, as they frequently are, of the 'rough handling' of events, it is the result not of personal factors which is the easily assimilable explanation but of 'the impersonal social process of newsmaking itself, as a professional practice . . . the routine mental orientations shared in a necessarily unreflecting way by busy people'. Assumptions, premises and pre-conditions which permit and sustain such routine orientations, however, might be 'made legible' through a critical reading of news stories as texts. This kind of reading also needs to be separated from what an audience decoding might look like; and, in some sense, it could be argued that 'acts of textual dissembly' (Goldman and Rajagopal 1991: 34) are actively worked against by the way that television news tries to position its 'reader', in terms of such journalistic imperatives as immediacy, authority, impartiality, accuracy, comprehensiveness and the desire to produce 'good television'. This is not to suggest, however, that the text simply works its ideological propositions on audiences unimpeded, as a 'perfect transmission'. It follows that at some point in a more general investigation of the 'other news' the moment of decoding has to be inserted into the research.

Still, there is the persistent 'issue of proof' (Hoggart 1979: viii). In reference to Erving Goffman's essay on advertising Hoggart (1979: viii) explains that the act of reading critically – 'the interpretation of meanings', to use his phrase – always confronts the possibility of alternative readings: '[t]hese would not necessarily be conflicting interpretations; they may be parts of compatible multiple interpretations. For any cluster of material there may be a great number of coherent patterns; and all may be in certain senses "true"'. To offer one reading as significant, to assert its importance in relation to other possible readings means to build up in the analysis what Hoggart calls 'a kind of "convincingness"'. Ultimately assessment related to the issue of proof may reside here. The way to convincingness is not in some final subscription to 'truth', but in the construction of a reading which is grounded and consistent.

There is another way to view this problem – from the tenets of a semiotic practice. As an analytical method semiotics argues that texts are always multi-accentual, never finally fixed; meaning is slippery and fluid, although certain discourses regularly seek to 'close' pluralizing possibilities. The message–text 'operates a continuing "multi-order" system of signification which moves from level to level, its denotations becoming connotations in a kind of infinite progression. As a result, we never arrive at a "final" "decoding" or "reading" . . . ' (Hawkes 1977: 142). Critical reading then is never replete and finished. Assessing an analysis, like this one on the 'other news' cannot be based on some notion of the search for, and successful/ unsuccessful discovery of, some pre-ordained core content in these stories which, with enough digging below the surface, is finally revealed. What follows then is *one* critical reading which utilizes a certain degree of rigour and evidence, offering a way both to understand the shape and structure of 'other news' story-types and to situate a politics imbedded in this ostensibly non-political news.

One final comment needs to be made before moving to the substantive sections of the study. Stated baldly, no matter what battery of methodological or theoretical tools is brought to the site of the text, the act of critically reading with one's own eyes and ears requires a leap of speculation – informed speculation, but speculation nonetheless. At a time when media studies has gone some considerable way towards dispelling accusations (at least in some quarters) of idiosyncratic conjecture in its textual readings and has established itself as a codified 'discipline' with discernible methodologies (see Berger 1991; Jensen and Jankowski 1991), this assertion may seem retrograde. Yet there is an important issue at stake: the relationship of the critical reader to the text and to the analysis attempted. Semiotics argues for imminence – texts contain in themselves the relations that need to be deciphered and this deciphering work always has to be done first (Burgelin 1972). Even if this were the case, and some might suggest otherwise (see Eco 1979), the critical reader/analyst still needs to mull and muse over where to make the first 'incision', where and how best to 'carve' a space into that text, to allow for 'probing'.[5]

At the end of his book on news Hartley (1982) has some advice about how to move from the position of news consumer to news critic.

Whilst there is little choice in the texts you're offered to read, you can choose several different ways of reading them. . . . For example, you can concentrate in turn on the way the news text is made to 'make sense'; on the ideological meanings it promotes; and on its appeal to your desire and pleasure.

(Hartley 1982: 154)

His comments are interesting because he presupposes sets of choices to be made about how to engage analytically with the news. The choices are framed within a particular paradigm but their application is filtered through speculation about where they might best be used. This is not a mechanical or 'scientific' process but one based on supposition, contemplation, testing, refining and so on. The capacity to accomplish this however, does not amount to an argument for the 'creativity' of the author, for clearly authors, even analytical ones, are positioned within discourses that have their own codes and ways of representation, but rather for the recognition that the act of critical reading, however objectivated by its methodology, has to also be contextualized in terms of certain speculations, disciplined and intuitive at the same time.

4

THE ESPECIALLY REMARKABLE

In his account of the social and historical conditions which give rise to the 'phenomena of stars' Francesco Alberoni (1972: 75) observed that in 'every society are to be found persons who, in the eyes of other members of the collectivity, are especially remarkable and who attract universal attention'. Typically, according to Alberoni, this applies to those 'who hold power (political, economic, religious)' but one also finds others 'whose institutional power is very limited or non-existent, but whose doings and way of life arouse considerable and sometimes even a maximum degree of interest'. This latter group constitutes what Alberoni describes as a 'powerless élite' which includes not just the stars of cinema but 'idols', 'champions' and 'divas'. If this formulation is used as a starting point for mapping the contours of this story-type it is clear that a significant number of 'other news' stories in the broadcast sample weeks had a very specific focus on the 'doings and way of life' of people who could qualify as 'especially remarkable'. Although there appeared to be a substantial diversity of individuals covered in these news reports, it will be argued that all these cases should be located as part of what Monaco (1978: 10) calls the 'calculus of celebrityhood', television journalism, as it were, factoring in its own particular equation, and facilitating, through the use of its own specialized methodology, the broader 'process by which fame is manufactured' (Boorstin 1963: 57).

According to Chibnall (1977: 27) because celebrity is increasingly the focus of the mass media, the news itself has been obliged to recognize and promote the cult of the star and while the serious news may do this indirectly, so that 'politics becomes a gladiatorial spectacle in which the conflict of policies is reduced to the clash of personalities', the 'other news', less constrained by obligations to report pressing or weighty matters, can construct élites, political or otherwise, as especially remarkable simply by featuring them in terms of their 'doings and way of life'. For example, in the broadcasts collected there were a substantial number of stories dealing with élite 'persons' who ostensibly did have some type of institutional power, but rather than being a major focus of the report, as might be the case in the serious news, this institutional power served merely as a backdrop. These stories were concerned with élites not in their roles as power brokers or decision makers but with informal activities, publicly ritualized displays of attention and 'private lives' (Lowenthal 1961: 118). A 'powerless élite' was also the focus of considerable 'other news' coverage: television personalities, theatrical performers, sporting champions, fashion designers, pop music stars, Hollywood directors, bon vivants, all of whom would, in Alberoni's terms, have little in the way of conventional institutional power but still qualify as 'especially remarkable' with the capacity to arouse a considerable 'degree of interest'.

A calculus of celebrity is relatively flexible and can be operationalized 'down' as well as 'up', in the direction of those who have neither power in an institutional sense nor any kind of élite standing as celebrities but who, through specific personal achievements – their doings rather than their way of life – gain an appearance in the news, and concomitantly considerable, albeit fleeting public attention. Here, the 'other news' may be engaged in promoting the actualization of Andy Warhol's utopian/dysutopian vision: a future where everyone would be famous, for fifteen minutes. In his discussion of 'symbolic leaders' Klapp (1964) provides some sense of what this vision might entail in an American, but increasingly a more globalized context.

> The chance of becoming famous might be called the great . . . jackpot. To be a celebrity, to appear on television, to be applauded . . . that is the warm and not-so-secret dreams of countless Americans in a society that is becoming more and more an audience directed by mass communication. And . . . it may be hard to avoid the impression that almost any kind of person can be a celebrity.
>
> (Klapp 1964: 26)

Reports on ordinary people as manifested in this story-type help to cultivate this impression – that becoming celebrated is a state of affairs virtually accessible to everyone. Indeed, some have suggested that the traditional version of mobility and success in an 'open society', once so closely associated and measured within terms that might have been economic or social, is now increasingly implicated in and 'ratified by publicity' (Lasch 1979: 60). In his commentary on the 'society of the spectacle' Guy Dubord (1983) suggests the historical development of this process, which may help to explain where coverage of the especially remarkable in the 'other news' on television might fit.

> The first phase of the domination of the economy over social life brought into the definition . . . the obvious degradation of *being* into *having*. The present phase . . . leads to a generalized sliding of *having* into *appearing*, from which all actual 'having' must draw its immediate prestige and its ultimate function.
>
> (Dubord 1983: 17; original emphasis)

46

The emphasis in this last cluster of stories needs to be seen not just in terms of how seemingly quite *un*remarkable people become remarkable, performing deeds of distinction, but how this process is inexorably 'ratified' by (news) publicity – in the present phase having distinction means 'appearing' with it and generating a maximum degree of interest.

NEWS VALUES

Hall (1973b: 183) points out that the news is constantly presenting the actions, situations and attributes of 'élite persons': 'the prestigious are part of the necessary spectacle of news production – they people and stabilize its environment'. According to Galtung and Ruge (1973: 66) there is a structure of access to news which is élite-centred and 'the more the event concerns élite people, the more probable that it become a news item'. Because the focus on élites is such a standard news gathering practice, élites become 'naturally newsworthy' simply for their 'very-being-as-they-are' (Hall 1973b: 183). Their place and status in the news comes from a place and status which is already defined elsewhere as part of other contexts – social, political, economic, and even in relation to a prior 'place' in the media discourse itself (well known for their well known-ness). In part then, the doings and way of life of such élites arouse a 'degree of interest' precisely because of these prior, established contexts – their already-known-ness as élites makes them qualify as especially remarkable anterior to the 'other news' story. The 'other news' report acts both to reconfirm these qualities and, on another level, to present the most recent occurrence where these qualities are put on display.

Elites featured in two ways in this story-type. There were items which dealt with what, in terms of Alberoni's framework, would be examples of attention given to individuals by virtue of their institutional power, but in each case it was not this power which was the concern of the coverage. Instead these were stories about Prince Rainier of Monaco 'contemplating the purchase of the Premier Rose, the richest diamond in modern history' for 'the wedding finger of Princess Caroline'; the announcement of the marriage of the Queen's cousin Prince Michael of Kent to a 'Roman Catholic Baroness' after receiving 'a special dispensation from the Pope to marry in church'; the Queen 'spend[ing] a quiet weekend' celebrating 'the twenty-fifth anniversary of her coronation'; 'the Queen and Prince Phillip mak[ing] the most of an informal tour of Denmark'; the visit to Australia of 'the Dutch royal couple, Princess Beatrix and Prince Klauss'. There were also a considerable number of stories across the sample bulletins centred on those others who for Alberoni would be part of a powerless élite, having limited institutional influence in a formal sense but still capable of generating 'a maximum degree of interest'. Connected with the culture industry, the sporting world and life-style markets, these especially remarkable persons could easily be located as the 'other news' descendants of the 'idols of consumption' uncovered by Lowenthal (1961: 115) in his study of American magazine biographies where 'almost everyone . . . is directly, or indirectly, related to the sphere of leisure time': 'The English comedian Ronnie Corbett arriv[es] in Sydney . . . to star in a show with his long time partner Ronnie Barker'; 'former Australian cricket captain Graham Yallop . . . launch[es] his book'; Australian 'actor Reg Livermore, star of . . . outrageous box office hits promot[es] his new one man act'; 'That famous British designer of tennis outfits, Teddy Tingling' whose 'clientele includes Billie Jean King . . . releas[es] . . . his latest summer collection'; champion [Australian] marathoner Tony Rafferty is 'off and running again . . . to set a new one thousand mile record'; 'Francis Ford Coppola, the man who made *The Godfather*, the movie that scooped the Academy Awards, arriv[es] in Sydney . . . to promote his thirty two million dollar epic, *Apocalypse Now*'; 'England's prestigious Old Vic Theatre Company' returns with 'its proclaimed production of *Hamlet* with Derek Jacobi in the lead role'. One crime item was included because the story's newsworthiness came not from the fact that there was a crime committed, but because those arrested were international rock stars: 'Two members of the touring American pop group Dr Hook appeared in Sydney's Central Court on drug charges today after police raided their hotel rooms and . . . marijuana [was] found'.

A further variation on the theme of the especially remarkable 'whose institutional power is limited' was found in the extensive coverage given to seemingly very ordinary people whose especially remarkable identities were constituted not by way of their 'very-being-as-they-are', because in news terms they are essentially 'nobodies', but in relation to what might be called their 'very-acting-as-they-do'. Unlike élites, powerful or powerless, whose actions regardless of how ordinary (marriage plans, gift giving, an overseas trip) are deemed newsworthy (remarkable) by virtue of an already overdetermined presence in journalism's discourse – 'the actions of élites usually, and in the short term perspective [are] more consequential than the activities of others' (Galtung and Ruge 1973: 66) – ordinary people must *become* especially remarkable. The emphasis in this case is on the value and outcome of action and deed, particularly as these are manifested in exceptional achievement and idiosyncratic preoccupation. Characteristically, this entails the operation of news values which emphasize the fracturing of the normal expectancies of the world: 'what is regular and institutionalized, continuing and repetitive at regular and short intervals, does not attract nearly so much attention. . . . Events have to be unexpected or rare, or preferably both, to become good news' (Galtung and Ruge 1973: 65). Ordinary people have to be positioned by the story as 'ordinary' while at the same time be shown to be engaged in breaching expectations by doing extraordinary things; and it is the scrutiny of this dynamic which admits them into the realm of the especially remarkable and allows their 'doings' (but not necessarily their 'way of life') to gain a degree of attention. Putting it more schematically, it might be said that stories focused on élites tend to be constructed around the ordinary routines of extraordinary individuals whereas stories dealing with ordinary people are built around the extraordinary actions of ordinary folk.

Once the reports that make up this story-type are specified like this a structure begins to emerge and attention can be directed to the way 'élite-ness' and 'ordinary-ness' as constructs are encoded, not in terms of some real life referent (this is what studies of bias might try to do) but with reference to the signifying practices of the news story itself. These constructs begin to make their appearance within individual stories, but they also need to be traced across stories as 'associative fields' of meaning (Barthes 1977c: 48). When stories about the especially remarkable are scrutinized more broadly, a set of relations can be detected which link élite-ness and ordinary-ness through a triangular structure of similarity and difference, the apex of which is provided by our own inscription in the story as viewers. The process works through a discourse which shifts between humanizing the subject and at the same time exalting it. Humanization acts to make the 'person' of the story like us in most respects. This is where stories of ordinary people start. Exaltation acts to make the story's 'person' different from us, and this is the point from which élite stories begin. Then each story reverses the terms. Those that are initially humanized are exalted – ordinary people made especially remarkable; and, those that are exalted are humanized – élites, especially remarkable to start, are made less so and therefore more ordinary. Each story alternates between moments of humanizing and of exalting, between that which is similar to us and that which is different. Elites are different, but examined more closely also human to a fault. Ordinary people are the same as us, but by their accomplishments also different.

Ordinary people then, start off being just regular folks but get observed performing and acting 'extraordinarily' in a number of different contexts. Sometimes this manifests itself through incongruous or unanticipated juxtapositions. Ordinary people, for example, can become especially remarkable for engaging in unexpected hobbies, preoccupations and leisure time pursuits: 'a schoolboy' builds a working hovercraft; an 'adult' is convinced that comics are 'serious'; members of an outback rugby club hold an 'annual crab race'; a man wins a boat race 'in his vessel made from two thousand beer cans'; 'a mother of three' becomes 'the first woman given a licence to drive on a major [trotting] track against men'; a man 'communicates with gnomes' and writes a book about it. Stories about ordinary people who make their mark by setting or breaking 'records' also share in this sense of the novel and the incongruous: a barber sets a 'world non-stop shaving record'; a 'cabinet maker' stays in a cage with 'two dozen deadly snakes' for 'more than thirty-six days'; a young man engages in 'an attempt to set a new world record' for 'domino toppling'; a 'world record' for 'motorcycle car jumping' is set;

thirteen firemen are training for 'the most gruelling non-stop endurance run in the world'. In some items ordinary people breach expectations by overcoming seemingly insurmountable physical disabilities: a woman 'confined to an iron lung' gives birth to 'a baby daughter'; after 'a near-tragic car accident' causing massive facial damage, a young woman 'expects to be modelling again'; 'the sole survivor of a light plane crash ... will be walking again'. Unexpectedly overcoming personal danger for the sake of others also qualifies ordinary people as newsworthy: twenty-six people are 'awarded for their bravery by the Governor General of Victoria'; a journalist swims across the Mekong River in a 'daring bid ... to help a Laotian girl escape from Thailand'. Ordinary people also get into the news when their unassuming and quite routine actions bring consequences much greater than initially anticipated: a truck driver who stops to 'fill out his log book and answer the call of nature' finds a satchel with 'ten million dollars worth of cheques inside'.

To start, perhaps one of the salient features to be noted about these stories – thirty-one on élites and forty-four on ordinary people – is their placement within the overall order of the news bulletin. If the bulletin's total number of stories is divided in half, these especially remarkable person stories tend to fall within the second rather than the first half of the broadcast and in several cases the item is the last one of the programme, confirming a pattern, noted in America (Epstein 1973) and in Britain (Glasgow University Media Group 1976), that reports placed near or at the end of the bulletin serve as the 'human interest' or 'soft news', offering a rounding out and a gentler finish to the harsher realities of the rest of the broadcast. However, there were some revealing exceptions. Whereas stories about élites consistently fell in the later part of the bulletin, a number of reports dealing with ordinary people were placed much earlier in the running order of stories – the schoolgirl air crash survivor, for example, was positioned as the fifth item in a bulletin of eleven stories, the iron lung mother was sixth in a line up of thirteen items. This suggests that at least some of these stories are more ambiguous in terms of their news value, tending to slide between soft news and hard news distinctions. The ambiguous news status of certain stories is also evident when the same event is covered by several bulletins. The teenage stunt jump story placed fourth on Channel 9's broadcast in a line up of fourteen items whereas it came last in a bulletin of nineteen stories on Channel 2, the public broadcaster, and seventh out of a total of eighteen items on Channel 7. Overall, it is also worth noting that stories about the especially remarkable are more numerous on commercial channel bulletins than on the government public channel and in this context it might be suggested that the frequency of such stories, along with their placement, may give some indication as to how a particular news service defines itself on the continuum of 'serious' as opposed to 'popular' journalism. It may also indicate how the service situates its constituency; that is, how it perceives and hence addresses its imagined audience.

HOW POWERLESS IS A 'POWERLESS ELITE'?

Let's end this section with a qualification. Although Alberoni's notion of a powerless élite is a helpful way of locating and grouping a range of television news stories it does have some limitations as a concept, not least of which is the fact that a clear separation between the especially remarkable with institutional power and those without it is sometimes a distinction difficult to sustain. A number of case studies have shown that although they may not directly exercise control or occupy authorized positions of power, stars have a significant part to play in the way that values and attitudes are assembled and disseminated at particular historical conjunctures (Dyer 1979, 1987; Fiske 1992a; Schwichtenberg 1993). For Dyer, the power of stars resides precisely in their apparent lack of connection with traditionally defined structures of influence. Klapp (1964) contends that the 'cult of celebrity' needs to be seen in relation to 'symbolic leadership' acted out in public dramas, 'providing models of what to do and how to behave'. Whether considered a member of an institutional élite, the powerless élite or merely an 'ordinary person' experiencing the obligatory fifteen minutes of fame, the celebrity can stand as a spectacular representational version of aspects of primary-lived realities and 'structures of feeling' and can operate as a site from which key ideological themes can be reiterated and played out.

Given their proliferation and continuous presence in the media in its various forms, celebrities come to take up positions as 'primary definers' (Hall *et al.* 1978: 58) around whose accounts and status contending perspectives must inevitably be located. The very force of representation itself gives their doings and way of life a kind of privileged moment of authority in a world which has become increasingly characterized as divided between those who are image-accessed and the rest. Celebrities as symbolic leaders are, however, not straightforwardly and automatically echoing the conditions for the production of dominant socio-cultural meanings. The especially remarkable can be as much symbolic leaders working 'against' primary lived realities as 'for them'. Gramsci's point is an important one here – hegemony is never given and permanent, but is always in the process of being struggled for and secured. But, it needs to be remembered that celebrity is intimately bounded by the process of representation – image–access as we are discussing it currently means particular reliance on the mass media of communication. Thus, there may be many genuine moments of subversion or challenge constituted around particular symbolic leaders, but even in this plurality of representational responses the tendency of the media, especially television is to offer a 'regulated latitude of ideological positions'. (White 1992: 190). Counter-hegemonic forces can be recuperated, normalized, contained (even Madonna loves being a mum) or be strategically marginalized and rendered ineffectual (Hebdige 1979; Gitlin 1980), perhaps turning into another moment of consumption, where 'dissatisfaction itself [becomes] a commodity' (Dubord 1983: 59).

ELITES

News does not merely take note of the especially remarkable, it actively participates in their construction: it makes them 'remarkable' and especially so. Once élites enter journalistic discourse as the subject for stories it becomes relevant to ask – how are they represented; which 'remarks, attributes, actions and possessions' (Hall 1973b: 183) are the focus of interest; how are élite 'persons' signified and given meaning as especially remarkable? A study of the 'William Hickey' gossip column as it appeared in the English newspaper the *Daily Express* during the 1950s and early 1960s (Smith 1975) offers some concrete suggestions in terms of ways to proceed. According to Smith (1975: 205) this particular gossip column is best understood in the way it provided its readership with a glimpse of a 'higher world', serving to build a contrast between the dull routines assumed to govern everyday life and a 'charmed spectacle' which was regularly paraded like a kind of 'theatrical show'. Interestingly, despite the apparent gap in years and the different media, a number of the rhetorical and stylistic devices which Smith's study of the gossip column uncovered are still very much in evidence in the coverage of élites and their 'doings and way of life' in television's 'other news'.

Subsidiary characters

Smith (1975: 207) found that the 'central characters' who perform in the theatrical show of Hickey's gossip column were regularly described in situations where they were surrounded by 'bit players'. For Smith these are the 'subsidiary characters' whose function it is to enhance activities and 'add lustre', some 'well known in their own right' while others simply mentioned by category or collectively, a 'second stratum of dependent and faceless people'. In 'other news' about élites, this convention seems to have been followed closely. Without exception, news talk made distinct reference to such subsidiary characters. This was particularly evident in the coverage of royalty where State Governors, an Acting Prime Minister, senior public servants, directors of cultural institutions, the Pope, all 'well known in their own right' were swept up into the proceedings. The dependent faceless 'stratum' also has its presence registered in news talk, sometimes in a service relationship – 'diamond experts' assess and cost the jewel that the Prince is about to bestow on his daughter; 'Danish security [get] distinctly nervous' as the royal couple take an 'informal tour' of the Tivoli Gardens – and in other instances taking part in the manufacture of the public gaze ('more than eighty people waited'; 'a crowd gathered').

If, as Mills (1956: 71) has argued, institutional and celebrity élites are becoming increasingly indistinguishable in the way they are portrayed in the mass media, sharing and exchanging the same publicity regimes and fame making apparatus, it may follow that these admirers, on-lookers, fans, hangers-on, and other manifestations of spectacle and the process of public looking, normally associated with more conventional forms of stardom, come to be shared in common as well. The 'service' offered to institutional élites by such subsidiaries becomes one of collective recognition or acclamation, functioning to enhance the main character's notoriety and thus the construction of the especially remarkable person. To take one telling example, when a count of all the 'characters' mentioned by news talk in the sixteen stories dealing with royalty was done a total of nineteen central characters were mentioned. In contrast to this relatively small number, there were an extraordinary seventy-five subsidiary characters cited, of whom forty-six could be designated as relatively well known in their own right and twenty-nine were part of the anonymous 'second stratum'. It would appear that the secondary character, at least in news about the doings and way of life of royalty, is an overwhelming condition which accompanies their going about in the world, one of the structuring 'terms' perhaps, in the way that élite-ness can be reiterated and the realms of the especially remarkable established.

This emphasis is developed further when connected with news film where the main characters can be seen (by us) being seen (by others). The use of photographic images has the potential to consolidate what is delivered as verbal commentary, or act in its own right to set out with pictorial conciseness some of the significant and visible properties signifying élites as especially remarkable. Common to all élite stories is the way that news film clearly registers the attention of subsidiaries – individuals shown in the process of watching, waiting, attending or serving. When the main character is the subject of the shot, images are regularly framed to register the presence of subsidiaries: Ted Tingling surrounded by admirers before the fashion parade; Tony Rafferty beseiged by supporters before his run; Graham Yallop flanked on all sides by cricket fans. When a clutch of onlookers is not obviously there, as in the case of the Ronnie Corbett story, news film still makes certain that some kind of subsidiary presence is established. As the newsreader finishes his introductory remarks about the English television comedian's arrival the first image in a news film sequence is a medium close up of Corbett, apparently with no one else around. Then the camera starts to slowly pan, and as it does clusters of reporters and camera crews are revealed – watching, attending, looking on *in public*. The Prince Michael story is even more parsimonious but no less committed to constructing the moment of the public gaze. Although the entire item's news film shows only the briefest glimpse of a single reporter, and he is tucked away in the right hand corner of the frame, the presence of a retinue of subsidiaries is still very much in evidence as the audio track prominently registers a chorus of clicking cameras off screen.

The Glasgow University Media Group (1980: 328–47) argue that in those stories that begin the news broadcast, what they refer to as the 'serious' news, the use of news film in its relationship to news commentary is highly 'symbolic'. Contrary to broadcasters' claims to show it like it is, news film in these stories rarely relates to what is being said in the commentary directly. Visuals often refer to news talk obliquely, so that 'intangibles' like foreign exchange markets, which become the subject of stories, can only be represented indirectly through a set of arbitrarily selected signs, shots of supermarkets for example. 'The results are often essentially journalistic essays with film merely added – sometimes in extraordinary ways' (Glasgow University Media Group 1980: 338). However, the further down the bulletin a story appears, they suggest, the more likely it is that news film will be used in an 'iconic' relationship, where 'the word simply repeats verbally what can be seen in the image' (Glasgow University Media Group 1980: 354). This, of course, is where the 'lighter items' tend to reside. The irony here is that the broadcaster rhetoric about the visual imperatives of TV news seems to find its fullest expression in those stories considered by television journalism's harshest critics to be least significant. The iconic relationship – the correspondence between word and image – may also have a special function in stories about élites, namely that we can 'see for ourselves', that what is being designated verbally as especially remarkable is *recognizably* the case. The cult of celebrity may get special benefits from this arrangement. A 'second order' relation is at work so that the especially remarkable are as much a particular kind of ritualized specularity as they are 'persons' in their own right. The opportunity which television news offers – not just to watch the celebrity but to watch the ritual of watching (and waiting) on a regular basis – may be a unique journalistic ingredient in the manufacture of fame.

Control

In his analysis of the gossip column, Smith (1975: 207–8) detects a pervasive admiration for the ability of its inhabitants to 'have a variety of places to live in or to visit', to 'appear to control their own time and environment on a large scale, to move around effortlessly', to regularly demonstrate an 'ease of possession', options that the column presumes no ordinary person has available so readily. Such control may simply be carefree movement from one exclusive setting to another or it can also refer to the effortless ability to gain an education, choose a career, rise the corporate ladder, host a party, enjoy a holiday, 'have difficulties . . . resolved':

> Hickey people, at work and play, enjoy a power over their own style of life undreamed of by other classes. The column's latent function is to

assert, and celebrate, the persistence of such power in the form of a daily serial.

(Smith 1975: 208)

A similar kind of regard seems to pervade 'other news' items about élites. In order to marry a woman who is not officially approved of – a Roman Catholic and a divorcée – Prince Michael of Kent has to take a number of crucial steps and make a number of seemingly serious sacrifices to obtain social, institutional and religious acceptance. These, the story implies, he is able to accomplish without the slightest difficulty or doubt: he gains the Queen's consent ('The Queen has approved of the marriage ... '), 'renounce[s his] claim to the throne', arranges a special 'dispensation from the Pope' and 'curb[s his] risky sporting activities' as a racing driver. Similar conditions seem to shape the events surrounding Princess Caroline's wedding gift: although the diamond is 'the richest ... in modern history' with one company 'offer[ing] ten per cent of its value merely for an option to see it', and its 'present owners pay[ing] around three million for the stone in its rough state', Prince Rainier of Monaco 'will present his daughter with the diamond when she marries'.

Stories about show business élites also rely on referencing a set of conditions which emphasize effortless control over time, environment and activities. Although the basis of some of these reports could not be anything but an exercise in public relations – Francis Ford Coppola is in Australia to drum up audiences for his new film; Ronnie Corbett gives interviews to ensure interest in his latest comedy enterprise – the context of this promotion is never observed as part of a pattern of work and effort. In this story type celebrities seem to inhabit what Brunsdon and Morley (1978: 24) call a 'private leisure-world', glimpsed as a 'free floating sphere from which the productive base has been excised'. From here promotional tasks like holding news conferences, can be constructed simply as an expression, perhaps even the epitome of 'a certain freedom and smooth control' (Smith 1975: 207). Ronnie Corbett then, is not in Sydney to labour like the rest of us do to make a living but 'to star in a show with his long-time partner'. To star in a show in this context implies a certain kind of power: taking up the option at will, effortlessly appearing rather than plying one's trade. As if this is not clear enough, the way his press conference is spoken about in news talk makes the point again – Corbett is 'meeting with reporters [at] Sydney's Australian Golf Course'. The implication is that this is not something formally arranged or commercially motivated, but a kind of spontaneous gathering, effortlessly organized and executed. The setting itself eludes the sphere of production and work – a golf course is a cultural icon of casual leisure and recreation. On Channel 9 the opening remarks of the reporter actually describe the event as 'time relaxing' before the stage show begins in earnest. If there are still any doubts, these are dispelled in the next sequence in the story when

55

Corbett seems to convert the gathering into an occasion to simply be, as news talk puts it, a 'funny man'. Promotion plays into one of the myths about comedy – it appears as though the comedian cannot help being funny. He does not have to work at it, he simply *is* it. His facility for banter seems so effortless, his repartee so spontaneous that even the newsreader on Channel 9 is barely able to contain his own mirth by the story's end: 'He's a knock-out, that guy'. A dour newsreader laughs on camera – clearly a sign that this individual is indeed one of the especially remarkable.

According to Channel 0's newsreader, for most of us, doing the same thing two hundred and ten times in a row would cease to be interesting, but for the Old Vic Theatre Company's lead actor Derek Jacobi this appears not to be the case. The especially remarkable are less prone to suffer, like we ordinary folk might, from boredom or the tedium of repetition in our job. 'How many more challenges can you cope with?', asks the reporter during an interview. The answer clinches it. A necessity becomes a virtue. If there is a difference between the first and two hundred and tenth performance, it is, explains Jacobi, that the most recent one is 'better'. The especially remarkable, it seems, are not weighed down by the regimes of repetitive work – the very thing that would deplete more conventional energies is converted into challenge, betterment and the search for excellence. This story is of course promotional, virtually an advertisement for the theatre company and its production, but it acts to do more than just promote. It turns publicity into an opportunity to display a degree of control, freedom and effortless endeavour of which the rest of us can only dream.

The organization of news film sequences can produce a very specific sense of that 'free floating sphere' from which the world of expended labour has been effortlessly banished. In the Reg Livermore story, for example, images are organized to alternate between shots of the actor in close-up during an interview where he talks about his career and shots of his performance on stage. And, just as effortlessly as the images shift from his face to his performance, the sense is produced that the creation of the performance and the performance itself are effortless. The performance just *appears* – it seems to emerge, coherent and complete, packaged to be consumed, first with our eyes as a part of a news story, and then perhaps again when we purchase our ticket for the theatre. This control over environment is remarkable: the visuals suggest that Livermore only has to speak and his 'one man act' happens, uncontaminated by the burdens of effort, routine and labour. By glossing the expenditure of effort the visuals can suggest that people like Livermore, *by nature*, create. It is just *in* them, part of their very-being-as-they-are, and from the point of view of those of us who toil every day, only the especially remarkable can produce something without working at it.[1]

Superlatives

A short placing phrase, the inclusion or omission of a definite or indefinite article, the first few words of an item, and the replacement of common usage with something having a grander ring all help the Hickey column to create some of the aura around the charmed spectacle. As Smith (1975: 214) explains: 'The people who have their being in [the higher world] are not simply degrees above us in the hierarchy, they are different in kind. That is why a different kind of language . . . is necessary to apprehend them'.

The commutation test, according to Barthes (1977d: 65), 'consists of artificially introducing a change in the plane of expression (signifiers) and in observing whether this change brings about a correlative modification on the plane of content (signifieds)'. This test can be usefully applied in order to situate some of the 'implied superlatives' (Smith 1975: 210–11) embedded in 'other news' stories about institutional and celebrity élites, and to demonstrate how this deposits yet another layer of meaning in relation to notions of élite-ness. For example, almost every item in this story-type utilizes a kind of linguistic 'flourish' when describing or discussing the actions or pre-occupations of royalty – an especially remarkable language seems to be required in news talk in order to register the especially remarkable qualities of these élite persons. The item on Prince Michael's wedding announcement is particularly notable, steadily building its picture of the higher world through such phrases as 'was educated at'; 'outside the home of'; 'was a contemporary of'; 'considered something of a daredevil in sport'; 'taken some nasty spills'. With the commutation test each of these fragments of news talk could be replaced by a more conventional type of usage: house instead of 'home'; went to school instead of 'was educated'; involved in some bad accidents instead of 'taken some nasty spills'. Such changes, however, would considerably alter and even destroy the preferred sense offered by each of these signifiers, the sense that these types of people inhabit a place not just above us socially but 'different in kind'.

In stories about celebrities however, well-bred, plummy descriptions are replaced by a rhetoric more conventionally accompanying images of stardom. Again, the news story and the advertisement are collapsed together through a language mobilized from billboards, newspaper entertainment pages, fan magazines and television commercials. Hyperbole and exuberance are the keynotes. Reg Livermore is proclaimed 'the star [of] outrageous box office hits', 'the master of the one man show', a 'huge success'. The story about Ronnie Corbett declares that his television programme is 'one of England's and indeed one of Australia's top comedy shows'; Dr Hook is 'the top American pop group'; Francis Ford Coppola 'the man who . . . scooped the Academy Awards'. To establish the higher world right from the start, these superlatives tend to be placed within the opening sentence of the newsreader's introduction to a story. This opening sentence also makes regular use of the special placement of definite articles before the celebrity's name or in relation to another noun in a descriptive position with regard to the name: *The* English comedian Ronnie Corbett . . . ; *the* touring American pop group Dr Hook . . . ; Francis Ford Coppola, *the* man who made the Godfather movies. The commutation test can be applied here, as well, to demonstrate how éliteness is produced in language: definite rather than indefinite articles produce a sense of superiority, uniqueness and recognizability ('*a* man who produced *a* Godfather movie' would hardly be newsworthy at all). Sometimes definite articles are dropped entirely ('Actor, Reg Livermore . . . '; 'Former Australian cricket captain, Graham Yallop . . . '), a journalistic practice designed to underline the importance of the person being described and to introduce a 'hot-off-the-presses factual urgency' (Smith 1975: 211). No explanation or context is needed for the especially remarkable, since their very-being-as-they-are is assumed to be an already established fact.

Is there a visual equivalent to the linguistic flourish punctuating the news commentary which helps to constitute élites as especially remarkable? In the case of the press photograph Barthes (1977b: 22) explains that there are always connotative procedures operating and 'special importance must be accorded to what could be called the posing of objects' whereby they become 'inducers of associations of ideas . . . or veritable symbols'. This would seem to be no less the case with television news film, where the objects which surround and seem to attach themselves to élites become a 'lexicon' for visually producing superlatives, an array of props on display through which remarkable-ness can be spoken. As they stroll leisurely down the path through the garden, Prince Michael and his fiancée are framed in full against a sizeable amount of the background. They walk towards the camera arm in arm, he in a double-breasted blazer adorned with brass buttons and she in a light blue dress, displaying a kind of understated elegance. The camera zooms in for a more intimate look and the shot ends with a medium close-up of the Baroness alone. Her head is now more fully visible and detailed: blonde, stylishly cut hair tastefully subdued, flawless teeth and skin, a single strand of pearls around her neck. All these 'posed' objects which attach to these élites work together to produce the visual superlatives. The setting itself acts as an indicator of superlative qualities – an enormous white house hovering in the background, imposing wrought iron gates, a plush green lawn cohere together and serve as a set of visual signifiers which remind us that we are in the company of those who inhabit 'the higher world'. The commutation test may work here as well: change the signifiers, in this case the objects posed, and the meaning changes. The Prince without his grand stately home, his wrought iron gates, his brass buttons becomes less princely; the Baroness without her pearls less aristocratic.

Codes of dress, fashion and setting are not the only ones at work in stories about élites however. In instances where celebrities are involved in interviews or press conferences specific visual conventions derived from the cinema can be mobilized to pose the celebrities themselves as connotative objects in order to produce superlatives. Here, editing, lighting, camera angle and camera framing can all play a part. The news film sequence used in the Francis Ford Coppola report consists of nothing more than a series of shots of the Hollywood director and the reporters on the scene. Coppola however is filmed from below, the severe angle of the camera accentuating his stature as he stands on a platform at the front of a room. In contrast, in a type of shot/reverse shot arrangement, the reporters are shown from an angle of vision which looks down on them seated in rows. In this same image sequence Coppola seems to 'capture' most of the available illumination in the room and is shown in close-up, individuated and personalized by the frame as he speaks, while the reporters appear in darker unlit areas, undifferentiated, silent, looking in the same direction and doing more or less the same thing. Edited together in a series of alternating shots which shift between the celebrity and the reporter subsidiaries an arrangement is produced which expressively sets out the terms of a visualized 'superlative'.

The twitch

Elites appear to be a 'natural' topic for news. Their 'very-being-as-they-are' becomes a readily available source of occurrences that can be used to generate news stories. Yet simply to follow their doings and way of life lacks the efficacy assumed to be the basis of good journalism. Some 'impact' is sought, some circumstances revealed, which can give the impression that this is indeed a news story. The gossip column, according to Smith, faces the same reportorial problem. To solve it 'Hickey has to make the most mundane activity arresting. His technique is generally to twitch our mild surprise at a discrepancy between what we expect of a character and what Hickey can actually tell us' (Smith 1975: 215). An item about Princess Anne taking her Brownie road test, observes Smith, may momentarily shake up the reader's deposited sense of how princesses ought to behave and simultaneously reveal an unexpected ordinariness in the aspirations of a member of the higher world. The strategy of the twitch stands in close proximity to a rhetorical manoeuvre commonly encountered in the *fait-divers* – bringing together 'terms' logically belonging to distant 'circuits of signification' in a relation of coincidence for surprising effect (Barthes 1977a). The seemingly incongruous relation – in this instance between royalty and road tests – can however work at another level and provide the scaffolding for another discourse about the especially remarkable. Starting with the formal arrangements of the *fait-divers*, the twitch ends by making an ideological point: namely, élites are different from us, yet the same. They are simultaneously élite and ordinary, exalted and humanized. The reduction of distance

59

between two seemingly distinct circuits of signification allows the higher world to become both more recognizable and more like our own. The privileged and those without it, the powerful and the powerless, the rulers and the ruled are shown to inhabit the same universe of small and ordinary things. Taking a Brownie road test 'brings a homely aura to the Princess, makes her seem lovely and suburban', but paradoxically, as Smith (1975: 215) explains, 'even as we pleasurably exclaim "Well I never"', our sense of her distance from us, her royalty, is reinforced by the fact that so commonplace an activity has won our attention'.

When ordinary people visit a 'fun park', listen to the resident band or play games at side shows, their activities generally pass unnoticed. When royalty is reported on the early evening news doing much the same thing the deposited expectations that are held about how queens and princes ought to behave are momentarily challenged. A relation of coincidence can be set up where two terms which usually operate at a 'kind of logical distance' – the formality of a royal visit and the informality of the fair ground – are 'found in the same realm' (Barthes 1977a). Our surprise arises because of the discrepancy between what we expect of such people and what the news story actually specifies about their doings (Queen Elizabeth and Prince Phillip 'took a ride in the tunnel of love'). In this juxtaposition a certain ideological inflection can be effectively mobilized as well – despite their place in the higher world, élites can play and have fun, just like us ordinary folk, even it seems in the very places where we disport ourselves. This informality and outburst of spontaneity demonstrates that underneath these individuals are really not all that different from us. Yet, even while it dwells on the playful participation involved in such 'ordinary' indulgences, the story paradoxically begins to recirculate the traditional image of royalty back to us. So commonplace an activity turns into a newsworthy event only because it is royalty who indulge. The story's language actually makes sure that the display of spontaneity is never less than appropriately decorous – out there, in the domain of popular entertainments, royalty 'try their hand at smashing crockery'; ordinary people, at least in Australia, would probably 'get stuck into it and break some plates'. The higher world remains intact.

When daughters are about to be married, fathers customarily buy gifts. When the daughter is Princess Caroline and the father is Prince Rainier of Monaco, an expensive gift is within the realm of possibility. This story about a relatively conventional occasion – the giving of a wedding present – can still create the conditions for the 'twitch', set in place this time by what Barthes (1977a: 190) describes as a peculiar kind of spectacle resulting from 'the surprise of quantity'. We know through accumulated stereotypes that princes can be wealthy, that they have the means to be lavish and even flamboyant in the use of their accumulated riches, but to be *that* wealthy – twelve million dollars for a wedding present – is unanticipated in its excess. The discrepancy between what we can 'reasonably' expect and what this story actually relays in the telling makes us 'twitch' as we exclaim in disbelief or wonderment. And, at the same time that the story sets up the 'terms' of its impact as a newsworthy occurrence, it also provides a way by which this can be appropriated as normal. The spectacle of the gift is lodged in a particular relationship which has to do with how fathers ordinarily behave towards their marrying daughters: despite his excess, the Prince is still behaving like a dutiful caring father. The act of giving brings the Prince, as part of the higher world into a place we all know – the world of kinship and family with its rites, duties and obligations. His excess is humanized and made ordinary – even in such extravagance, he still acts like a father towards his daughter. Yet, as we recognize this familial gesture and all its mundane implications, we also find out about the cost involved in being a dutiful father and a wealthy prince at the same time, and our distance from the higher world is once again confirmed.

The story of the American rock group, Dr Hook, appearing in court on drugs charges also plays on a 'disturbance' arising out of the conditions of unexpected coincidence while at the same time hinting at the ordinary qualities of the especially remarkable. It is not uncommon for rock stars to get into trouble in connection with the use of drugs. In one respect the use of these 'substances' comes with the job, an established part of the professional and sub-cultural baggage of contemporary musicianship and this is what we have come to expect, at least as it is sedimented through the layers of media representations of the rock world. What surprises and seems incongruous, however, is when trouble with drugs is encountered, it is initiated, not by the musicians themselves, but by those who we might suppose would do anything to keep them out of trouble – their adoring fans. A 'symmetrical' reversal of this kind Barthes calls the 'acme' and it is a regular form of story-telling in the *fait-divers*:

> it is precisely when she has invested her savings in an annuity that the seventy-year-old woman is strangled; it is precisely the blowtorch manufacturer's safe that the burglars manage to open with a blowtorch; it is precisely when they are summoned to a reconciliation session that the husband kills his wife.
>
> (Barthes 1977a: 193)

And, it is precisely when the American pop group are at the pinnacle of 'an extremely successful trip', due to their popular following in Australia, that they manage 'to spend their final few hours in the country [in] Sydney's Central Court' because of this following.

> During the tour the members of the group are often given gifts and letters . . . the two half Buddha sticks found by the drug squad detectives early this morning had been slipped in their pockets by admiring fans.

According to Barthes (1977a: 193) the acme is an expression of 'mischance' which can be seen in mythic terms. It suggests that although life has no real direction, wherever 'a symmetry' like the one in the television story is produced, 'there has to be a hand to guide it', and this hand is what we think of as fate. Indeed, the story itself produces this reading when the reporter summarizes events by saying: 'as they put it, they were just victims of circumstance'. But it is also this situation of mischance which can be inflected ideologically, placing these élites on our level and positing them as ordinary after all. Despite their place in the higher world, celebrity élites, it turns out, are as much the subject of caprice as any of us might be: as the tee shirt says, 'shit happens'. We are all susceptible to being 'just victims of circumstance'. Yet as the story produces Dr Hook's acme as if it could mirror our own, it simultaneously feeds back to us qualities that make these celebrity élites especially remarkable. Members of the higher world may be vulnerable like us to the fateful organization of the world, but, hotel rooms ('police raided their hotel room'), limousines ('as their limousine waited outside'), barristers ('the barrister representing Ray Sawyer and Dennis Le Perrier'), a popular following ('the group are often given gifts and letters . . . by admiring fans'), acknowledged success ('up until today it had been an extremely successful trip throughout Australia'), and unlimited mobility ('the men then raced off to . . . catch a flight home') clearly illustrate that their circumstances are not ours. The higher world of celebrity, like that of royalty, is affirmed once more.

ORDINARY PEOPLE

Another cluster of stories needs to be examined in order to cover fully all the news items that constitute the story-type dealing with the especially remarkable. In these stories, focused on ordinary people, a discourse is produced which locates individuals as 'no one particularly special', certainly having no place in the higher world, but still qualifying as especially remarkable by virtue of distinctive deeds and achievements. Whereas élites are newsworthy simply because of who they are, ordinary people tend to be given entry to the news as especially remarkable on the basis of what they do. The weight of news value leans, in the first instance, towards activity and performance. Notions of novelty, unusualness or unexpectedness play a crucial role in allowing 'just regular folks' access to news. The novel and the unexpected as news values tend to give these stories their shape, consequently, the twitch of mild surprise comes to be a more prominent feature in the reporting. While stories about élites rely on a kind of seriality effect – the report on this day is another episode in the doings and way of life of these especially remarkable persons, with more to come in the future – stories about ordinary people, reliant on the more foregrounded device of the twitch, tend to be narratively self-contained and circumspect, frequently 'refer[ring] formally to nothing but itself'. As a result of this structure of 'immanence' (Barthes 1977a) these particular stories are able to offer a special significational space for the textualization of Andy Warhol's prediction about everyone's fifteen minutes of fame. The self-bounded news story is the way journalism can provide potential sites for such a prediction to be inscribed on a very regular basis: celebrity for a few glorious media moments where, like the *fait-divers*, 'everything is given', and then the slide to obscurity. There are of course exceptions; how else would the cult of celebrity survive and have continuity? As Galtung and Ruge (1973: 62) have pointed out once a news channel is opened up, it can be very difficult to close it down completely. Writing this some time after the sample stories were collected gives the opportunity of seeing how these channels are kept open, and how seemingly ordinary people are 'taken up' again after their initial moment of media notoriety. In the sample there was an item on an Australian teenager attempting a world record motorcycle jump, a suitable rival for celebrity stunt man Evil Knevil according to the news commentary. Several years after his 'astounding jump', he appeared again in a news report – this time as a suicide in a motel room. Even though stories about ordinary people seem, at least initially, to be self-contained, there is always the potential for the narrative to expand into another episode.

Subsidiary characters

Confirmation of an enabling story-type is provided when early evening news stories about ordinary people doing extraordinary things are examined and found to be governed by the same meaning production strategies as those operating in stories about élites. Again, the rhetorical inclinations and the stylistic practices typical of the Hickey gossip column are at work in the organization of sense-making. Like stories about élites, the especially remarkable qualities of ordinary people can be signalled and enhanced by the visible presence of a retinue of subsidiary characters who can function as a form of public acclamation. This was particularly apparent in items dealing with record-breaking stunts, where performances were always filmed so that 'dependent and faceless people' could be shown watching. In this case, subsidiaries seem to function textually in a way similar to those making appearances in élite stories – the especially remarkable are seen (by us) to be seen by others in the public domain. The capacity to have the watchers watched (by the viewers) is a way of designating the extraordinary aspects of ordinary people, separating them off from the normal and the mundane. Most stories allow the visuals to carry evidence of the public gaze, however, in some cases news talk will convey the 'maximum degree of interest' by supplying certain specifications: 'Twelve thousand fans looked on . . . for the motorcycle jump'; 'three thousand people turn[ed] out' for the rugby team crab race; 'two hundred proud friends and relations' attended the 'bravery awards'.

In some stories the watchers can shrink away completely leaving instead a single well-situated individual in a special kind of subsidiary relation. Here it is the reporter in the field who acts to 'add lustre' by attending to and framing the story's orientation towards the central character. Reporter interest itself stands as a sign that these people, although they may seem ordinary, are at some level remarkable, and where interviews take place ordinary people are given a discursive space to reveal motives, assess achievements, reflect on feelings and offer explanations for their newsworthy actions. The reporter as subsidiary acts textually as a 'way in' to the main character, providing the moment in the story for the construction of 'the person' behind the occurrence, positioning us to get closer to an actual 'identity'. What may be a remarkable feat can be a perplexing one at the same time. Through the interview however, we are offered an attendant individualization which can articulate and make intelligible the dynamics of intention and outcome that at first may seem distinctly odd. The reporter as subsidiary, questioning on our behalf, produces a privileged moment in the story which 'quickens' the category of the subject.

The report on Joe Italiano, the 'man . . . who collects comic books' demonstrates this process well. After the newsreader's introduction, the story is handed over to the reporter who first lays the groundwork for the interview. The emphasis here is on Italiano's attempts to organize 'the first ever comic convention to be held in Australia' and his efforts to 'show more people that comics are a serious art form and shouldn't be considered childish'. The reporter's commentary ends with some further information about the collector's special interest: of the 'more than eleven thousand comics' in his collection, 'Italiano has read ninety-nine per cent of them [and] fifty mail order comics [arrive] every month'. This is not neutral information however. Although it does not directly say so, such statistics speak not just about the collector's special interest, but about his obsession, an involvement so profound as perhaps to be bordering on the abnormal. But the interview which begins directly after these comments gives the collector a chance to explain his eccentricity, to provide a personal statement for what is first situated as 'a children's fad' and then as the behaviour of a deluded individual.

ITALIANO: I started [collecting] when I was twelve years old . . . I had a short break when I wasn't collecting for a few years, but otherwise it's been fairly solid.

REPORTER: I understand also that you believe comics are more entertaining than television.

ITALIANO: One thing about them is that when you pick it up it's there in front of you. You miss nothing. You can always go back, whereas if you miss something important in a film you miss everything.

REPORTER: So it's a serious business to you and not really childish?

ITALIANO: No, definitely not childish. Comics are for all ages.

With the guidance of the reporter's questioning what initially appears as 'odd' is explained and provided with motivation and a personal history. The collector even gets the opportunity to 'theorize' about the aesthetic merits of comics compared to television. His account does not explain away the especially remarkable quality of his preoccupation; rather, it is placed within the realm of the personal. By doing this, the story invites a certain kind of identification: we may not completely approve of this sort of activity – 'most of us would never consider comic book collecting as much more than a children's fad' – but once it is situated in biographical terms and in relation to our own cultural activities ('more entertaining than television') the remarkable behaviour is, if not normalized, at least located within the realm of the recognizable. Rather than an undersocialized adult, the collector becomes merely quaint or eccentric. Potential deviance is recuperated for the norm through common sense understandings, because, as we all know, and the story positions us to re-appreciate, there's none so strange as folks.

Control

If what Smith designates as 'freedom and smooth control' is the higher world's apparent ability to manipulate and co-ordinate its own time and environment on a grand scale in seemingly effortless fashion, then ordinary people, as they appear in this story-type, are not given this ability. Instead, control is always circumscribed, narrowed to particular specialities, talents or predispositions. Where control seems to pervade all corners of existence for élites, for ordinary people it is posed in terms of a single, limited domain – comic books, harness racing, the world of gnomes, old aeroplanes, barbering. Nor is control for ordinary people ever simply a given state of affairs, as it tends to be for élites – it has to be strived for and won. The especially remarkable qualities of élites are connoted by the relatively fluid ease with which they proceed in the world. In contrast, to be rendered especially remarkable, ordinary people need to be seen to 'make the effort' – their very-acting-as-they-do does not 'come easy'. However, the expenditure of such effort is not a drawback but appears in these stories as a distinct asset, a testament to these individuals and their ability to persist, to sustain a degree of determination and strength of conviction. In order to 'show more people that comics are a serious art form and shouldn't be considered childish', Joe Italiano expends considerable energy organizing 'the first ever comic book convention to be held in Australia'; 'to set a new world record [for] domino toppling' Michael Kearny 'spent fifteen days and ten hours setting up the intricate formations'; in order to build his hovercraft Peter Broome had to be 'tucked away in the garage [while] most of his class mates were out on the town at weekends'; his absorption with 'a vintage Tiger Moth' meant that Jim Riley had to spend 'a number of years scrounging around Australia' for airplane parts to assemble it. For élites, effortlessness seems to be a given part of the condition which makes them especially remarkable, whereas ordinary people are caught up in the expenditure of time, energy, money, resources, reputation in order to finally become especially remarkable, and they become so precisely when such effort 'pays off'.

Ordinary people can also be subject to degrees of variability with regard to the control they are capable of exerting over their special domains. Where control for élites seems much less problematic, it can be inscribed in stories about ordinary people either as initially absent, or prone to unpredictable fluctuations as the event unfolds. The obstacle that appears to be at work preventing the exertion of smooth control is frequently attributed to the play of fortune, where external unforeseen circumstances interfere, in varying degrees of severity, with the effort of action. The chance setback, however, is only momentary and with perserverance, and occasionally the right type of ingenuity, control is restored, the challenge met. What might be called the circumstantial reversal can serve as an important component in stories about ordinary people. In the midst of effort being exerted fortuitous happenings intervene to make completion of the task or performance an elusive affair. This reversal, however, also produces the conditions of redemption and finally, adulation: the less control to start, the less smoothly things run, the more remarkable the achievement appears when control is finally secured. Paradoxically, then, in ordinary people stories lack of control rather than its effortless execution becomes one of the conditions upon which especially remarkable qualities can be built.

The story of 'London's fastest barber' explains that he 'beat his own non-stop shaving record', but 'only by a whisker':

> The intrepid volunteers, students from University College, were pre-lathered with razors at the ready, to save time, and as Jerry set off at terrifying speed all seemed to be going well. But then came the problem. Some students had backed out at the last minute and Jerry was running out of willing victims.

As it turns out, the barber does succeed in breaking his own world record, but only after the dialectic of ill-fortune and effort has been played out. The momentary loss of control which comes, not from some failing on his part, but through the unpredictability of others is recuperated back into the story as a testimony to the man's accomplishment. The ill-timed withdrawal of volunteers, which might have proven a lesser person's downfall, becomes the fortuitous moment with which to demonstrate tenacity of purpose and quick thinking. Instead of floundering in the face of these desertions, the barber resourcefully shaves the same people again ('one hapless student was shaved ten times'). Bad luck is turned into good. The reversal is reversed, so that even in all its apparent banality and inconsequentiality, the reporting of this record event produces a powerful statement about the individual's will to succeed which can, with the right sort of determination, even conquer mischance and turn it to advantage.

The story about Peter Snyman, the cabinet maker who spent 'more than thirty-six days alone in a cage with two dozen deadly snakes' also includes intimations of faltering control and the playing out of this dialectic:

> Surrounded by giant mambas and cobras, Snyman told reporters by telephone he hadn't decided how many days he'd add to the old record. His initial goal was forty but Snyman said if the snakes behave themselves he might extend his target to fifty days.

The success of his performance resides partly with himself and his own efforts, but also with his accomplices, the snakes. He reminds us that his fortunes ultimately depend on external circumstances beyond his control i.e. the snakes behaving themselves. Yet, in the collision of effort and chance, in the shadow of a possible reversal, the story gives Snyman the opportunity to declare his determination and to assert his control – surrounded by giant mambas and cobras he might *extend* the target of his 'death-defying record'.

Even that 'special kind of person' who has the capacity 'to risk his or her own life to help someone else' and get 'awards for their bravery' is not immune to the play of fortune in the course of their extraordinary actions. Efforts are finally recognized ('they were given special certificates by the Governor'), but control is less than unwavering. 'Retired flat owner Hector McKenzie ... received high praise for his attempt to rescue two trapped passengers in a burning car'; but, exerting control over this situation was not automatic. News talk explains that:

> Mr McKenzie crawled into the front seat of the car where there was a clearance of only eighteen inches. At the time the flames in the rear of the car were coming forward. He managed to pull the injured to safety.

And just at the moment of maximum effort and determination (there was, after all, only a clearance of eighteen inches) Mr McKenzie is faced with a reversal due, not to any personal inadequacy on his part, but to the force of external circumstance, as the flames came forward. Despite this unforeseen adversity he succeeds in his mission; but achievement in this case is not completely decisive. Mr McKenzie does not give a triumphant performance; rather we are told that he 'managed'. Perhaps one of the most equivocal terms in a journalists' vocabulary is the verb 'to manage'. Used in this context it suggests that the play of fortune, which has already produced the circumstantial reversal, is still hovering close by during the final execution of the deed, this time working in a helpful rather than a hindering capacity. When Mr McKenzie manages to pull the injured to safety he does so with the fates smiling kindly on him. This, however, should not be taken to imply that these stories are representing ordinary people as merely buffeted about by the whims of fortune; the situation is more complex. Although he may not make his fate directly, Hector McKenzie does make the effort ('crawl[ing] into the front seat of the car') which in turn makes his fate. The proverbial expression 'the gods help them that help themselves' comes to mind. Here, the dialectic of effort and fortune mingle in the word 'managed'.

If control and fortune are taken as recurrent variables, stories about élites and ordinary people might better be understood, on one level, by situating them on a continuum, with unqualified control at one end and the undiluted play of chance at the other. In terms of the stories examined so far, those focused on institutional and celebrity élites seem to be most easily placed at the end where the oscillations of fortune are least likely to have a major influence. It is also near this end where some stories about ordinary people can be situated – where full control is exerted but over narrowly defined spheres (barbering, motorcycle riding, rescuing). As shifts along the continuum are made, fortune is increasingly introduced into stories. These are items about ordinary people who perform extraordinary deeds, but who are subject to the dialectic of fortune and forbearance, with some items giving priority to the play of luck, while others emphasize the persistence of effort. Now, as we shall see in the next chapters, news about victims and communities at risk are found even further along the continuum in a region almost entirely dominated by fortune. Reports about victims are always posed in terms of fortuitous circumstances which wrench subjects out of their everyday activities, and over which they appear to have no control. Community at risk stories work in a similar fashion, but at the level of collectivities: sudden inexplicable circumstances play havoc with the orderly procedures of community life. Of course, there is a good deal of variability here. Reversals which take place in victim stories can be overturned with the aid of strategically placed 'helpers' and 'donors' and community at risk stories connect the cessation of misfortune with the determined efforts of rescue agencies. Regardless of these variations there still seems to be a critical thread which runs through and binds these apparently very different news stories together into a particular kind of unity based on shifts between agency and fate. The continuum on which these stories could be located ranges through circumstances handled with effortless control at one end (the Prince gets a 'special dispensation from the Pope'), which in turn moves to control with effort (the barber 'was running out of willing victims'), then a struggle between effort and fortune (the flat owner 'managed to pull the injured to safety'), and eventually sliding into situations where fortune takes control (the girlfriend 'will be flying to Noumea to find out more about [the] fate' of the missing school teacher) .

When news talk refers to the conditions of control which permit ordinary people to enter the realms of the especially remarkable, news film becomes the site from which these conditions can be observed. The effort expended, which is discussed and explained in a story's news commentary is demonstrated to have results in the visuals. News film functions in these items to *show* ordinary people acting, performing and doing extraordinary tasks. If élites in the 'other news' tend to get depicted in news film merely being-as-they-are, ordinary people appearing in the visuals are given the opportunity to act-as-they-do, displaying their virtuosity or revealing the results of their personal accomplishments. Their especially remarkable qualities are made manifest and 'real'-ized in actions that can be documented by the camera and shown to us. The fifteen-year-old schoolboy is witnessed deftly gliding his hovercraft over an open field; the record-setting barber is shown hard at work on his chins; the man with the beer-can boat is seen winning the race. Sometimes the exercise of control is deemed to be so conclusive that its visualization in news film is given special treatment. The shot of the 'young stunt rider', Dale Buggins, making his 'record breaking leap at one hundred and forty five kilometres per hour' over twenty-five stationary cars is shown first at normal speed, and then replayed in slow motion. As the footage is repeated the reporter's voice-over suddenly ceases – a rare occurrence in television news which tends to favour 'covering' all actuality footage with commentary – the remarkable leap apparently leaving the newsmakers speechless.

Superlatives

News talk is punctuated by superlatives which proclaim the achievements of ordinary people and assign especially remarkable qualities. A particular kind of emphatic language is employed to characterize performances and their outcomes as well as to underline and counterpoint the normal. As in celebrity stories, the choice of words tends to favour a rhetoric drawn from the world of promotion and marketing. This mode of address overflows with the extravagance and the enthusiasm of an advertiser's grand claim: Jerry Harley is labelled 'the fastest razor in London'; Michael Kearney wants 'to set a new world record for domino toppling'; thirteen firemen set out on 'the longest and the most gruelling non-stop team endurance run in the world'; Dale Buggins is 'one of Australia's youngest ever world champions'; Margaret Cross is 'the first woman given a licence to drive on a major track'; Joe Italiano has organized 'the first ever comic convention'. Through the strategic deployment of such constructions, news talk can assert the remarkable qualities of these occurrences and their initiators. Superlatives are also set up by 'the surprise of numbers' (Barthes 1977a: 190) where enumeration, either large or small, is used to give remarkable substance to action. For example, Peter Snyman spends 'thirty-six days alone' in the cage with snakes, and 'he might extend his target to fifty days'; Dale Buggins jumps over twenty-five cars whereas 'the best Evil [Knevil] has managed is nineteen'; Joe Italiano 'has a collection of more than eleven thousand comics [and] receives fifty every month'; Howard Gerd's vessel 'is made of two thousand beer cans';

Michael Kearney 'spends fifteen days and ten hours' setting up 141,000 dominoes; the hovercraft 'only cost Peter and his Dad a little over five hundred dollars to build'. When not dealing in specifics, quantification is simply presented through globalizing claims: world records, world champions, world competitions are the reference points which help define ordinary people as especially remarkable.

Superlatives applied to ordinary people are also established through the regular use of the narrative of personal triumph in which individuals are essentially cast as characters in one of life's 'dramas', progressing through a series of obstacles or dangers from which they emerge successful, usually with a reward of a tangible kind – money, public recognition, status, renewed physical well-being, even life itself. These narratives are formed around a sequence of codified 'moments' which include the setting out of obstacles or deficiencies to start, a 'theory' of motivation which helps to explain why 'protagonists' have been able to overcome barriers and engage in remarkable accomplishments and a final testament to acknowledge the actual triumphant performance of the deed. News talk is essential for constructing such narratives, although sequencing is unlikely to follow in a strictly chronological order – the story is reassembled from 'the plot' (Bordwell and Thompson 1979: 52) – and important detail and emphasis can be provided by visualization, especially where the successful performance itself is recorded and offered as the culmination of endeavour.

The story about the 'iron lung mother' follows this pattern closely, even referring to this narrational approach in the opening moments of the newsreader's introduction to the report: 'Mrs Rosina Grosse gave birth to a baby daughter, and that's quite an achievement. Mrs Grosse has been a polio victim for twenty years . . . this is her story'. The reporter comes in at this point to provide more elaboration on the unfavourable background circumstances and then to counter these with a theory of motivation:

> Rosina Grosse was stricken with polio at the age of sixteen. Today she has only two per cent mobility and spends her life in a wheel chair or an iron lung. But with courage and determination Rosina has overcome this enormous handicap.

The story closes on the personal triumph as we are told that 'for her and her husband Ron the dream of having their own family is now a reality'. News film confirms the especially remarkable achievement by showing the 'new mother' lying prone in her iron lung behind a glass window while her husband holds the child so that she and the viewer can see the victory of motherhood over physical adversity. The item about 'stunt boy Dale Buggins' uses a similar narrative pattern to assert superlatives. Background hardships are set in place – '[during] his last attempt at the world record . . . he made it over twenty of the twenty-five cars but hit the last few . . . end[ing] up with the motor bike on top of him and a couple of broken bones'. Motivation and psychological cueing are given strategic placement – 'for a successful jump Buggins knew that he would have to top one hundred and sixty kilometres an hour by the time he left the ramp'; and ultimately a triumphant success – 'twelve thousand fans looked on as he set off on the ride of his life'. News film provides visual authentication for the narrative by showing Buggins as he performs his 'amazing leap', once at normal speed, then again in slow motion.

The twitch

Whereas the twitch in stories about élites tends to operate in the singular – one story, one twitch – in the coverage of ordinary people who become especially remarkable the twitch can be manifested through a number of mutually reinforcing mild surprises. Possibly the most prominent of these occurs as result of a 'relation of coincidence' (Barthes 1977a: 192). This catches us out with an unexpected juxtaposition: a technologically sophisticated hovercraft is built . . . by a fifteen-year-old schoolboy; an adult likes reading . . . comic books; a man builds a boat . . . made from beer cans; a rugby team holds races each year . . . using crabs; a veterinarian goes to work . . . flying a bi-plane.[2] As in stories about élites, our surprise is twitched because the reduction of distance has collapsed together elements normally encountered in 'autonomous circuits of signification' (Barthes 1977a: 192) – schoolboys and advanced technology, 'terms' logically separate, are now part of the same realm. Surprise is also generated because the structure of such stories asks us to 'look for one cause, and it is another which appears' (Barthes 1977a: 190) – a hovercraft is designed . . . by naval engineers? No, by a schoolboy; a boat is made . . . from wood, steel, fibreglass? No, from beer cans.

Elites enter the news simply for their very being-as-they-are; but as we have seen, reports on their doings and way of life may not always contain sufficient news value, so these items set about to construct a twitch of mild surprise within the story, to give it that 'little extra' which meets the criteria of newsworthiness: the formality of a royal visit is 'unexpectedly' made informal when the Prince takes part in side-show games. What stories about élites need to insert into themselves in order to gain value as news – the unexpected in the routine – stories about ordinary people used as the basis for the item itself: inconguity serves as the *starting point* of these stories rather than merely an additional effect. Stories about élites begin with their very-being-as-they-are and insert a derranged casuality; stories about ordinary people are news precisely because their initial premise is a fractured causality. However, once the relation of coincidence is set in place certain propositions can unfold which generate especially remarkable qualities. Despite their apparent ordinariness (their nomination in news talk makes this clear: *a* schoolboy, *a* cabinet maker, *a* barber) these individuals turn out to be just the reverse. Initially presented as an incongruous set of circumstances by the organizing principles of the story, the relation of coincidence actually proves the means by which the ordinary person can be judged extraordinary. So, for example, the peculiarity which attaches to the fractured causality of schoolboys and hovercraft also becomes the source of extraordinary achievement. Peter Broome's connection with advanced technology may seem strange and surprising but he 'win[s] an award for . . . design' and he 'hopes that [he will get a] job . . . as an engineer, and thanks to "The Blowfly" he will be well prepared'. Similarly, Joe Italiano's 'childish' attachment to comics may be curious, given that he is after all a 'grown man', but this peculiar obsession is the very condition which gives rise to the possibility of the first ever Australian comic book convention. Rugby and crabs may be an odd combination but that does not prevent a crab race run by a rugby team from becoming 'one of the highlights of the year' in the town of Mount Isa.

Further conditions for surprise have as their basis what Barthes (1977a: 190), in his analysis of the *fait-divers*, refers to as the relation of 'disproportions' – the results of an action seem to greatly exceed what could be expected given the causes of such an action. A boy is given a school project so he ends up building a hovercraft; firemen want to raise money for charity so they engage in the longest non-stop marathon run in the world; a man wants to demonstrate that comics are not childish, so he holds a national conference to prove it. These examples often surprise us because, as Barthes (1977a: 190) explains, causal relations are demonstrated to be 'peculiar; the slight volume of a cause in no way diminishes the scope of its effect; a little equals a lot'. Moreover, if seemingly inconsequential causes can produce great effects this fractured causality might be found anywhere: 'it is not constituted by a qualitatively accumulated force but rather by a mobile energy, active in very small doses' (Barthes 1977a: 190). This opens up a particular paradoxical situation with regard to ordinary people and their remarkableness. On the one hand ordinary people are constructed as especially remarkable for what they do. How they act to breach expectations, their remarkableness, is lodged in the extraordinary acts that they perform. This separates them from us, makes them different and transcendent; they start where we are but then move beyond. On the other hand, the causal logic of disproportions postulated by Barthes which is operating in stories about ordinary people can be found everywhere – the empirical minutiae of causality, those 'very small doses', makes it fluid and mobile, capable of turning up in all kinds of places. The implication is that, although these people are assigned especially remarkable qualities based on what they do, such qualities and performances could just as easily be within our grasp. If those seemingly mundane occupations and enthusiasms – barbering, drinking beer, tinkering in a garage, raising money for charity, having a love of horses – can become the springboard from which those ordinary people ascend into the realms of the especially remarkable it could just as easily happen to us as well. At any moment 'minor causes' – our hobbies, our work, our indulgences – could yield up 'great effects'. This may be in part one way of specifying what Andy Warhol's aphorism about fifteen minutes of fame was alluding to, and in this context, television news 'factors' itself into the calculus of celebrityhood on a nightly basis.

5

VICTIMS

This chapter and the next will focus on those types of news stories often referred to as 'accidents', 'disasters', 'chance events', 'mishaps', and sometimes 'personal tragedies'. Although these labels are imprecise I wish to retain them for the moment in order to make some initial comments on the contours of these stories, how they have been handled by some news studies and in more general commentaries on news. Once this has been done, there will be an attempt to refine these terms, not necessarily changing them, but offering a more systematic analysis of the news stories to which they frequently refer.

Television news studies regularly acknowledge the presence of these types of stories but tend to slide around when trying to specify what actually constitutes such reports. For example, in the news item profile employed by Bell, Boehringer and Crofts (1982: 149–51) for their study of Australian television news and politics, content categories related to these types of stories included 'accidents and chance events', 'disasters' and 'weather'. A later Australian television news study made use of a single, encompassing category called 'accidents and disasters' (Gerdes and Charlier 1985: 12–13). In Britain, the Glasgow University Media Group's analysis (1980: 420) of news content on the BBC and ITV simply located news stories of this type in a broad unitary category they called 'disasters' while Hartley (1982: 39), in his study of British television news, employed the term 'occasional stories', a classification broad enough to incorporate items as diverse as disasters, celebrities, the Royals and 'topical talking points of the day'. Although its presence and continuance has been well documented, not much by way of detailed study of this type of news has actually taken place, particularly as it ordinarily appears in everyday news bulletins. When analysis has been done either it tends towards a series of cursory remarks which act as backgrounding for what is ultimately a discussion of the serious news (Windschuttle 1984; Bonney and Wilson 1983) or it focuses exclusively on 'big news' oriented around 'crisis coverage' – the San Francisco earthquake (Pearson 1992), the 'Challenger' space shuttle explosion (Mellencamp 1992). As a result attention has been deflected away from normal journalistic practices as they work in relation to what might be described as, if I can be excused such terminology without sounding too glib or cynical, the 'routine' accident and personal catastrophe – that is, reportable occasions of misadventure which have a consistent place in news bulletins between the grandiloquent crises. Even basic questions like what makes the terms 'accident' or 'disaster' appropriate labels for such stories have not been explored in any detail. This chapter and Chapter 6 are attempts to fill in some of these gaps, examining these types of news reports as meaning-producing texts, paying particular attention to their organizational features, the way they construct and narrativize notions of 'accident', 'disaster' or 'tragedy' and the assumptions used to make sense of the occurrences which they represent.

As we have seen, these types of stories are commonly among the first to be condemned by critics of television news, singled out as symptoms of the worst excesses and trivializations of television journalism, frequently described as 'sensationalistic', 'ghoulish', 'exploitative', certainly unworthy of our time and attention. If negativism and personalization are two primary news values (Bonney and Wilson 1983: 301), the lament would argue that these have been promoted in the extreme in catastrophe-oriented coverage. Regardless of such disapproval, these types of stories play a prominent role in the constitution of the news bulletin as a totality, and this seems especially the case in an Australian context. As Bell, Boehringer and Crofts (1982) discovered the amount of time devoted to various types of news and the general sequencing of items in the overall bulletin structure was virtually invariant over time. Even during an Australian federal election when the conditions for wider political coverage were readily available, stories about 'accidents', 'chance events' and 'disasters' were still among the most frequently appearing news items. When comparing television news content between 1980 and 1985 Gerdes and Charlier (1985: 96) found that 'accident and natural disaster' stories were among the few types of reports which had actually increased in frequency. This may suggest that, at least in the Australian instance, this type of news is an essential generic ingredient of the television news format; that television news *must* include such stories in order to retain its *modus operandi*.

Disaster, accident and personal mishap reportage has a long, if inglorious, history in journalism. These types of stories have a lengthy pedigree, certainly preceding television and perhaps even journalism itself. The general subject matter of such stories (the events themselves or the representation of such events) can, and frequently does, serve as the basis for other cultural narratives and other forms of representation. There are books for example, published for the popular market, which specialize in making 'great disasters' of the past their entire focus – a chapter each on train crashes, derailments, misadventures at sea, bridge collapses and so on (see Mackay 1982; Kartman and Brown 1971). Mishaps of this kind have also emerged as the subject of an identifiable genre in the cinema, notably the Hollywood cycle of disaster films of the 1970s (Gans 1977). Events of misadventure, however, do not have to be selected in terms of an agenda which only stresses magnitude – seemingly small disasters or individual misfortunes, sometimes referred to journalistically as the 'personal tragedy', can also be the topic of both news and elaborated narrativizations. In the sample stories collected for this study, 'the release' from an inner city hospital of Ann McDonald, an eighteen-year-old 'severely handicapped girl' was featured as a major report on all bulletins over several days. Subsequent to this coverage, an Australian feature film called 'Annie's Coming Out' (1984) was made based directly on the events surrounding this release.

Given the wide range of cultural texts which focus on disaster and misadventure, some might be inclined to argue that this is as it should be as these themes are some of the key recurrent and universal preoccupations of humankind – the struggle for life, disturbance and dread, the play of fate. And when these themes make an appearance in television news stories, there is sometimes the temptation to read them as up-dated archetypal expressions of the human condition (see Rutherford-Smith 1979). But, if news stories such as these seem to adhere so easily to notions of the transhistorical and the timeless it may be even more important to read them socially and historically, in order to demonstrate how, precisely through their apparent eternal concerns, such stories are able to contribute to one of the crucial hegemonic achievements of broadcast journalism, the winning of consent (Goldman and Rajagopal 1991).

CONTOURS OF A STORY-TYPE

We come now to the point where these kinds of news reports need to be allocated to particular story-types in order to proceed with the more detailed analysis proposed. Until now I have been employing terms for these stories which have been in circulation both journalistically and analytically. Although it may be readily apparent the type of story about to follow when the newsreader proclaims ' . . . and there were accidents in Sydney . . . ' – conjuring up mangled bodies of automobiles, ambulances on the scene, flashing blue police car lights, perhaps someone being carried on a stretcher – the boundaries, diversity and 'form[s] of thematization' of such stories may need to be looked at a little more closely. The tendency has been to simply use a convenient or conventional label to classify a range of stories without taking into account possible variations in emphasis, internal organization, thematic orientation and modes of explanation. In order to build a more comprehensive picture with regard to the kinds of events on which catastrophe coverage is focused, and to be more exacting with regard to story content and structure, it might be useful to begin by dividing such stories into two broad story-types. The first of which is distinguished by a primary focus on the plight of individuals caught up in circumstances of adversity beyond their immediate control, the second by an emphasis on communities or social aggregations suddenly threatened with some form of collective danger. The first grouping will be referred to as victim stories, the second community at risk stories. The rest of this chapter will deal with the former story-type while Chapter 6 will be concerned with the latter.

Victim stories can be characterized by their insistent focus on individuals who, in the process of going about their daily affairs, encounter an unanticipated turn of events which ensnares them in a state of crisis from which they cannot emerge using their own efforts and resources. If these individuals can be situated as 'characters' in an unfolding drama, their principle role is constituted primarily as that of victim. From the news stories collected, examples included a 'pre-dawn fire . . . one of the most tragic in [the state's] history' which 'claim[ed] the lives of a mother and four of her children'; the 'tragedy' of a twelve-year-old boy 'mauled and killed by a lion at the . . . [l]ion [p]ark west of Melbourne'; and 'a distraught wife and mother of two children' outside the court where 'her husband is on trial for murder'. Usually victims are depicted as thoroughly ordinary people, but becoming a victim can befall anyone regardless of position or prestige, so an item about the Premier of New South Wales who was 'subject of a scare . . . when the light plane [he] was travelling on had engine trouble and looked in danger of ditching at sea' was considered a victim rather than a political story because its dominant form of thematization focused entirely on aspects of the misadventure and individuated psychological consequences and nothing more. Other victim stories tended to focus on the severity of a particular medical condition: an 'Adelaide girl with a rare muscular disease'; the 'total paralysis' of a Sydney rugby player, the result of an injury during a game. Places of work or leisure in relation to modes of transportation featured prominently as well: a truck driver has a 'close brush with death' when his 'brakes . . . failed'; a construction worker 'lay[s] trapped under a giant sewage pipe thirty feet below the ground'; 'a light plane crash . . . claim[s] the life of an experienced aviator'; a police constable is run over by a truck; a crop duster pilot is 'recovering in hospital . . . after crashing during an air show'; a Melbourne school teacher is the 'subject of a search' after his 'mysterious disappearance . . . from a Russian passenger ship off Noumea'. And animals are not only the cause of personal tragedy, but can also be tragic victims: rangers discover 'a mass slaughter of wallabies on Queensland's South Stradbroke Island'.[1]

The victim story also has two important narrative variations. The first involves stories which begin with typical conditions of victimage – individuals trapped in unanticipated circumstances of adversity over which they have no control – but follow through with a report on how these conditions are partially or completely alleviated. In terms of the story however, this process is only made possible with the assistance of a strategically placed benefactor or 'helper' (Propp 1968: 39). A female 'trainee pilot . . . being vindictively assailed in the most inhumane and unforgivable manner [by her] airline employer' is provided with the key figure of the helper in the form of 'the chief representative' of the national pilot's federation whose function in the story it is to 'rescue' the victim 'hero' so that the initial conditions of misadventure can be overcome. The story about 'the release' from hospital, after fourteen years, of the 'physically and mentally handicapped girl' assigns a caring 'ward attendant' the crucial role of helper.[2] The second narrative variation can best be explained as a 'fool making encounter' (Klapp 1964: 90). If stories about victims emphasize the inability of individuals to help themselves or extract themselves from entanglements not of their own choosing, fool-making encounters rely on individuals attaining the status of victim mostly through their own misjudged actions: a bush walker is lost for several days in 'some of the most rugged mountain country' because he got separated from his companions, wearing hiking boots that didn't fit.

Unlike especially remarkable person stories, reports about victims are not lighter items appearing in the later half of the bulletin. Their overall place-ment is closer to the top of the bulletin than the bottom and in several instances – the missing school teacher, the house fire, the lion park death – the story will lead the bulletin. Victim stories are apparently 'hard news', yet there is not complete agreement about how much news value this kind of coverage should be accorded. Discrepancies are most obvious if story placement is compared between the commercial and the public news ser-vices. For example, although the missing school teacher item is the first story of the day on the commercial bulletins (Channels 7, 9, and 0), it is placed tenth in the running order on Channel 2, the public broadcaster. An item about 'the fate of the lion' ranks first, second and third on the commercial channels, but is located well down the bulletin in tenth position on Channel 2. The New South Wales Premier's plane emergency resides in second, fourth, and sixth position on the commercial news but in fourteenth on the Australian Broadcast Commission bulletin. A preponderance of victim stor-ies appear on the commercial news bulletins, however, it also needs to be noted that although the ABC bulletin does not run as many of these stories, it still includes some, and of those that do appear some seem to have as much news value as those on the commercial channels; for instance the house fire and the wife and children outside the court stories both appear as lead items.

GOOD VICTIMS AND THE REFLEX OF TEARS

In order to understand the ways by which the 'other news' selects victims and reports on their misadventures, the work by Klapp (1964) on the 'dramatic encounters' of 'symbolic leaders' is a useful point of departure. Importantly, Klapp (1964: 91–2) explains, the 'good victim' is produced by way of sym-pathy, and certain 'objects' and 'dramatic relationship[s]' are likely to have more 'symbolic advantage' than others. Smallness or infirmity, a sense of helplessness or vulnerability, the inability to fight back, the 'style of encounter' between the one who evokes sympathy and a villain who provokes misfortune, the unexpectedness of the circumstances, and the 'magnitude' of the misfortune all make a difference. Conditions which produce good victims must be understood to 'approach disaster' shattering everyday experience socially and psychologically. It is also 'crucial that the trouble be suffered but not chosen' (Klapp 1964: 92) – victims cannot be seen to be capable of helping themselves or remedying the situation by means of their own resources, a state of affairs favourable to the possible introduction of a 'dramatic partner' who acts as a rescuer providing special resources or know-how in an attempt to get the victim 'out of trouble'.

The concept of the good victim has an interesting connection with what literary theorist Northrop Frye (1957: 33–9) called 'low mimetic tragedy'. According to Frye, European fiction can be divided into epochs or periods characterized by 'the different elevations' of the protagonist: 'the hero's power of action . . . may be greater than ours, less or roughly the same'. Through the progressive evolution of the fictional form the action of the hero moved from a position of superiority (the mythic mode) towards a position of inferiority (the ironic mode). Low mimetic tragedy sits somewhere in the middle where the hero is posited as one of us and we are asked to 'respond to a sense of his [sic] common humanity' (Frye 1957: 34). Typified especially by the realist fiction of the new English middle class, extending from Defoe to the end of the nineteenth century, Frye (1957: 34–8) contends that: 'the best word for low mimetic or domestic tragedy is perhaps pathos, and pathos has a close relationship to the sensational reflex of tears'. Without becoming overcommitted to his general theory of modes, Frye's observations, nonetheless, provide another useful entry point for understanding news stories focused on victims. Pathos, Frye goes on to explain (1957: 38–9), often requires protagonists to be 'isolated by a weakness . . . [which] is on our own level of experience'. Sometimes this process is generated by the 'inarticulateness of the victim', 'the catastrophe of defective intelligence' or flawed bodies, or through a reliance on a strong contrast between a 'ruthless figure' and some type of 'delicate virtue'. Frequently the central figure of pathos is a woman or child, sometimes both. Frye describes pathos as tapping into some kind of 'queer, ghoulish emotion', a comment, it will be noted, not dissimilar to the way the lament characterizes unworthy news.

The perspectives offered by both Klapp and Frye seem to be underscored by some notion of identification, which for our purposes means exploring the relationship set up between the viewer–reader and the news text: in constituting good victims, news items in this story-type must offer the reader a position, not of pure spectatorship, but of involvement or affiliation. The news story has to facilitate, in a very short interval of time, a way by which the viewer can enter into a relationship of sympathy with individuals caught up in the event. In order to investigate this process it will be necessary to uncover the framing devices and methods of 'story-telling' systematically deployed in this story-type which attempt to illicit the requisite sympathy from viewers. These are techniques learned by journalists which aid in the ordering and emphasis of certain aspects of an event, and in the constitution of the good victim.[3]

A 'good victim' is above all a person, 'character' to whom one can relate. As Frye (1957: 38) points out our sympathy is evoked because the action and character stand on 'our own level of experience'. In terms of this process of identification, it might be argued that these stories function differently from the serious news where reportage is primarily concerned with the worlds of politics, the economy, international affairs and so on. Although the serious news does offer points of identification – politicians are discussed in personal terms (see Bell, Boehringer and Crofts 1982) and the 'economy' is shown visually via the everyday reality of the supermarket check-out counter (see Glasgow University Media Group 1980) – overall, serious news stories posit a position for the reader/viewer which is detached and observational with occasional forays into positions of identification. Victim stories work the other way around. The points of identification which are offered seem to proliferate and become more frequently available within stories and across stories. Serious news is often not about those on 'our own level of experience', but concerns the power brokers and decision makers, whereas the majority of victim stories, at least from the sample at hand, begin in the everyday and its 'background expectancies', with which it is assumed we are all completely familiar. This is not to suggest that the powerful and the influential cannot become victims. The point worth noting is that it is the moment when these individuals do become victims – the New South Wales Premier on a routine airplane journey is the 'subject of a scare' – that they can be most personalized, made most like us, brought down to 'our own level of experience'. However, news stories about victims do not, in fact as television news cannot, exclude positions from which to simply 'look on' (see Connell 1979) but unlike the serious news the possibilities for identification are much more extensively produced. Consequently, it could be suggested that one of the basic structuring operations in victim stories is a constant shifting from positions of detachment to involvement, distance to sentiment – we are both surveying the site of victimage and, at the same time, being led into it by way of its placement at our level.

IN-THE-NORMAL-COURSE-OF-EVENTS . . .

Victim stories attempt to establish an ordinary, routine world which we are encouraged to assume is trouble-free and stable. Studies of news show that journalism implicitly relies on some notion of consensus in order to do its reporting – a what-everyone-knows 'organizing principle' (Hartley 1982:

82). This is necessary in order to explain and classify the world as well as to allow for the selection of newsworthy events. Victim stories also offer a version of consensus, but in terms of the most mundane of everyday affairs – the consensus in this context emerges out of the 'background expectancies' which make it possible to carry on the normal routines governing our waking, eating and sleeping lives. (These particular routines are worth a special mention here because victim stories are known to begin with a logic like this: the family was eating their evening meal, in bed asleep, etc., when . . . the truck hit the house, the wall caved in, the fire started.) Mundane routines are established, only to be disrupted. This disruption can be gradual, but it is more likely to be depicted as sudden, unexpected and importantly not something chosen by potential victims. Grounding victim stories in such ordinary aspects of everyday life can act as one of the narrative facilitators for producing pathos and sympathy.

The normal course of events, when referenced, is not situated at the start of the story. The ordinary state of affairs is often placed inside the body of news talk, sometimes spoken about by the newsreader, sometimes by the reporter, or even by a witness or rescuer. News stories about victims seem to work from a state of actual harm or crisis back to the normal state of affairs that has been disrupted. The first statement of news talk might be heard this way: 'A twelve-year-old boy was mauled by a lion at the Bacchus Marsh Lion Park, west of Melbourne today'; 'A truck driver had a close brush with death today when his semi-trailer came to rest hanging . . . over a twenty-five metre drop'. Details of the normal taken-for-granted world of mundane routines are retrieved in flashback, later in the story. The opening sentence of the news commentary, however, is a first hint that something has been disturbed – 'in-the-normal-course-of-events' twelve-year-old boys are not mauled, nor do truck drivers have a brush with death – and only later are disturbances fully contextualized. The first statement seems more concerned with immediately posing a series of unanswered questions, opening up puzzles to which we desire answers – How? Why? Under what conditions was it possible that a twelve-year-old could get mauled?

When it does arrive, the reference to normal consensualized routines is sometimes foregrounded quite directly in order to produce a forceful juxtaposition between the regular and the unanticipated. In the story about the 'plane emergency' involving the Premier of New South Wales we are told that the pilot 'was about to eat a slice of fruit cake when trouble struck'. The report about the truck driver who 'had a close brush with death' foregrounds the routine order of things when it is explained that 'the driver, Geoff Baker, aged twenty-eight from Elwood was delivering steel channelling in Church Street' (something he would be doing in-the-normal-course-of-events), 'when the brakes on his truck failed'. In addition, this story contains a number of other indices which assist to produce the sense of the normal, deriving from the journalistic convention which insists on identifying the who, the where, and the when in news copy. However, placed in the context of victim stories, these seemingly straightforward details extend beyond mere information and act as another gesture which locates the occurrence in relation to what would exist in the normal course of events. The particularity of the driver's 'co-ordinates' in time and space – he has a specific age, he lives in a specific suburb, he is driving in a specific street and so on – marks him and his routines out as nothing but ordinary. Yet, the very particularities with which this ordinariness is established also stand in for a series of more abstracted possibilities. Not only are his biographical details particular, they are also arbitrary – his age could be any age, his suburb could be any suburb, his job any job, his fate could be anyone's fate, *in-the-normal-course-of-events*. The mobilization of identification and sympathy can begin in these strategic story-telling moments.

ACCIDENT AND AGENCY

To effectively secure the victim's status and the concomitant sympathy response from the audience, a number of complimentary strategies are used to enhance the sense that disruption, when it occurs, is unanticipated and outside any individual's control. This kind of emphasis is notable in light of research on accidents and accident-related behaviour which suggests that, despite conventional wisdom, there is a certain degree of individual and community control involved in the development of accidents, the contention being that although accidents may not be entirely preventable, there can be a degree of anticipation, predictability and even preventability at work when the complete accident dynamic is examined (see Turner 1978; Malik 1970). This point is raised, not to argue that news 'distorts' the realities surrounding accidents in the real world but that victim stories in the news offer particular narrativized versions or transcriptions of accident 'realities' that need to be accounted for in their own terms, and read in relation to the framing devices upon which these versions are built. Two operations seem to be at work at this level. The first addresses the question of human agency – how do these stories attempt to offer, or explain, causal sequences leading up to the crisis in terms of human action or its absence? The second relates to the way that a story typifies the build up to the crisis, focusing on the inescapable preconditions of ensnarement.

For example, stories concerned with workplace or transportation related accidents have a strong tendency to evacuate human agency. Through the use of certain phrases in news talk, the impression is created that some greater design is at work, a process that gives power to inanimate objects which seem to manifest a life of their own, immune to the control of human agents. The report on the 'air crash' near Goulburn in New South Wales explains that 'once again a light plane crash *has claimed* [a] life', while the story about the crop duster pilot describes how 'the plane *hit* a tree and *ploughed* into the ground only one hundred metres from the nearest spectators'. The item about the truck driver's out of control vehicle puts it like this: '[w]hen the brakes *failed* on his truck . . . his prime mover *kept going, went over* the drop only *to be halted* by the channelling on the tray'. It could be countered that too much significance is being placed on such phrases and imagery, that these expressive strategies are part of common usage and are not exclusive to news talk. The point here, however, is that these phrases and modes of expression are being used in particular signifying contexts – news stories about victims – and as a result usage has to be seen in connection with this emphasis. If good victims cannot choose the course of their actions and must suffer accordingly, such modes of expression work as rhetorical devices to secure the status of the constructed character in the story as a victim.

In some stories the evacuation or glossing of human agency will appear as a reference to the notion of ill-fortune or luck. Filling in the details of the crippling spinal injury sustained by the Sydney footballer, the reporter explains that the 'twenty-one-year old . . . is one of at least ten footballers to suffer that fate this year'. An explanation of the school teacher's demise is implicated in something other than human agency when it is reported that his brother and girlfriend 'will be fly[ing] to Noumea to see if they can find out more about his fate'. And, the girl with the muscular disease is given 'her last chance to live a normal life'. Outside the possibility of human intervention, a victim's destiny seems to be haphazard and beyond their own control, making the story's protagonist both more vulnerable and also more pitiable, a worthy focus for concern. When the idea of fate or luck is not directly referenced, some stories rely on what might be called the invocation of the inexplicable, further diverting explanations away from causal sequences governed by human agency or error. The strategy works by producing incongruence between what is known about the victim and what actually takes place. The story about a fatal accident involving a light plane near the town of Goulburn does it this way: first, the unforeseen mishap – 'a light plane crash has claimed [a] life'; and then the appeal to the inexplicable – 'of an *experienced* aviator. At the controls, forty-one-year-old Graeme Kenneth, owner of an established charter business based in Sydney, and a well known figure among Sydney's flyers' (emphasis added). The item about the 'school teacher missing from a Russian cruise liner' dwells almost obsessively on the incongruence between the occurrence and available information about the victim prior to the mishap. To start the invocation the victim is located in terms which juxtapose what has happened against what is known – the incident is designated a 'mysterious disappearance'. And the mystery apparently deepens when it is revealed that 'Kevin [was] an outstanding sportsman . . . with many trophies for football, athletics and tennis'. To punctuate this point a series of close-up shots of the victim's trophies is provided, and then to make certain that the invocation is thoroughly thematized, in an interview with his friends on the same cruise, the teacher's athletic ability is highlighted once again:

REPORTER: Do you think that he could have fallen overboard?
FRIEND: It's a remote possibility.
REPORTER: He would have been a strong swimmer.
FRIEND: He is very fit, he would have been a good swimmer.

Seemingly, the victim possessed the resources to facilitate his own rescue – the emphasis is on why he inexplicably did not do so.

Another strategy which appears to divert agency in order to enhance victim status and potential solicitude is to suggest that the circumstances unfolding happen so quickly that escape or counter-action is virtually impossible – human intervention of whatever kind, by the victims themselves or their potential rescuers, is just not an option. The implication here is not that these types of occurrences do not happen rapidly as described – anyone who has ever had even a minor automobile accident knows that they do – but to evaluate this kind of emphasis in conjunction with a news report's attempt to construct a good victim. The reporting of the fire in the town of Gordon explains how the 'house was *quickly engulfed* in flames'; and an item on the mauling describes how the 'lion *burst* through the fence'. Becoming a victim, it appears, can be only a matter of seconds: as pilot Paul Keece was 'about to eat a piece of fruit cake trouble *struck*' (emphasis added).

ACCOUNTS AND WITNESSES

As well as strategies used to set up the conditions for unenvisioned occurrences, each report has to offer an account, to present 'the story' of the victim's plight. These accounts are offered from a number of differing yet overlapping points of view so that the viewer is able to take up a number of positions from which to relate to the victims and their circumstances. In this sense these accounts may be referred to as renditions, something like musical 'variations on a theme'. Renditions act as explanations of the chain of events leading to an individual becoming a victim and make available some crucial details of the occurrence which testify to the actuality of the event, opening another space for additional identification and sympathy.

Accounts of events are multilayered and might be divided or separated out from one another in terms of a number of features. For example, there are the accounts 'internal' to the bulletin itself; primary here is the newsreader whose position in television news is so central. His/her rendition of events remains detached, neutral, impersonal and totalizing in contrast to renditions offered by participants or witnesses to the event, whose perspective is just the reverse – their accounts remain personal, partisan, and partial. In between stands the reporter, whose position swings from being internal (part of the bulletin itself) to external (on the scene) and whose account is offered as both partial and particular in relation to that of the newsreader but also totalizing in relation to those of the witnesses. Renditions also vary in terms of access to certain registers of address and to the camera. The newsreader's access is optimal in the sense that he or she delivers the account directly, looking at 'us', having access to our gaze, whereas witness accounts are mediated through the interview structure or simply through the use of reported speech. Accounts of how victims come to encounter unforeseen crises begin with the totalizing view offered by the newsreader, who provides a concise version of the chain of events. In Brunsdon and Morley's terms (1978: 58–61) the newsreader 'frames' and 'focuses' the story, establishing the topic and its relevance:

> The New South Wales Premier, Mr Wran and two of his staff were the subject of a scare this morning when the light plane they were travelling in to Lord Howe Island had engine trouble and looked in danger of ditching at sea.

> A crop duster pilot is recovering in hospital after crashing during an air show . . . late yesterday. The plane hit a tree and ploughed into the ground.

> Today the small township of Gordon, 90 kilometres west of Melbourne is mourning the deaths of a mother and four of her children in an early morning fire . . . when their weatherboard house on the main street burst into flames.

Once these introductory comments are made, offering an overview, the story moves to the reporter who provides his rendition which reiterates and then embellishes providing additional detail about the circumstances of the victim's plight.

> The twin engine Cessna was 200 kilometres over the Tasman [Sea] at 23,000 feet when the engine started sounding rough.

> The pilot, Graeme George, had already completed one successful demonstration earlier in the day but on his second flight the right wing of his Piper Pawnee clipped a tree at the edge of the airfield and the plane spun to the ground.

> The fire started around 5.30 this morning and the late nineteenth century house was quickly engulfed in flames.

With the entry of the reporter's rendition, the chain of events begins to take on depth and actuality – the use of description itself is a formal device which produces realism. Circumstances become more palpable, more concrete partly as a result of these descriptive passages. The newsreader explains that the plane hit a tree; the reporter offers details about what went on 'earlier in the day'. The general becomes the particular – the plane becomes a 'Piper

Pawnee', the pilot is now 'Graeme George', hitting the tree becomes 'the right wing . . . clipped a tree at the edge of the airfield'. As if in chorus with the realism of the concrete produced in description, it is at this point where news film is introduced. The reporter's first words correspond with the introduction of news film 'on the scene'. Although this structuring of news can be explained in terms of the pyramid convention of news reporting, the point here is that the reporter's embellishments, synchronized with the visual 'embellishments' can also be understood in terms of the way that the structure of story-telling takes us out of the distant studio into 'direct' contact with the site of victimage, a powerful device for securing a sympathetic reading of the incident.

Two other points are worth noting about accounts offered by newsreaders in victim stories. First is the use made of the 'hermeneutic code' (Barthes 1974: 19), which operates in conjunction with the totalizing view provided by the newsreader. In the above examples, the first statement sets up the terms of a puzzle to be solved in the unfolding of the rest of the story. The New South Wales Premier and two of his staff being subjects of a scare leaves the listener with a series of questions: Why? How? What happened? What was the result? The answer is partially provided in the second half of the sentence when it is revealed that the incident occurred 'when the light plane they were travelling in . . . had engine trouble'. Arguably victim stories are not unique in their use of this code; indeed most, if not all television news stories rely on this device. However, if sympathy through identificatory involvement is a necessary condition for the production of good victims, this strategy may have a special place in this story-type. To offer the viewer unanswered puzzles may serve as a way of initially opening a space from which involvement can be arranged.

Second, statements given in early accounts rely heavily on a particular kind of well rehearsed news language which is both expansive and reductive, paradoxically saying a great deal and very little at the same time: 'the subject of a scare'; 'recovering in hospital'; 'mourning the deaths'; 'seriously injured'; 'a close brush with death', 'last chance to lead a normal life'. Because of the distinct quality of this language it has the ability to construct victims readily with very little elaboration, but also because of its generality it can offer a totalizing view broad enough to include almost anyone. So, we can all potentially be 'the subject of a scare'; 'recovering in hospital'; 'mourning the deaths'; and possibly worse. In the very insubstantiality of such language and the dramatic sweep of its clichés, these stories not only place us close to the event, requiring us to 'respond to a sense of . . . common humanity' (Frye 1957: 34) but also to recognize that becoming a victim is as much a possibility for us as for the people whose victimage we encounter in the news.

In order to obtain the requisite amount of sympathy for victims, these news stories tend to load at least one of the renditions of the event with a certain emotional charge. Inclusion of accounts by witnesses on the scene commonly serves this function. These witnesses are summoned to provide testimony on behalf of victims, to actualize the reality and the trauma of the misfortune. Victims become more authentically sympathetic and worthy of our 'reflex of tears' when an ordinary person located in the real world, rather than someone from the potentially manipulative world of professional newsmakers, can guarantee the details of the misfortune. In this sense, newsmakers hand over the story to witnesses, temporarily suspending themselves from the tale so that events can be scrutinized from a point of view less distant from the victim. The story provided by witnesses becomes a tale within a tale, a first-hand account which positions the viewer in a more direct relationship with the events and those involved. If newsreaders offer us a point of view which is essentially detached, non-partisan and seemingly objective with regard to events, witnesses do the opposite – providing a position for involvement, partisanship, and emotional engagement.

This sense of engagement can be intensified if witnesses are also implicated in rescue attempts. In these instances, the witness serves not only as a sub-narrator of the story giving personal accounts of the cause and consequences of the event, but also functions as an 'expert' on the victim's plight by virtue of a first-hand involvement. This provides victims with a 'dramatic partner', the rescuer who tries to get them out of trouble. The relationship between the rescuer and the victim further contributes to securing the protagonist's status as victim. Rescuers take on a special heroic role trying to save victims from approaching disaster (with varying degrees of success) and victim's misfortunes are highlighted even further in relation to these acts of bravery. It also means that our own position in relation to the occurrence is made less distant. Hearing and seeing someone who was personally involved means that we are given an additional place from which to enter the story. Identification at this point starts to work at two levels – at the level of victims who in most cases are ordinary people, like us, going about their daily affairs before being caught up in misfortune, and at the level of witnesses, who offer a second order of involvement by being on the scene or by participating in rescue bids. If the sweeping clichéd language of the story implicates us all as potential victims, then the presence of the witness provides us all with the potential to become dramatic partners.

The Channel 2 report on the weatherboard house fire clearly situates a particular neighbour as a witness involved in victim rescue. In an interview he is called upon to give his account of the unfolding events and his part in them. He explains that there was:

Nothing, nothing that anybody could do. We were hampered by a blaze that was beyond any means of control. Apparently it was an old dwelling, the fire went through it very quickly. . . . You couldn't get within twenty feet of the fire. It was that hot. It was just a red ball inside, just a

87

glow, you couldn't get near it. When I got here my wife had taken the husband and the elder son away. We could do nothing.

During his testimony the neighbour's face fills the screen in a very tight shot. His hair is dishevelled and wind blown across his forehead, his eyes are cast down, looking up only occasionally, his chin is bristling with early morning stubble and his voice is flat with weariness and defeat. If his version of the attempted rescue is at all in doubt, his presence before the camera gives his testimony complete veracity. Clearly, here is a man who has witnessed and taken part in an event which has affected him deeply. The framing of the shot, which specifically excludes details of the body and setting and high-lights the face and eyes, culturally taken as the most expressive parts of the body (Hall 1973b: 178; Dyer 1979: 16–17), lends both authenticity and emo-tion to the magnitude and effects of the disaster. Although the neighbour provides a rendition already made available by the newsreader and the reporter, more importantly, both in image and in speech, he is the bearer of the emotional payload of the story, the nodal point of identification which most directly encourages a 'reflex of tears'.

The story about the 'tragic death of young Neville Vance' at the lion park uses a similar strategy when the park's manager is asked for his rendition of events. His first-hand account also carries the story's most powerful emotional change because it is the closest point of identification we have with the occurrence:

> we had a new section under construction within the boundaries of the main compound . . . and Neville was up there with his father, during the school holidays. He was obviously helping . . . and as it is normal for children to like being with their father when they have a holiday break . . . unfortunately this was where he was when it got him.

Like the neighbour's story, the manager's tale is fraught with the visible and audible signals of distress. His eyes are puffy, he squints towards the inter-viewer off screen, his hair is out of place, his speech is slow and haltingly delivered. And as he proceeds through his account the camera is used to accentuate the emotional intensity of the moment. Beginning in a relatively wide shot with a sizeable portion of his body showing, the camera slowly zooms in so that by the end of the shot the manager's face is held in extreme close-up. Now a convention begins to reveal itself: a relation between wit-nessing and seeing the witness speak about what has been seen. Camera work acts as a parallel for viewer involvement, echoing the pattern of the intensify-ing emotion and revelation of the witness's spoken account. The emotional charge is heightened as a result of the use of the calibrated image: it is the close-up which plunges us into the crisis, the mid-shot will not do.

The story about the 'girl with a rare muscular disease' uses the girl's mother as witness. Her testimony comes in a shot where she holds the young girl in her arms, while kneeling in a garden. The girl wears a frilly dress, and has a bow in her hair, and she is curled up apparently asleep on her mother's lap. As the mother speaks, the camera stays fixed on the resting child, and then slowly pans upward to a close-up of the mother's face as she finishes her rendition (a move narratively similar to the zoom in on the manager).

> They give them a toxic poison and it burns all the cells out because it is her own cells that are doing this. And when you get an infection your cells kill that infection, and with Shelley it doesn't. It eats away at Shelley.

As medical information, these statements by the mother are vague and in one sense virtually meaningless. They explain nothing in particular. The earlier part of the news commentary also offers no clue as to the real nature of the disease, just that the girl will be seeing 'a specialist who has cured six similar cases'. What the testimony of the mother as witness does offer is a position from which the spectator can enter into the situation. A space is opened for us to step into a relationship with the hapless victim. The charged image of the distressed mother with the very vulnerable looking child is crucial: as an image it succinctly holds in itself a number of the key features of pathos (the inarticulate victim, the catastrophe of the defective body, the 'ruthless figure' posed here as the disease itself, the delicate virtue of the victim signified in her dress and ribbon) all of which prepare the way for securing sympathy, even from the hardest of hearts. This 'scene' is played out even further by camera work and the quality of the light in the setting. The first shot in the garden has the camera angled up towards the greenery of the trees; the light filtering through the leaves is muted and soft. There is a kind of serenity that momentarily washes over the scene. The camera then pans down to reveal the mother holding the child – it is a visual tableau with an almost religious quality to it. The quasi sacred connection between mother and child conjured in this shot makes the 'personal tragedy' all the more profound and deserving of our feelings and sympathy.

In some instances, however, involvement by means of witnesses is not available. In this case, another order of 'testimony' may be provided – the camera itself can be summoned to give evidence, the image delegated to 'speak' on the victim's behalf. In conjunction with the narration of the story by the reporter or the newsreader the camera can offer a rendition in its own right which like a story 'character' can reveal and confirm the status of the victim and brings us 'close' to the occurrence and its emotional possibilities.

A lead story on all four channels, ostensibly about a man appearing in court on a murder charge, employs such a procedure. News talk, which includes the newsreader's introductory comments followed by a reporter's voice over the news film, explains in some detail the events leading up to the court appearance and the specifics of the courtroom hearing. However, the major inflection of the story comes from what Channel 9's reporter describes as 'dramatic and emotional scenes' taking place in the street (in front of the camera), set in motion by the suspected murderer's wife. The visual sequence begins with the wife running to her husband in tears as he is escorted to the courthouse by plain clothes policemen. She tries to embrace her husband but the police intercede and move her aside. The husband and the police, with the wife directly behind walk down an alleyway. The camera stops at the entrance to this alley but frames the figures in a wide shot as they move together towards the courthouse door. The wife is now weeping loudly. Still in the same shot the husband is led into the courthouse through the door which closes before the wife can enter. At a distance now, she is seen pounding on the door, crying out desperately. She then staggers across the alleyway and leans against a wall, her arm covering her face. Then a final image: the children sitting on the steps outside the courthouse. Hunched over and silently looking at the ground, their body language, accentuated by the angle of the camera, readily conveys a sense of isolation and 'inarticulateness' which, according to Frye (1957: 38), are optimum conditions for constituting the good victim who can make a strong appeal for our sympathy. Through its pictorial construction, which is strikingly cinematic rather than journalistic, this becomes the story about a wife and children as victims of inexplicable circumstances rather than one about a man accused of murder. The production of the wife and children as 'good victims', is shaped and given meaning almost exclusively by the witnessing 'eye' of the camera. The drama that has engulfed the victims seems to unfold before the camera, naturally and unpremeditatedly. The ability of these images to 'speak for themselves' is confirmed when the voice-over of the reporter stops entirely to allow the woman's desperate screams to be heard unimpeded as she is seen pounding on the closed courthouse door.

The act of witnessing – offering personal, partisan renditions of events – seems to be crucial for the structure of victim stories, whether these events are recounted by those close to the victim or the institutional 'figure' of the news camera. Summoning witnesses acts in two ways. It lends truth value to the story, giving it validity in the realm of personal experience; and, it creates a position for the audience to enter into the tale – through the 'eyes' of the witness – enhancing the possibilities for a sympathetic response, one of the conditions for the production of 'good victims'. The galvanizing moment invoked by witnessing however has to be framed carefully as these stories profess to be governed by news values and not those of melodrama, and as such 'the tale' has to be managed in a way which does not tip the balance so that the viewer becomes 'overwhelmed by emotion'. Here, we encounter another sphere of witnessing, inscribed this time in the role of the reporter. Like other television news coverage, victim stories can be characterized by conventional 'on the scene/eyewitness' reports, usually delivered by journalists who have placed themselves in close physical and/or temporal proximity to the site of the newsworthy occurrence. The placement, delivery and exposition provided by reporters also makes possible another order of witnessing which provides one further rendition of the victim's circumstances. This reportorial role is ostensibly not unlike ones encountered in all types of television news stories. Where the function of reporters becomes more individuated and specialized with regard to victim stories, so also is its placement in relation to the 'reflex of tears'. Situated on location, reporters can witness at close range but also maintain critical distance. They can organize our entry into the world of emotions by easing us towards first-hand witnesses but also offer us a way out of the intensity of a first-hand account. Reporters can also stand between the totalizing but impersonal view of the newsreader and the overwhelmingly personal but partial account of witnesses. So, for example, the on-camera reporter on Channel 7 in explaining the circumstances of the house fire can be sufficiently close to the event to understand it as 'tragic' in its impact, yet be distant enough to discover that the tragedy 'may have been avoided – if the town had a proper water supply'. On Channel 9, during the coverage of the lion park accident, the reporter can organize the conditions of our entry into the crisis by explaining before the interview with the park's manager that 'it is obvious that the tragedy has deeply affected the staff'. He can also facilitate the way out by replacing a personal response with an institutional one when he indicates after the interview that 'a coroner's inquest will be held . . . at a later date'. The position of the reporter – both close, yet distant, internal to the news, but outside in the real world – offers us a special position from which to assimilate untoward occurrences: safe yet still concerned; sympathetic without getting overwhelmed; engaged but at a distance.

EVIDENCE, IMPACT, CONSEQUENCES

Stories about victims are structured by 'looking backwards' – the occurrence that becomes news has happened already somewhere in the recent past with the result that the process of story presentation necessarily relies on reconstructing the event on the basis of remaining evidence. What survives from the event and is available for scrutiny is submitted as a sign for what has taken place. The actual occurrence which created the victim is absent. What remains available, however, are physical and psychological 'facts' which can be shaped and used as evidence to reconstruct the occurrence and at the same time demonstrate its effect. The status of 'good victim' is, in part, secured by a strategy which offers an exposition of the aftermath of the occurrence. News film is extremely important in this context. Renditions of misadventure rely primarily on verbal explanations – versions of events are covered by language used as story-telling devices. In contrast, the submission of evidence to reconstruct events and substantiate the victim's plight relies more heavily on the visual register. Acts of witnessing where verbal accounts

91

are given and the submission of evidence where physical 'facts' are shown are not necessarily separated within the story – just before the end of his account of the house fire the close-up of the neighbour's face is intercut with shots of the smoking ruins and the fire trucks on the scene, the *visible* evidence of 'the magnitude of the tragedy'. However, once they have been contextualized by news talk the power of these images 'to testify' is their capacity to do their connotative work relatively autonomously, leaving the linguistic register to become 'only a kind of secondary vibration' (Barthes 1977b). Images selected for such stories serve as condensation symbols (Graber 1976) and can be very compelling in the activation of sympathetic responses since they are often chosen to represent highly evocative emotional and personal realities.

The placement of evidence through news film will frequently proceed by documenting taken-for-granted conditions of the physical and social world in various states of disarray and decomposition. The news film used in the house fire story is particularly striking in this regard. The story appeared on all bulletins on the same day and in each case the images employed dwelt at length on the smoking blackened remains of the house and its contents. Incorporating numerous camera set-ups and angles a central pictorial trope develops around a shift between the recognizable and the unrecognizable; everyday objects are observed both in their allotted place and yet not quite there as well: a blackened bath tub, a charred stove, a burnt-out car with its windows and headlights shattered, the fragments of a child's school note book, a toppled refrigerator, twisted water pipes, a partially standing wall. Each story spends time isolating such objects in the frame, and then proceeds to build image upon image, in alternating patterns of close-ups and wide shots. In each case the additive effect of the shots produces undeniable evidence that something profoundly disturbing to everyday life has happened, that something 'tragic' has taken place. These objects resemble our objects, what 'we find in our own experience', part of our 'common humanity' (Frye 1957: 34). They are what we know, share, and touch, yet in their disarray they are strange at the same time. Most important perhaps is that this shifting between the recognizable and the unrecognizable offers us yet another 'place' from which we can sympathize, perhaps identify with the victims and engage in the unfolding of their misadventure. Equally striking in these images is the use of light which, despite the view suggesting news film is governed primarily by a journalistic logic, has a distinct aestheticising and cinematic quality. A bluish haze seems to hover in the air, perhaps the aftermath of the fire. Several times shots are taken, especially on Channel 7's report, of the house from a distance, so that there is a kind of silhouetting effect, which highlights the misshapen ruins of the dwelling and creates an atmosphere of desolation and finality. The alternation between these longer 'atmospheric' shots and close-ups of blackened, deformed everyday objects produces a forceful set of visual signs, seemingly independent of news talk which places us 'psychologically' very close to the victims' plight.

In the report on the truck driver's 'close brush with death' more cinematic possibilities are explored as part of the evidence submitted to show a world skewed. The opening image of the news film sequence is one that could have been lifted out of a Magritte surrealist painting: the truck cab implausibly projecting out over the twenty-five metre drop, as if suspended in mid air. The shot is a wide one which gives a full view of the evidence. The shot also establishes how in the realm of the victim taken-for-granted objects can become perilously disordered and out of place. The second shot in the sequence extends the disorienting quality of the first – a close-up of a wheel fills the whole screen, so we cannot be sure of the position of the truck, the drop, or indeed the camera (hence our viewing position). Suddenly the camera zooms back at a ferocious rate, revealing the entire underside of the truck's cab hanging over the edge of the precipice, and we realize that the wheel has been shown looking up from the ground below. This shot seems to encapsulate the transformational process at work in victim stories. In one moment we are looking at what is apparently a quite ordinary truck wheel at close range, an object in our physical world which has no special significance, its place in the order of things is recognizable and routine. Almost with a magical gesture (and indeed, the zoom lens, from the point of view of the spectator, is a process that transforms perspective 'magically', with no cause we can *see*) the object is transformed, now hanging over the precipice, out of tune with its normal place in the world. Two more shots allow a closer inspection of the truck and then another kind of transformational 'drama' takes place. Again a shot of the wheel (with a larger proportion of the truck revealed) similar to shot two. We know 'where we are' now. And again the rapid zoom out; but, this time another 'twist' is given to the camera's trajectory. Literally, it tilts on its axis, so that what is in the frame starts to topple sideways, giving us a feeling of vertigo, loss of control, and loss of the viewing position and perspective that we normally take for granted. In this very brief moment news film is offering some kind of visual evidence of what the accident 'might have been like' subjectively, a kind of visual reconstruction of the mishap from the point of view of the truck driver.

Instead of being strictly governed by a journalistic logic, the unfolding of the images in this story seems to gesture towards the conventions of the action sequence in the narrative cinema. And indeed we have encountered it before: the 1940s; a car driving along at top speed; the breaks fail; the car skids; it starts to tilt and roll off the highway; a point of view shot from inside the car, 'tilting' and 'rolling'; cut to the driver, now on a bed somewhere, holding his head saying something like 'wha' happened?'. The submission of visual evidence both suggests the destruction of the natural order of things and provides the opportunity to re-enact that destruction, albeit in a rather truncated form – a visual coding, distinctly filmic, of the subjective 'drama' that accompanies a 'close brush with death'.

Affirmation of victims' ordeals can receive additional support with references to the emotional and psychological states of others who are close enough to victims to register a personal response. Our place of identification, in this instance, is inscribed not with victims directly ('that could have been me') but at one level removed, with those intimate with and knowledgeable about victims ('that could have been someone dear to me'). Although these others are not witnesses in the direct sense, their reported reactions can lend authenticity to the victim's plight and connect it with another set of subjective perceptions. The item about the missing school teacher explains that 'Kevin's parents are deeply shocked by his disappearance'; the story about the boy killed by the lion states that '[the] family are still suffering deeply from shock'. Sometimes an entire community is enlisted as a source from which to gauge the magnitude of the mishap: 'there is a sense of shock and disbelief amongst the residents [since the fire] . . . as they look at the aftermath of this tragedy'. Like accounts of events discussed earlier, the attempt to register these reactions in news talk tends to operate through a language of cliché. These clichés should not, however, simply be dismissed. Their importance resides in their ability to act as a shorthand which both overstates yet says very little. The 'hollowness' of such language is precisely its generalizability – this time it is Kevin's parents, but next time it might be us. This insubstantial language becomes another rhetorical device through which to insert our sympathies, now as potentially traumatized associates of victims.

Consequences can be expanded further by a story's use of what might be referred to as doom-saying, where it is implied that whatever misadventure has taken place, it may have been even worse; the fact that it is not is accounted for by the intervention of something fateful, even miraculous. Describing the effects of the house fire, for example, Channel 9 reported that 'it is a miracle [the father and son] survived' and in the same story we are told that the next door neighbour is 'lucky to be alive'. This tactic of expanding the accident and potentially implicating others is also evident in the crop duster crash story: 'the plane hit a tree and ploughed into the ground only one hundred metres from the nearest spectators'. The truck driver's close brush with death is not a confined misadventure either because, 'unable to stop his . . . semi-trailer, he careered along the street heading towards the partially-built Greensborough shopping centre'. As if things were not bad enough with a quarter of East Stradbroke Island's population of rare golden wallabies destroyed, an interview with a park ranger reveals 'thousands of tourists . . . come here everyday . . . people firing shots at random – someone could quite easily be killed'. In these cases our inscription in the story begins to progress beyond mere attempts to gain sympathy for victims but is posed in terms which suggest potentially any one of *us* could become victims as well. At some time or other, we are all neighbours, house dwellers, spectators, shoppers, tourists. The tragedy may not be ours directly to start, but its reverberations could fatally touch any of us. No one can be absolutely assured of being out of peril.

THE NARRATIVE OF THE VICTIMIZED HERO

With little more than a passing aside Klapp (1964: 92) notes that good victims are often a standard feature in older cultural forms like folk tales, and that a recurring plotting device in such stories is the relationship set up between victims in seemingly hopeless situations and the presence of a dramatic partner who attempts to get them out of trouble. It is worth considering the implications of these few remarks in the light of Hughes's observations about the human interest story (1968: 184) where she points out that what makes for the 'good one' is its linkages with what made good ones in the past. In this context, it might be suggested that the perennial quality of victim stories, the reason why they keep cropping up in news, despite regular criticism, is not necessarily because journalists are indulging in some unsavoury preoccupation with suffering but because, like the folk tale, these stories offer the possibility for telling such 'good ones'. If some victim stories in the 'other news' have a genealogical link to a tradition more commonly found in the narrative domains of folk lore and folk culture, one pertinent question may be how to delineate some of the ways that the reporting of 'factual' occurrences employs devices more characteristic of 'telling tales'. Utilizing the morphological approach developed by Propp (1968) in his analysis of the folk tale, it can be demonstrated that victim stories, in at least some of their narrative manifestations, approximate remarkably well the structural properties of this older cultural form. The construction of the good victim turns out to be not only a matter of thematic inflection, but a consequence of the organization of the news 'tale' itself.

The narratives which concern us here are what Propp (1968: 36) calls 'victimized hero' tales. Typically, these stories begin with an 'initial situation', where the hero is introduced and family members are enumerated, and progress towards a 'disturbance' which comes about through an act of 'villainy' or by way of an 'interdiction' given but not heeded (dare not enter this room). The disturbance forces the hero from home and eventually contact is made with a new character who acts as a 'donor' or 'provider' from whom the hero obtains some magical 'agent' which will assist in the eradication of misfortune. A donor can also play the part of a 'helper', being placed at the disposal of the hero, and sometimes acquiring such a prominent role in the story that the hero is temporarily displaced as the focus of the tale, the 'helper accomplish[ing] everything' (Propp 1968: 50). At this point the hero journeys to 'another kingdom' where engagement in 'direct combat' with the villain ensues. The villain is ultimately defeated. Now, the hero is involved in some kind of 'return', and as the tale closes a 'new appearance' may be granted or a prize given, in the form of a 'monetary reward or some other kind of compensation' (Propp 1968: 64). Propp calculates a system of thirty-two 'functions' which constitute the folk tale, but makes it clear that every function does not appear in every tale and that the sequential order of the functions is variable.

Several early evening news reports could be described as descendants of the victimized hero tale. A number have already been mentioned. The 'assailed' trainee pilot story provides a villain (her employee), a 'helper' (in the form of an executive member of the air pilot's association who takes over the defence of her case), 'another kingdom' (the appeals tribunal) and a situation of 'direct combat' with the villain (the case currently being heard). The item on the 'handicapped girl' duplicates a number of these 'functions': a ward assistant who takes the role of the helper in arranging the girl's release from hospital, parents and medical practitioners perpetrate the act of villainy by putting her there in the first place, the court case where the villains and the hero with the helper engage in direct combat, the 'return' to a new home and the 'reward', as news talk puts it, of starting a new life. In the sample broadcasts the conventions of the victim–hero tale also give shape to several other items: the girl with the rare muscular disease; the injured rugby player; the girl who is the 'sole survivor of a light plane crash'; and a custody case involving two young Aboriginal sisters and their stepmother.

In an overall profile of the 'other news' the number of these types of stories is ostensibly limited, however all channels carried these stories, coverage sometimes ran over several consecutive days, and in certain instances some were allocated notably 'advanced' positions in the bulletin order. It is also worth noting that there is a tendency to focus on females or children and in one case on the 'catastrophe of defective intelligence'. For Frye (1957), these features would qualify the protagonists in these stories as excellent candidates for the 'reflex of tears'. These reports tend to concentrate on what could be called the social victim. Accidents, in a conventional sense, are not so much a thematic concern here; rather, misadventures of an unpredictable social kind are the focus: disruption through villainy, in these instances, takes on all too human, but no more explicable, form (corporate rigidity, uncaring parents, bureaucratic bungling). The other major difference in this version of the victim story is the strong emphasis placed on the power and capabilities of rescuers, whose actions actually become the centre of attention as the story progresses so that, like the folk tale discussed by Propp, the victim–hero is temporarily displaced as the key character in the narrative's development. One extended example might serve to illustrate how the structure of the traditional folk tale is appropriated and reproduced in the early evening news. A 'breach of promise' case being 'played out in the courts' was covered over three consecutive days and given substantial prominence especially on the commercial channels' bulletins (this was the last 'breach of promise case' in the state of Victoria, which may account for the sustained coverage). Using a Proppian-derived model and focusing especially on news talk as the register where the narrative is essentially codified, 'the breach of promise tale' was constituted as follows:

Initial situation

This is not described directly but can be inferred from news talk. Driving instructor Mary Harrison once lived (happily) with her mother in the Melbourne suburb of Sunshine (sic).

Interdiction

This is supplied during an interview outside the courthouse with the victimized hero, Mrs Harrison, after the trial where she explains that 'she [her mother] always said to me not to go . . . on with it [the relationship with the defendant/villain].'

Interdiction violated

According to Propp (1968: 27), at this juncture the villain enters the tale in order to disturb the peace of the happy family: 'The defendant, Uro Visovitch told the court that he met Mary Harrison . . . when he was learning to drive'. This was the prelude to an 'intimate relationship which lasted thirteen years'.

Villain uses deception to take possession of the victim's belongings

'[Mary Harrison] devoted twelve years of time, effort and money and had been looking after Visovitch in the belief that a wedding would take place [and] had loaned him five hundred dollars when he was building a house'.

Victim submits to deception

One way this can happen, according to Propp (1968: 29), is that the villain's 'deceitful proposals' are agreed to by the victimized hero: 'Mary Harrison claimed that Visovitch . . . despite a sixteen-year age difference . . . often introduced her to friends as his fiancée'.

Villain plunders the victim

During the coverage 'plunder' is posed this way – ' . . . because of promises, she had given sexual favours'.

The hero leaves home

News talk does not refer to this directly, but because of the villain's deceptions it has to be assumed, in order for the tale to make sense, that Mary Harrison leaves her home and mother ('she always said . . . not to go') in order to be involved in the 'intimate relationship'.

Encounter with the first helper

At this point, another character is introduced whose function in the tale is to provide the victimized hero with the opportunity to eradicate the misfortune. This character materializes as 'Counsel for Mrs Harrison, Peter Gallbaly'.

Hero is delivered to another kingdom

Arranged by the helper, the hero now enters the 'kingdom' of the law court to do battle with the villain face-to-face.

Hero and villain join in direct struggle

Because this is a journalistic discourse and not a genuine folk tale, the news story includes this function near the start rather than building towards it. 'Fifty-six-year-old Mary Harrison of Sunshine, a driving instructress, is suing the builder Uro Visovitch for breach of promise' is the second sentence in Channel 9's three-day coverage of the event. This kind of story sequencing may be explained, in part, as the result of the pyramid structure of news writing, but Propp (1968: 39) anticipates sequential reordering, even in the folk tale, when he explains that 'elements peculiar to the middle of the tale are sometimes transferred to the beginning'.

Encounter with the second helper

During the courtroom 'struggle' the first helper's efforts continue – 'According to Counsel for Mrs Harrison, Peter Gallbaly, Mr Visovitch, has, as he put it, treated Mrs Harrison and the court with contempt. This was a picture, said Mr Gallbaly, of a woman who had been exploited for material and sexual gain'. As the struggle gets underway another helper emerges, this time in the figure of the presiding judge: 'After giving evidence, Visovitch was warned by Mr Justice Brooking that perjury is a very serious criminal offence'; 'Mr Justice Brooking accepted virtually without reservation the evidence presented by Mrs Harrison'; 'Visovitch was described by the judge as an unmitigated liar who sought to mislead the court'.

Hero acquires the use of a magical agent

Although not possessing what we think of as 'magical' properties special objects do make an appearance in the story, and importantly for the structure of the tale, these work to bring about the downfall of the villain: 'A gold ring, photographs of the couple together and copies of love letters were produced in court . . . '.

Villain is defeated

News talk puts it this way: '[a] breach of promise case has ended in victory for a middle-aged woman'.

The hero returns

The news story does not literally have a 'return' as Propp specifies it, but this function is alluded to during the interview with Mary Harrison when she indicates that '[her] mother will be pleased with the result'. The 'return' in this case takes the form of a personal reconciliation.

Hero receives a reward

The last function of the traditional folk tale is the provision of a bride or a kingdom to the hero but monetary compensation can sometimes be substituted: 'Fifty-six-year old Mary Harrison of Sunshine has been awarded five thousand dollars'.

THE NARRATIVE OF THE FOOLISH VICTIM

Becoming a good victim worthy of our sympathy and possibly our reflex of tears is a precarious exercise. Certain conditions of helplessness have to be met and certain spaces have to be opened up for us to enter into an identificatory mode with regard to individuals caught up in untoward occurrences. These operations, however, are tenuous and capable of shifting or devolving into another perspective, so that what might have passed as unchosen helplessness can also be taken as self-inflicted misery, and what may have been a way to attract sympathy becomes a source of disapproval, even derision. The dynamics of such ambiguities have an interesting resonance with what Klapp (1964: 90–1), in his discussion of the 'dramatic possibilit[ies]' surrounding 'performance' of symbolic leaders, has termed 'the fool-making encounter'. Often deflating or comic in its consequences, the fool-making encounter is essentially based on the kind of reversal which leaves public figures without their 'advantage' and robbed of their credibility. In one sense the encounter can be likened to a fall from grace. Klapp investigates a number of ways in which this can occur, two of which concern us here. Simply by behaving in what is perceived to be an inappropriate or undignified way in a particular situation one can be made to look the fool. However, fool-making, Klapp observes, can be manifested in more intricate forms like 'the fiasco' which occurs when an undertaking, however well meaning or deftly executed, fails because of a rather untimely blunder, or because of the naïveté or insensitivity of the main actor. If harm is done as a result of the fiasco it usually occurs to the fools themselves rather than to others and generally does not involve serious personal injury – 'real pain' moves the mishap into the realms of 'martyrdom or tragedy', according to Klapp (1964: 199). Being the initiator of the fiasco, however, considerably diminishes the possibility of that individual receiving serious attention, or sympathy. Fool-making is the narrative variant in this story-type which works to turn potentially good victims 'bad', the status of victim given and repudiated at the same time.

There are four stories where this process of fool-making takes place, and although not a particularly large part of the sample, these items are important because they illustrate the precarious quality of victimhood. In order to examine how they work, each story will be loosely retold to provide the tenor of the item and to situate the logic of the reversal.

A student goes for a hike with some friends 'in some of Victoria's most rugged mountain country'. He gets separated from them and has no food. They 'raise the alarm', a search is mounted involving 'fifty people – police, search and rescue, state emergency and local volunteers'. Found two days later, the student confesses that the separation resulted because his shoes were 'a bit too small'.

A snake handler has 'a narrow escape from death' when he is bitten by a 'pygmy rattle snake'. After an 'emergency flight' to the hospital he is 'given two massive doses of anti-venene especially for rattle snake bites'. Doctors caution him that 'next time he might not respond to treatment'. Despite the warning he 'is going back to the job'.

An American tourist is 'reported missing' in the Flinders Ranges in South Australia. His disappearance 'sparks off a big search'. He 'turns up unharmed' and tells the police that he 'just went for a walk in the bush'.

'Local resident Thomas Snell' crashes his car into a railway level crossing gate. He goes to telephone the police for help. While he is gone his car is involved in more trouble: 'he might still have his car today, the coal train would be undamaged, the level crossing signal box wouldn't be laying on the roadside and the local signal box would never have been demolished [if], instead of calling the police, he had called the Department of Railways'.

Taking the stories together, there appear to be a number of strategies in common with the more 'conventional' victim story. The insubstantial language of accounts finds a place: the snake handler has 'a narrow escape with death'; the lost university student encounters some 'anxious moments'. The function of rescuers as dramatic partners is also evident: a doctor's 'quick work with special anti-venene' permit the snake handler his 'narrow escape'; two of the student's 'mates raised the alarm after a logger found them'. The submission of evidence by way of filmed images is also at work: the destruction caused by the car is illustrated fulsomely (all six shots of news film concentrate on the wreckage), and 'from search headquarters atop the Snowy Mountains' a series of images of mountain ranges, perilous looking gorges, the rescue team in blue uniforms, a fleet of four-wheel-drive vehicles is delivered to give credence to the student's plight.

Unlike conventional victim stories however, these reports also reverse a number of strategies, turning them on their heads, with the result that devices typically used to confirm 'genuine' victimage tend to work against these protagonists so that evidence of their plight also becomes evidence of their foolishness. For example, what tends to be presented as inexplicable about the onset of the occurrence in other victim stories becomes completely straightforward in these, especially in terms of personal responsibility and human agency. These victims seem to have *placed themselves* in untoward predicaments, not because they could not help it or were powerless to act, but because of their own inappropriate planning and actions – in short, their own foolishness, the consequences of which modify the usual invocation of a sympathetic response. Instead, we are positioned as judgemental observers who 'look down' on these victims and their seemingly self-inflicted troubles rather than being on the same 'level', one of the central conditions, according to Frye (1957), for eliciting the 'reflex of tears'. The position we are offered is specifically framed in terms of a type of remonstration which arises out of what the news story assumes we would all take as 'just plain old common sense'. Common sense tells you that you don't go hiking in rugged mountain country with shoes that are too small; it also tells you that in Australia, especially in the Flinders Ranges, you don't 'just [go] for a walk in the bush'; that once bitten (especially by a pygmy rattle snake) twice shy; that abandoning a car on a railway track spells trouble. The result of this structuring process is that what would characteristically pass as part of the conditions for producing good victims is turned against them, and used as evidence of their sheer foolishness. Shots of an emergency squad and its vehicles perched on a mountain side – conventionally one way of situating the rescuers as dramatic partners helping victims out of difficulty – now becomes evidence of wasted resources, unnecessary expenditure of time and effort, and all because of shoes that were a 'bit too small'.

Nor is a victim's foolishness allowed to pass without comment – within each story, directly or indirectly, a kind of reprimand or admonishing gesture is applied which follows from the common sense perspective framing the occurrence. In the item about the lost hiker the reporter sums up by taking the point of view, not of the victim, but of the searchers – 'and yet they ask, was it all really necessary' – and stressing that 'these hikers broke two vital rules ... allow[ing] their party to split up [and not] allow[ing] police or friends to know their plans. ... Now that could have spelt disaster'. The snake handler story ends by explaining that 'for him, it's ... back to the snake pit', but this action is not taken as a sign of admirable persistence or undaunted courage, rather as an indication of the man's unreasoned folly because ' ... doctors say next time he mightn't respond to treatment'. Common sense warns that it will be on his own head, next time. Thomas Snell's futile phone call is also reprimanded as the story closes: 'It seems the Department of Railways also wished Mr Snell had called them first, for if he had (acted less hastily, with more common sense [my addition]) none of this would have happened'.

For Klapp, fool-making encounters are often underscored by 'comic possibilities'. There is always the potential in these situations for the comic to overtake the serious, to open up a seemingly sombre happening to comic resonances. It has been noted that humorous stories are often used to close the news, strategically placing the 'lighter item' at the end of the grim and gruelling serious bulletin. But the stories examined here are not the items at the end of the bulletin; they find a place squarely in the middle. Yet, these stories have potentially 'lighter' comic undulations. To take one example, Thomas Snell's unfortunate encounter with the railway via his automobile has distinct parallels in what Mast (1974 : 460) describes as the *reductio ad absurdum* comic plot found in the cinema where 'a single mistake in the opening minutes leads inexorably to final chaos'. Thomas Snell becomes the television news version of Laurel and Hardy. The single inappropriate action – crashing his car into a railway gate – progresses through a series of increasingly larger forms of physical demolition, the final results of which are revealed to us on news film.

If these stories offer the spectator a position from which to look down judgementally upon a hapless victim, a position governed by an assumed commonsensical response, they also offer a space which surveys events in terms that might have a connection with Freud's explanation of the production of the comic:

A person appears comic to us, if in comparison with ourselves, he makes too great an expenditure on his bodily functions and too little on his mental ones and it cannot be denied that in both cases our laughter expresses a pleasurable sense of the superiority which we feel in relation to him.

(Freud 1965: 255)

Freud goes on to say that a comparison takes place 'between the movement I observe in the other person and the one that I should have carried out myself in his place'. If, however, the relationship between these two instances is reversed where 'physical expenditure' is less than ours and mental 'expenditure' greater, 'we no longer laugh, we are filled with astonishment and admiration' (Freud 1965: 255). Stories about ordinary people as especially remarkable and those concerned with victims as fools may have a bi-polar and reversible relationship to each other – the 'triumphs' of the former are the fiascos of the latter. We admire one, and find amusement in the other.

6

COMMUNITIES AT RISK

Whereas victim stories hold in their centre some notion of the particularized and psychologized 'character', helpless and entangled in occurrences not of their own making, this story-type builds its narrative primarily from a concern with the communal and the social rather the personal. Included here once again is coverage of accidents, disasters and chance events, and conditions of helplessness are still crucial to the story, but in these instances it is likely to be more collectively based, spreading to engulf entire institutions, districts, suburbs, and regions. The preoccupation of these news items is misadventure on a grander scale – the community at risk. What these stories provide, and use as a base from which to offer description and explanation of events, is a view of community analogous to an assumed living entity. This is characterized primarily by the capacity of its various parts and instrumentalities, under normal circumstances, to work in a kind of integrated harmony, without discord, conflict or interference. Periodically, however, the communal 'organism' encounters unanticipated and destabilizing occurrences, unwanted and unpalatable intrusions which disrupt the tranquility and balance of the overall design. A tangible crisis ensues, which may adversely affect various sections of the collective 'body', placing the community's smooth operation in danger. The crisis must be dealt with. Characteristically, this is accomplished by those 'reactive' components of the organism which function explicitly as its guardians and protectors, reflexively deployed to contain and expel the disturbance, after which time stability and cohesion once more return, all traces of disruption gone from view and recalled only as a memory fragment which serves to enhance a restored present.

Let me illustrate with an example. In 1974 the town of Darwin in Northern Australia was devastated by a cyclone which caused widespread damage and community dislocation. Ten years later, a lengthy feature article (Goldie 1984) addressing the question of how Darwin had recovered since the 'disaster' was published in the *Australian Women's Weekly*, a large circulation national magazine. The most striking rhetorical device in the article is constructed out of two juxtaposed sets of images. The first uses black and white photographs and shows clusters of buildings apparently torn apart by the wild wind and rain. These images convey a strong sense of placement and space – where the buildings, even in their state of disarray, are located and how they are positioned in relation to the surrounding environment. Following these images, taken from the same angle of vision and distance, offering the same sense of positional and spatial co-ordinates are a second set of photographs, this time of recent reconstruction. These are in colour. The signs of nature abound – green grass, a sky wide and blue, the trees tall, the whole scene tranquil and calm, particularly as its ambiance bounces off the 'chaos' depicted in the first set of photos. Indeed, it appears as if the damage caused by the storm has never happened at all; the world seems to have been remade exactly as it was, perhaps even better (the vibrant colour seems to testify to that). The organism, it would appear, has restored itself, repelled the invasive forces of disorder and healed the 'wounding' crisis of disruption to return magnificently to its 'natural' state of being. Darwin resumes its old shape and form; and these most recent images, so replete and lush, proclaim its continuity and its permanence, as if these are given for all time.

This progression through normality – disruption – renewal – return, provides the core of community at risk stories as news. As an extended analogy, the emphasis on the organic nature of the assumed community may not be all that precise, and is perhaps overdrawn, but for the discussion here, it can provide us with a way of finding some of the cultural codings in these types of stories and their underlying assumptions. The analogy also provides an orientation for investigating some of the signifying strategies upon which these stories, as they make regular appearances on early evening news, seem to depend. If victim stories can be described as 'micro' narratives detailing the intense and individualized consequences of untoward occurrences, community at risk stories tend towards the 'macroscopic', documenting crisis as it is expressed through broader social and physical conditions. Community at risk stories structure meaning by framing events and their consequences in relation to a chronology of action and process. A cycle of occurrences is posited which begins with conditions of stasis – ordinary circumstances governing the on-going affairs of everyday life, not dissimilar to the conditions alluded to in victim stories. Disruption of the routine course of activity ensues with the sudden arrival of unanticipated interventions, rendering social aggregations incapacitated, virtually powerless to respond on their own behalf. Stasis is replaced by crisis. Documentation is now offered of the aftermath of disruption, or sometimes of the disruption itself (as in weather and fire stories, for example, where the disturbance is still on-going and can be observed at first hand). The final phase of the cycle concentrates on attempts to reclaim order and return to a renewed stability.

The thematic focus of these news reports concentrating as it does on the shifts between the ordered and disordered community (stability and disruption) has an interesting resonance in what for Todorov (1977) are the basic requirements of the proto-typical narrative.

> Every narrative is movement between two states of equilibrium which are similar but not identical. At the beginning there is always a balanced situation; the characters form a configuration which may be in movement but which nevertheless preserves unaltered a certain number of fundamental traits . . . then something comes along to break the calm, and creates imbalance . . . the equilibrium is restored, but it is not the same as at the beginning; the basic narrative therefore includes two types of episodes: those which describe a state of balance or imbalance and those which describe the transition from one to the other. The first type contrasts with the second as stability with change.
>
> (Todorov 1977: 88)

Thus, an application of Todorov's syntactic model to the Darwin disaster story might offer the following schematic structure:

STATE: Equilibrium A – community past
  [Darwin before the cyclone]
ACTION: Movement to disequilibrium – onset of disruption
  [The cyclone hits]
STATE: Disequilibrium – impact of disaster
  [The aftermath: black and white photos]
ACTION: Movement to new equilibrium – reconstruction and recovery
  [Restoration]
STATE: Equilibrium B – community present/future
  [Darwin today: colour photos]

If this type of approach is used as a possible reference point it might be suggested that the apparent pre-occupation with disaster and accidents, so much a target for the lament's disaffection with broadcast journalism, may not be the result of some ghoulish attraction for and sensational exploitation of death and destruction (although these cannot be entirely ruled out). But because such untoward occurrences lend themselves so well to the production of commendable narratives, allowing the story form at its most proto-typic to be expressed so reliably and unerringly, and because in the moment of resolution, such narratives can be engaged in presenting testimonials which ritualistically confirm again and again the possibility of the survival and persistence of communal life.

Once again we need to confront the kinds of reports to be included in a particular story-type. In one respect what the stories in this context are about, and what binds them together seems relatively apparent. There is one pre-eminent thematic concern – the sudden and unexpected disruption to variously constituted communities and the attendant risk to social harmony and order. However, modes of disruption take a number of forms. In the sample broadcasts there were, for example, a variety of items dealing with large scale fires and collective danger: a fire 'ripped through [a] cinema's generating plant . . . sending patrons fleeing onto the streets'; 'a fire in a nursing home . . . threatened the lives of . . . patients'. Sometimes the fire is cited as part of a sequential chain of destruction: 'eleven workers died and twenty were injured in an explosion and fire in a Japanese coal mine'; at a Texas oil refinery 'petrol storage tanks caught fire following an explosion [resulting in] many of the city's 40,000 inhabitants [being] evacuated'. In some instances, explosions are reported without the presence of fire before or after: '[a] hospital explosion has killed at least seven'. A wide range of weather and climatically induced community disturbances were also a focus for numerous stories: 'Early morning fog and drizzle were responsible for many accidents'; 'Melbourne's notorious weather has struck again'; 'weather took a hand [in preventing] the historic completion . . . of Australia's longest bridge'; in England, 'Bank Holiday hot weather' caused 'long traffic jams . . . one hundred and fifty miles of queues and ten million drivers on the roads'; a 'freak storm which hit Sydney last night left a trail of destruction in the city's western and southern suburbs'; 'flooding in Eastern Victoria . . . isolated . . . [the] beach resort of Malacoota'.

Multiple aspects of transport were also implicated in a range of risk-producing disruptions: suburban trains 'were halted' when a semi-trailer 'rolled its load . . . against bridge pylons'; ' passengers were stopped [from boarding an airplane to Singapore] when structural corrosion was found'; 'army aircraft' were involved in 'two separate mishaps'; a roadside telephone pole 'claim[s] seven victims in an eight month period'. Occasionally, an ill-timed transportation mishap is merely the prelude for more pervasive aspects of danger: 'there was a threat of an explosion at Sydney Airport today when a fuel tanker . . . carrying the highly dangerous liquid methanol . . . turned over'; in Canada 'about 250,000 people have been . . . evacuated following a series of explosions aboard a derailed goods train . . . carrying chlorine, propane fuel and caustic soda'; in Florida 'seven carriages' of a train 'plunged off the line . . . leaking gas caught fire . . . [and] . . . several hundred people have been evacuated'; a 'ship exploded after colliding with a small freighter . . . burst[ing] into flames just outside Istanbul Harbour, sending tonnes of blazing oil floating towards the city'.

While a partial listing of reports such as the above provides the general thematic contours of the community at risk story-type (there were sixty five in total in the sample) it does not shed much light on how these reports might begin to portray occurrences as risk inducing. Work by Britton (1986) on what he calls 'collective stress situations' might help to examine these stories in a somewhat more systematic fashion, and more significantly, reveal at least one of the general tactics that this story-type uses to construct the incidence of risk. According to Britton, situations of collective stress can be divided into three general categories – accidents, emergencies and disasters.

The accident is comparatively localized, restricted to a relatively small group of individuals with disruption being minimal and of short duration. The emergency involves a gain in scale. Effects are felt more extensively, the impact covers a wider area, substantial numbers of people are involved, and sections of the community are rendered inoperative. The time between the event and its resolution increases but broadly there is no marked breakdown of social organization. The disaster is distinguished from these other conditions primarily by the quantity and quality of disorder and levels of destruction, 'social organization . . . become[ing] disrupted to the extent that human existence within a particular location is severely jeopardized' (Britton 1986: 268).

Although this schema is directed at categorizing events themselves (and despite the slippery imprecision of these categories) it remains a useful entry point for ordering and clustering news representations of such events. There are four factors in Britton's system working along a binary divide which might look like this:

		More	Less
Numbers	(N)	+	−
Area	(A)	+	−
Disruption	(D)	+	−
Time [to fix]	(T)	+	−

In the sample weeks many reports in this story-type would loosely qualify as accidents (N −; A −; D −; T −), some are emergencies (N + or −; A + or −; D + or −; T + or −) and only one, a brief item on a cyclone in India, would qualify as a disaster (N +; A +; D +; T +). Yet what is worth noting in relation to this schema is the way that certain stories, particularly by way of news talk, attempt to push lower level untoward occurrences through what might be termed a risk threshold, making events appear more threatening or dangerous than they actually might be − transforming accidents into emergencies and emergencies into disasters.[1] So, for example, a transportation mishap occurs in the form of a collision between two ships in Istanbul Harbour (− D), but this becomes a prelude for a series of reported effects which ripple out incrementally from the initial incident. The collision results in 'violent explosions' (D +) which in turn causes the 90,000 tonne oil tanker 'to burst into flames . . . sending blazing oil floating towards the city' (A +). 'The blasts' proceed to 'rock . . . the central business district' (A +) and 'break windows up to six kilometres away' (A +). There is a 'heavy loss of life among the tanker's . . . crew' (N +). The Turkish government is called in (N +) to 'immediately close (T +) . . . the sea lane linking the Mediterranean to the Black Sea' (A +) and ' . . . naval vessels join . . . rescue party boats'

(N +). What might initially have been classified as an emergency hovers dangerously on the edge of a disaster as news talk works to enhance the magnitude of the event extending its reverberations out from its source. A similar process can also turn accidents into emergencies. A truck overturns, lodging its load against some bridge pylons (D −). The result: a major arterial road is 'blocked (A +) . . . for more than two hours' (T +); 'hundreds of motorists' (N +) are kept waiting 'for the wreckage to be cleared'; 'the safety of the bridge' used by a commuter train (A +) is in doubt as 'inspectors were called in' (N+); police are summoned (N +) and they 'block off the intersection' (A +); traffic is 'blocked up (N +) . . . for more than three kilometres' (A +). 'Tow truck drivers (N +) . . . took several hours (T +) to pull the semi back to its wheels'.

Perhaps the most revealing story in this context is Channel 0's report on the road tanker which overturned near Sydney Airport (A −) spilling its load of liquid fuel (D −). News talk begins its move to push the incident through the risk threshold by describing the liquid as 'highly toxic methanol' (D +). More danger is presented when it is disclosed that this liquid has the capacity to 'kill simply by being absorbed into the skin' (D +). The report compounds the peril further, explaining that 'thousands of litres of [the] flammable fluid ran into the drains that criss-cross the airport' (A +). The pinnacle of the crisis is reached when it is revealed that 'the smallest spark could have turned the entire area into a raging inferno' (A +, D +). Yet, as the risk is augmented and spread from the initial scene of the occurrence, news film does not reveal, as might be expected, a vacant roadway with a few heavily clad specialists gingerly trying to deal with the predicament as best they can, but dozens of curious spectators hovering around the edges of the scene, watching intently as a crane truck rights the overturned vehicle. The discrepancy between image and sound in television news has been noted before (see Bonney and Wilson 1983: 21; Fiske 1987: 302) but here it provides one clear indication of the way that community at risk stories can use a type of 'signification spiral' (Hall *et al.* 1978) to 'up the stakes', attempting to transform the accident into an emergency by means of textual operations − news talk manoeuvres us through the scene, directing our reading of the images in terms which propose ever widening circles of risk.

Now the argument being offered is not that news is or can be deceitful − the possibility of lying, even inadvertently, is endemic in communication and this commentary/image conflict does not in itself indicate which is telling the lie, the voice or the visuals. The point is rather to recognize the tendency of these types of news stories to shade at least the verbal aspect of their reporting towards the more cataclysmic of Britton's categories. The search for striking visual material relating to 'disasters' has commonly been noted and bemoaned by the lament for television news but less remarked upon is the possibility to exaggerate or amplify the scale of untoward occurrences verbally, even when the visual material seems unsupportive. Here too, we may be confronting broadcast journalism's pre-occupation with making a 'good story' more than its malignant intentions (apart from the malignant intention of increasing ratings and profits): a good story *is* exciting and, narratively considered, the more catastrophic the disruption to equilibrium, the more exciting the story is likely to be. 'Sensationalism', in this understanding, becomes a function of the narrative concerns of television news and precisely not a 'media effect' deriving from the supposed superficiality of the visual image compared to the analytic 'depth' of words. What narratively makes for a good story also has a connection with the professional practices of journalism in terms of the constitution of news value. The more negative an event, the more likely it will be that it is included as news (Galtung and Ruge 1973); hence, stories which push accidents towards emergencies and emergencies towards disasters are more likely to be seen as having news value and be included as part of the bulletin. Simultaneously, those reports having most news value are also the ones having most efficacy as news *stories*.

Whatever might be said about their journalistic production, even a cursory glance at these stories cannot fail to detect how their general thematic focus bears an uncanny resemblance to that taxonomy used by ancient mythologies to divide up the cosmos into what were thought to be its constituent parts – the 'elements' of earth, air, fire and water. From here it would be easy enough to subscribe to a version of the Jungian 'collective unconscious' thesis and to assert that at the core of such news stories lies the re-figuration of some ancient culturally embedded archetypal system reasserting itself in contemporary guise, still having appreciable resonance in the culture (see Rutherford-Smith 1979). Again, we are faced with questions of pedigree and longevity as they pertain to sections of the 'other news'. Community at risk stories formed as they seem to be around the machinations of 'the elements' reach back, like the victim tale, through the history of journalism and further. Yet the persistence of such stories can also be examined in terms of specific historical conjunctures, the way, for example, Susan Sontag (1974) attempts to do in her essay on science fiction films of the 1950s. Although Sontag points out that this cycle of films can be located as a direct descendant of one of the longest standing traditions in art, 'the imagination of disaster', she avoids the temptation to see these films as merely a contemporary manifestation of archetypal universalized predispositions. Instead, for her, these cinematic musings on disaster should be read historically as part of the emergence of a post-war technocratic culture which accelerates the process of de-personalization and community break-down, and maintains its political ascendancy by way of the apocalyptic possibilities of atomic science. While some might argue that Sontag's analysis could be too sweeping and speculative, her insistence on locating disaster narratives socially and historically is suggestive, and even far-reaching enough to connect productively with an examination of the community at risk news story. In what follows, the discussion will initially concentrate on the stories themselves, their internal narrational organization and thematic emphases, leaving broader issues such as their link to an imagination of disaster until later.

HARMONY, EQUILIBRIUM, COMMUNITY

Like victim stories, reports concerned with communities at risk are structured around implicit assumptions about a place and time where the events of everyday life run smoothly. A certain kind of stability from which individuals can proceed and venture forth into the business of life's everyday affairs is projected as taken-for-granted: herein lies the social organism's state of harmony and the narrative's point of equilibrium. As in victim stories, the consensus of the mundane as 'absence' is the reference point from which the untoward occurrence and its narrativization begin – where events can be signified as unanticipated and a narrative equilibrium tipped off balance, giving the story momentum to commence. What is being offered as a newsworthy happening is made meaningful in relation to a state of affairs implied rather than specifically stated. Stories about the forces of nature illustrate this process well. In an item about 'sudden floods . . . isolating a beach resort', a statement about 'access to the town' being 'cut off' becomes meaningful in relation to an implicit assumption that under ordinary circumstances access is usually available. Another story explains that 'flash flooding has cut off several roads on the outskirts of Sydney'. The meaning of the statement as news derives from absent, but crucially informing knowledge which recognizes that routinely the roads would *not* be cut off, that passage would be unimpeded and that these conditions would be taken for granted. As a result of this structure of absence the forces of nature can be situated and offered as the undisputed cause of the disruption while in the same moment what constitutes the normal expected conditions of the world can also be asserted. In the case of the 'sudden floods', a once accessible beach resort has now become inaccessible and the fact of inaccessibility highlights both the taken-for-grantedness of its reachability and the cause of its unreachability. This kind of story structure is important for positioning us to make the 'preferred reading' in terms of community risk and for situating the forces of nature as the central cause in altering the harmony of everyday life.[2]

As well as constituting a routine world taken-for-granted which gets disrupted, these stories tend to locate this world in relation to social aggregations which are designated as types of communities. This operation must be done quickly and effectively since what these stories are actually interested in most is the disruption and its consequences. Sometimes geographical regions or social collectivities are nominated in news talk in a way which suggests that disturbance and impact are broadly based and shared uniformly. This tendency is particularly evident in stories concerned with the weather: '*Residents* in the South Australia town of Renmark are still cleaning up in the wake of Wednesday's storm'; '*The city's* first major alarm was at North Sydney' (emphasis added). In other instances stories use a more selective form of nomination, offering details of location to produce a sense of community out of an assumed mutual knowledge which pre-dates the disruption. For example, in a report about the effects of the weather on the traffic, news talk first explains that 'morning fog and drizzle were responsible for many accidents in Melbourne' and then goes on to specify: an 'elderly man was killed on the corner of Clayton and Ferntree Gully Roads [and] a sixty-eight-year-old woman [was killed] on the corner of Hotham and Dandenong Roads in St Kilda'. From the point of view of journalistic practice these details of place (the 'where' in the who, what, where, when, why, how of the news story formula) are merely providing the information needed to describe newsworthy happenings in a reliable fashion. But such 'facts' go beyond their information function in this context by inscribing 'us' as knowledgeable members of a particular community who it is assumed share some sense of place both in relation to one another and the reported events. A story about the disruption to the 'historic completion' of an important freeway bridge picks up this theme even more strongly when it explains that '*our* weather took a hand . . . [and] the great moment had to be postponed'. This mutually shared positionality binds 'us' together as a social collectivity and allows a discursive space from which to enter into the story as community members.

DISRUPTION

A discussion of disruption needs to refer to those moments in the narrative which fracture harmony and stasis and progress towards discontinuity and crisis. Some strategies used to convey disruption have a degree of similarity with the protocols employed to produce good victims, but there are others which seem to have their own distinctive regime of signification in community at risk stories.

The dangerous double

Todorov (1970) explains that narratives are characterized by statements about balance, imbalance and the shifting relations between the two, the latter unfolding as situations of transition or transformation. This condition of transformation in the community at risk news story is eloquently realized in what might be described as the manifestation of the dangerous double. Here, the materiality of the object world – all the 'stuff' that plays a part in our routine comings and goings – normally taken-for-granted as benign, helpful or merely present, to be used and not particularly dwelt upon, turns with unexpected speed into something 'other', and once in this condition becomes a dark purveyor of harm, threat and risk to the social organism or its parts. Consider the story about the overturned road tanker on Channel 0. The ordinary objects which contribute to the ultimate crisis include a 'metal crash barrier', a 'drainage system', 'the smallest spark' and a 'discarded cigarette'. The tanker, we are told, made 'a right hand turn into Qantas Drive', a temperate enough action it would seem. But now a roadside 'barrier', normally connected with safety and protection turns into the exact opposite: a weapon of destruction. When the tanker overturned it 'ended up *impaled* on a metal crash barrier (emphasis added)'. And this is only the beginning of (double) trouble. Normally underground, not really noticed or noticeable, taken-for-granted as part of everyday life, a drainage system is suddenly capable of inflicting widespread harm: '[The tanker] was carrying 28,000 litres of methanol alcohol when it slammed into [the] . . . barrier. Thousands of litres of flammable fluid ran into the drains that criss-cross the airport . . . the smallest spark or a discarded cigarette could have turned the entire area into a raging inferno'. Barthes (1977a: 191) uncovers something remarkably similar to this process at work in the narratives of the *fait-divers* – the story which 'revels' in the 'false innocence of objects [where] the object hides behind its inertia-as-thing . . . only to emit an even stronger causal force'. By exhibiting their own malignant purposes, unlike anything we supposed, the objects in these stories display a double life and, in turn, subject causality to a 'fundamental astonishment' (Barthes 1977a: 191).

Stories focused on communities at risk also seem to revel in the possibility that the innocent objects which surround us can emit a 'stronger causal force'. Ordinarily, airplane toilets are not the objects of contemplation, worry or fear (you may dislike flying, but the toilets are neither here nor there); simply to be used, functional and not particularly significant. But in a report where one hundred and fifty passengers are stopped from boarding an international flight, 'the lavatories' take on new and sinister meaning. News talk explains that 'structural corrosion [was] found in the aircraft'. This finding however begins with the discovery of an 'unidentified blue liquid' escaping from the fuselage. Traced to its source, a leak is located – in the lavatories. Airline officials 'refuse permission to take off'. The life of objects is doubled; destruction is imminent in all things. Oxygen in hospitals may be a wonderful medical aid, able to help work marvellous cures, but mostly taken-for-granted in this context. But oxygen too has a double. It can save lives but also destroy them: 'seven people [are] dead and more than twenty missing following an explosion which ripped through a hospital in the city of Parma', and the cause, a 'canister of oxygen . . . kept in hospital wards'. Moving goods from one place to another requires the work of special transportation vehicles, skilled drivers, adequate roads and so on. These arrangements are simply part of everyday life, experienced by most of us as 'traffic', to be coped with and negotiated: 'a semitrailer truck [was] carrying a full load of containerized aluminium as it attempted to turn left and pass under the Dandenong Railway bridge at Caulfield this morning'. Ordinarily there would be nothing untoward about this procedure, perfectly routine and in keeping with the function of such vehicles, but sometimes other more unsuspected developments can occur: 'as the driver tried to negotiate the corner, the weight of the two containers pulled the semi off balance. As the truck rolled, its load fell heavily against the bridge pylons'. Once again, the objects of ordinary life turn out to be less than innocent, to take an active and, so it would appear, even malevolent part in disrupting the harmony of the social organism. The results: traffic 'blocked for more than three kilometres', 'motorists [with] no option but to wait' and the community put in jeopardy ('railway inspectors were called in to determine whether trains should continue to run').

Stories about communities at risk construct disruption at two levels – one is the actual destruction or disruption: four thousand evacuated from the airport area, seven dead and twenty missing. But also, and perhaps more central for understanding the way these stories work as stories, there is disruption which is attached to the disintegration of normal causality. What is, in routine circumstances, simply designated as functional, useful and above all innocuous can for no apparent reason transform into the reverse. The very smallness or insignificance of the objects (the smallest spark) at the centre of such disturbances suggests that these occurrences can happen anywhere, at anytime, and indeed these stories seem to posit just this condition: driving a truck, boarding a plane, visiting a hospital, living in a suburb. There is no place that is really immune and no object that cannot suddenly mutate into something 'monstrous' and unleash a variety of forms of devastation. Sontag (1974: 425) has argued that the modes of destruction in the science fiction film can best be understood by reference to their scale and ingenuity. The process of doubling in community at risk stories is a constant reminder of how ingenious the object world can be, always finding interesting ways to create disorder and 'astonish' causality.

Once the notion of the dangerous double and the 'monstrous' is raised, it may be possible to situate these news stories inside a broader cultural context. There is at least one cultural form which relies heavily on the idea of the dangerous double, the relationship between normality and its nemesis. This is the genre of horror, especially as manifested in the cinema. Film critic Robin Wood (1985) explains that:

> the relationship between normality and the Monster . . . constitutes the essential subject of the horror film . . . and that relationship has one privileged form: the figure of the doppelganger, alter ego or double, a figure that recurred constantly in Western culture especially during the past hundred years. The locus classicus is Stevenson's Dr Jekyll and Mr Hyde, where normality and Monster are two aspects of the same person.
>
> (Wood 1985: 204)

The community at risk stories in the news, especially as they treat the doubling/duality of everyday objects, may be a variant of this horror tradition – the benign objects of everyday life contain within them something monstrous which, given the right conditions (sparks, drainage systems), is unleashed to cause havoc. White's discussion (1977) of the cinematic 'structure of horror' seems to lend additional support to this argument. The horror film genre for White (1977: 131) is characterized by 'uncontrolled causation' where events seem to unfold in a 'continued revelation of the random' creating a 'foreboding sense of insecurity and defenselessness'. Although the obvious manifestations of this are monsters and nightmarish situations 'there is no reason to assume that horror is synonymous with the supernatural. It is not necessary to go beyond conventional situations to find ingredients for horror' (White 1977: 132). Stories about communities at risk seem to be dealing with a version of such 'conventional situations'. Furthermore, the relationship of the monstrous to the normal is also the relationship of imbalance to balance, the condition identified by Todorov as fundamental to the production of a narrative. In this context news reports reliant on the convention of the dangerous double could indeed be specified as an exemplary prototype for the 'good story', which may help to explain the lengthy pedigree of such 'tales' in news and why journalists persist in 'telling' them despite attacks by critics.

Wood (1985: 205) goes on to suggest that certain types of horror film can be linked with the Freudian thesis concerning 'the return of the repressed' – 'in a society built on monogamy and family there will be an enormous surplus of sexual energy that will have to be repressed and that which is repressed must always strive to return'. Through the monster the horror film can give expression to this return, especially in the arena of forbidden sexuality. If Wood's observations are expanded, community at risk news stories might qualify as further adaptation of that cultural tradition which, in its story-telling, plays out the drama of the return of the repressed. In this case, what is repressed is not immediately related to the dynamics of sexuality but to questions of order and causality. To have a world that is taken-for-granted, to allow for the possibility of a 'normal-course-of-events', material objects and their relations to one another need to have what appears to be a kind of immutability, something fixed and invariant which allows the social organism to run smoothly and harmoniously. Our conviction in the social organism, its credibility as a system which provides the basis for our everyday lives in part depends on the operation of this orderliness and the causal links which give rise to it. What then has to be repressed are the 'vulnerabilities of the organization of our experience' (Goffman 1974: 439). But these news stories, through a focus on the sudden transformations of the everyday world, open a space for the repressed to return. These are narratives of vulnerability, and if the 'tale' offers a 'moral' or a 'lesson' to be learned, it is that all things contain a negative charge, a sinister type of 'surplus energy', and it is this which must be repressed for everyday life to proceed as normal.

These types of news stories also signal another domain of repression and return – what Barthes (1977a: 191) has referred to as 'the infinite power of signs'. In the constancy of routine and custom things as objects are essentially taken for what they are within the pragmatics of everyday life – water in airplane toilets, oxygen canisters, discarded cigarettes are defined in their most fundamental and functional terms. Running counter to this established taken-for-granted order, these stories have the capacity to unleash the repressed meaning-potential of objects. Things are made 'infinite' in their power to signify: no longer inert, functional or innocuously ascribed to a particular domain, they are able to signify well beyond their regular place in the ordered universe of objects – the smallest spark can now 'spell disaster'. The return of the object as sign has the potential to create a 'panic sentiment' for now we find that 'signs are everywhere . . . anything can be a sign' (Barthes 1977a: 191), and that we should be alert and 'reading' all the time because what we assumed to be merely an insignificant and innocent part of the order of things is potentially the part which can also undermine that order. These possibilities are taken slightly further with Sontag's observations about the 'naïve' ability of certain 1950s science fiction films to combine 'the grossly familiar' with a 'sense of other-ness' during their most dramatic moments.

> In particular the dialogue . . . which is of a monumental but often touching banality, makes them wonderfully, unintentionally funny. Lines like 'Come quickly, there's a monster in my bathtub' . . . are hilarious in the context of picturesque and deafening holocaust.
>
> (Sontag 1974: 437)

If it was not delivered with such straight-faced high seriousness one might ponder whether television news was actually engaged in a type of reflexive self-mockery, stepping into parody through some of its own conventions and the conventions of other texts. Is there, for example, an affinity between Melbourne's 'killer pole' or Canada's 'killer gas' and the dangerous double in the Z-grade horror-comedy film *The Attack of the Killer Tomatoes*? After all, each narrative neatly tempers an exaggerated incongruity between the thing that is utterly ordinary and its 'monstrous' transformational possibilities.

Animation

In order to secure a sense of risk which can be readily attached to the inert object world (or the world of 'forces', like the weather) these stories, like those about victims, tend to evacuate signs of human agency. What might be called the animation of the object world, however, is not just a matter of absenting human instrumentality but of providing the inanimate domain with what seems to be an almost palpable 'consciousness' which manifests intentionality, wilfulness, a kind of disruptive volition that ultimately has to be confronted and forced into submission. For stories about victims, this strategy helps to engage sympathy; for community at risk stories it is crucial for building a sense of powerlessness and vulnerability at a broader social level. Rather than providing 'background expectancies' for human affairs, the inanimate world is made to appear an active and unaccountable participant. This process becomes even more threatening when connected with the dangerous double. For not only do objects contain the tendency to transform, but once the change has taken place, other equally invigorated forces are likely to come into play – the train jumps the rails only to set off a blaze which '[shoots] flames 150 metres into the air'. Whereas victim stories emphasize the psychologization of the individual, community at risk stories seem to require the anthropomorphization of the inanimate world (a device perhaps parallel to the psychologizing of 'character').

This strategy is especially evident in reports concerned with transportation mishaps. Here is the story about the tanker accident near Sydney's airport, carried by the three commercial channels on the same day:

The tanker was carrying . . . highly dangerous liquid methanol when *it failed to take a bend and turned over.*

The tanker had overturned *while making a right-hand turn* . . . and ended up impaled on a steel crash barrier.

The tanker . . . *slipped into the guard rail, . . . and tipped on its side.*

(Emphasis added)

Well placed verbs can carry out the work of breathing unexpected life into the object world: 'a train derailment *released* deadly chlorine gas'; 'the freight train *jumped* a rail' (Emphasis added). The following is an example of the direction news talk will take in order to produce the requisite sense of risk through animation. 'Plans were made two years ago to remove Mordialloc's killer pole from the roadside . . . but red tape and lack of finance have left it standing to claim seven victims in an eight month period'. No one made the plans; red tape and lack of finance seem to act on their own; and the result – a monstrous killer pole left to snatch life indiscriminately from seven victims.

Stories about the weather typically situate it, not as a background feature for human activity, but as an active player seemingly with enough intentionality to be wilfully disruptive and cause disorder. Just from the first week of sample stories, such phrases as:

our weather took a hand . . .
weather permitting . . .
Melbourne's notorious weather struck . . .
bad weather again held up . . .

117

hot weather has brought people out . . .
weather has caused . . .

seem to define the weather as a newsworthy event in a personifiable form. When weather is made 'notorious' or 'bad', it is attributed with a persona, a distinguishing identity which sets it apart and allows it to 'act' in a variety of communicable ways. The use of the transitive verb provides the weather with a means for actively participating in the world, for becoming an agent of discontinuity in human affairs. When weather turns into something 'nasty', its characteristics are transformed as well and there is an incremental leap in the power attributed to it. Again there is remarkable consistency in the inflection of news talk across stories: '[the] storm *slammed* into Adelaide; 'storms *lashed* the city again'; 'the storm *carved* its way' (emphasis added). A particularly vivid description is provided on Channel 2: 'the storm picked up these wine storage tanks and dumped them about one hundred metres from their stands, and crumpled them like paper cups'. Fire is also provided with a lively set of anthropomorphized possibilities, equally active and disruptive, as it 'roar[s]', 'race[s]', 'rip[s]', 'reach[es]', 'erupt[s]'. In one report the fire described does indeed start to assume the persona of a monstrous creature as it might be encountered in the cinema: displaying its power and tenacity ('the fire had a strong hold'), devouring voraciously to stay alive ('fed by these highly flammable materials'), being fearsome and wantonly destructive ('roared through the warehouse bringing the roof down'), deflecting valiant efforts at control ('making the fireman's task even more difficult'), eventually revealing its weak spot ('the heart of the fire'), and like all respectable monsters, refusing to die with equanimity ('firemen are watching the scene in case of flare ups').

It becomes apparent that by assembling together these phrases and sentences a particular discourse about the inanimate world runs through news talk. The linguistic instances used to designate the activities of the object world and the forces of nature – preventing, causing, plunging, roaring, lashing – seem to be produced in terms of a highly conventionalized 'inferential framework' (Glasgow University Media Group 1976: 23) duplicated across a whole range of stories. That the inanimate world is situated linguistically as an activated subject in this inferential framework allows the news story to specify a type of mobile power which can exercise negative forms of interference and create large-scale disorder in everyday life. This process is further consolidated through references to the speed at which events unfold. For victim stories this device serves to enhance the status of the victim; for community at risk stories it assists in building the sense of the unpredictable vigour with which the inanimate world can unbalance the harmony of the social organism. If a 'fire *raced* through two . . . factories', not only is the threat provided with a kind of intentionality, but it is one which will be hard to catch or contain. However, such acts of seemingly uncheckable disruption, narratively speaking, *are* contained – these stories frequently finish as news talk explains that the danger has been 'brought under control'. The matter of producing powerlessness and setting the context for risk also acts in part as a story-telling device. The breakdown of community harmony leaves a way open for someone or something – a narrative agent – to step in and restore a disturbed equilibrium, to act as rescuer and move the narrative from one state to another. This narrative moment brings these stories close to the structure of the victim story where the weakness of the victim creates the opening for the dramatic partner to enter for the rescue, but here this process works at another level – the collectivity rather than the individual is vulnerable and communally based agencies take up bids for deliverance and restoration. In both cases, weakness or helplessness provide a logical opening for the next phase of the story.

IMPACT AND AFTERMATH

News relies heavily on the pre-arranged event (Bonncy and Wilson 1983; Epstein 1973). The press conference or the political campaign, are carefully timed so that news professionals can be in attendance. Routine stories about emergencies or accidents on early evening news rarely have that luxury, hence the initial action, the moment of impact is frequently missing. That moment – when the road tanker hits the crash barrier, when the train plunges off the track – is held in absence, recalled only in the telling of the tale. Community at risk stories are, in this sense, like victim stories, told looking backwards, reiterating the point of impact and proceeding up to the present. Like victim stories, many community at risk reports rely on submitting evidence for the actuality of the event from what remains at the scene, indicators of disruption to everyday life. If however, 'direct contact' with the occurrence is made before its cessation ('the warehouse fire [is] still burning . . .') some visual evidence in the form of news film gets tendered to concretize the 'battle' taking place between the monstrous possibilities of the inanimate world and the specialist defenders of the community at risk. If contact is made after the event – the storm 'hit', did its damage and moved on – visual evidence is submitted in a similar fashion to victim stories: what is filmed is what is left as the aftermath of the occurrence. Whichever 'contact' scenario unfolds, three story-telling strategies are at work sketching out the magnitude of disruption.

The inventory

One of the most effective devices used in this context is a straightforward listing of various objects, places and relations which have been disturbed. Stories about communities at risk simply take an inventory of the sites of disruption. These sites are spoken about as well as 'sighted' in news film so that each 'item' of the inventory becomes one of a number of significant examples cumulatively arranged to demonstrate the extent of impact. The story about the collision of the oil tanker in Istanbul Harbour compiles its inventory this way: 'the vessel . . . burst into flames on impact'; 'a series of three explosions . . . shattered windows as far as six kilometres inland'; 'burning oil spread over the surface of the Bosporus Sea'; 'marine traffic was halted'; 'fifty seamen are feared to have died'. The report about the overturned road tanker on Channel 9 offers this tabulation: 'planes were stopped, aircraft [were] moved' [and] 'people evacuated'; 'all roads around the area were closed'; 'traffic was thrown into chaos'; 'a train carrying . . . petrol was prevented from crossing a rail bridge'; 'workers from cargo and maintenance sections were evacuated'; 'some aircraft . . . remained with fire crews standing by'. By far the most extensive use of the inventory occurs in stories focused on the weather and the forces of nature. The report on the storm in Sydney on Channel 9 is typical of the way the inventory accumulates and arranges information about disruption: 'the whole roof section and ceiling' of a hospital were 'peeled away'; a house 'roof was simply plucked off . . . and dumped in the street'; a coastal suburb was 'hard hit as well'; 'the entire frame of [a] partially built house simply collapsed'; 'chimneys . . . toppled onto cars'; 'entire trees yielded in the gusts'; 'gale force winds [whipped] up the seas'; 'concrete sections of a [beach] retaining wall were wrecked'. As news talk (and accompanying news film) accumulates site upon 'sight' it begins to feel as if no aspect of everyday life has been left unscathed. One of the notable outcomes of the use of the inventory is the way such an aggregation of sites of destruction can push an occurrence through the risk threshold into what appear to be escalated zones of danger.

Negative disruptive power can also be constructed through other rhetorical devices in news talk which add further weight of evidence to the inventory. According to the Glasgow University Media Group (1976: 22), a central aim in the production of scripted news commentary is to create 'preferential hearings' which close off questions about evidence and causality. Preferential hearings are formulated in part through use of the consistency rule which operates to 'gloss' ambiguities and contradictions. Although the use of a category or sentence may be ambiguous, the consistency rule will direct the audience to 'hear it this way rather than another and not [to] notice the problem in using this category' (Glasgow University Media Group 1976: 25). For example, the story on Melbourne's weather states that the wintry conditions caused flooding, traffic accidents, the closure of an airport and the postponement of a bridge's historic completion. The word 'caused' is thus used simultaneously to gloss four diverse phenomena. The preferred hearing is clearly that we interpret all of these instances as merely the consequences of the notorious winter weather. A closer look at this segment of news talk, however, reveals that the consequences resulting from the actions imputed to the weather may not in fact have a uniform, coherent 'cause'. The weather may indeed be one factor contributing to the onset of traffic accidents but there could just as well be others – careless driving, faulty car maintenance, punctured tyres, early morning drowsiness. The simultaneous treatment of potentially discrepant happenings in terms of some preferred causal equation related to the weather shuts down questions of evidence. Membership categories such as flooding, accidents, closed airports, and incomplete bridges are not necessarily instances predicated by the weather. Each can have several distinct and quite different referents. Preferential hearings, however, operate by grouping these categories so that the possible ambiguity of causal explanation is neither noticed nor questioned.

Another example to illustrate this point comes from news talk in the story about the Sydney storm.

> Two people are now dead as a result of the heavy rain and wind which has battered Sydney for the last two days. A middle-aged man was drowned today when he fell into a swollen creek . . . and on Wednesday night another man was drowned crossing a flooded river.

The preferred hearing is coded so that we unproblematically accept the evidence as it is presented – two people have died 'as a result' of the disruption and disorder set in motion by the forces of nature. The consistency rule directs us towards a causal message suggesting that both drownings belong to the same category of phenomena and that both were the immediate consequence of 'the heavy rain and wind which has battered Sydney'. The two drownings are associated unambiguously so that the blame for the deaths can be interpreted as consistent with the effects of the raging elements. No attempt is made to consider human error as a factor or to situate the floods as a product of inadequate preparation, bureaucratic bungling and so on. The fact that a man drowning in a creek and another man drowning in a river may have little to do with each other as events or even with the rain and wind is selectively ignored, and issues of evidence and causality can be confidently fixed to the power of the natural environment.

Images of discontinuity

Community at risk stories rely on documenting visually the consequences and scope of disruption. Out of sixty-five reports in the sample weeks there are only seven which had no accompanying news film and these were of extremely short duration. News film is offered as the necessary 'eyewitness' evidence to support claims about the problematic and unpredictable actions of the inanimate world. This process of visualization is generated through a recurrent system of images – a type of pictorial iconography – which seems to have stylistic consistency across stories. This programmatic system of image production operates in large measure by emphasizing the multitude of ways that everyday, commonly encountered objects, situations and routines have been disturbed or transformed by the malignant power of the inanimate world. What appears before us represents a familiar taken-for-granted environment, particularly its physical and spatial characteristics, dramatically altered, and in some cases literally turned upside down. The images that predominate are ones which seem to 'play' with and on inversions and reversals. Roofs, brick walls, flagpoles, telephone lines, chimneys, trees are repeatedly shown in their various states of collapse: 'toppled', 'tumbled', 'tipped' is the way news talk explains it. Inside now becomes outside: the roof blown off in the storm allows the hospital's interior, normally concealed, to be revealed like the inside of a doll's house, walls, beds, floors all on view. Things belonging in one place are illogically found in another: sand dunes are piled on freeways; the top of a telephone booth is surrounded by a lake of water; a light plane perches on top of a petrol pump. The visual evidence provided to indicate disruption consistently testifies that the logic governing space, objects and even perspective, and the relations between these, is inverted or destroyed. In one sense the incongruities and inversions relayed in these images echo some of the structured improbabilities contained in the *fait-divers* where circuits of signification, normally separate, are brought together (Barthes 1977a: 192) – floating in a rowboat beside the back window of an automobile. These juxtapositions give such images their efficacy as news because they are novel, but at the same time they act to supply the startling visual evidence of 'disruption'.

Two other points are worth making about the construction of these images. First, their organization in the story is primarily cumulative rather than narrative. That is, they tend to build one from the other in something like a montage of fragments where the meaning 'disruption' is produced both by what is contained in the single shot and in the way that one shot relates to others around it, especially where the disruption is claimed to be widespread and the camera 'travels' from site to site. Metz's concept (1974: 127) of the descriptive syntagma is appropriate in this context: images in sequences producing what is meant to be read as a generalizable 'description' of the state of disruption. Second, images used as news film in these stories tend to change with great rapidity, even when a report concentrates on only one site of disturbance. In these instances the sequencing of shots can itself act as a kind of equilibrium breaking device. The act of editing one image with another in quick succession and the movement in space from one angle of vision to the next creates a type of rhythmic discontinuity in the visual register which can operate effectively to correspond with the inventory of disruption presented in news talk.

Scale

News film images can register another type of juxtaposition by setting up a visual relationship between what we recognize as ordinary objects in the world and the sheer physical size of the manifestations of disturbance. This might be designated the surprise of scale. Not all community at risk stories can use this pictorial device, however when it is available as part of a report, it provides a form of visual condensation symbol which can mark succinctly the overwhelming presence and power of the inanimate world. In the item about the Sydney storm the opening shot of the news film sequence is taken from an airplane, looking down on a streetscape. From this very high angle the houses are, naturally enough, small, squarish boxes neatly arranged in curving symmetrical lines. But, surrounding these objects – identifiable as dwellings in a suburban setting – is water, slate grey in colour and stretching as far as the camera eye can see. The shot from above which makes those familiar houses seem so small, is precisely the one that makes the flood so astonishingly large.

The scale of community risk can also be figured by news talk in portentous comparisons:

A fire aboard a chemical loaded train . . . forced the biggest peace time evacuation in Canada's history.

Methanol alcohol . . . is one of the most dangerous substances . . . to deal with.

The collision occurred in one of the world's busiest shipping lanes.

In numerical specifications of destruction:

A series of three explosions . . . shattered windows . . . as far as six kilometres away.

Three hundred holiday shacks were destroyed and another two hundred damaged.

In the enumeration of the agents necessary to contain the risk:

Fifteen appliances, including two snorkel units and thirty-five firemen fought the blaze.

Hundreds of firemen were rushed to the area.

In an economics of damage:

[The] storm . . . left a trail of destruction estimated at somewhere between ten and fifteen million dollars.

And through environmental effects:

Flaming oil . . . stretched across the water for more than two kilometres.

The George River reached a height of three metres . . . wind gusts up to one hundred and thirty kilometres per hour were recorded.

Waves up to fifteen feet high battered the beaches.

RESTORATION

Concerns have been raised by critics about whether stories such as these have a genuine place in television news, especially when the reports in question are seen to be overly focused on what some would say are community 'risks' of dubious news value. Censure of broadcast news in this context frequently concentrates on the suitability of content. However the reason for the perennial appeal of such stories as news, even in the face of strongly voiced disapproval, perhaps needs to be looked for, not in terms of what stories are 'about' (the fire, the accident, the flood) but in the narrative symmetry that such events 'out there' afford the act of story-telling. The issue then, may need to be taken up, not by way of questions about whether what happened rates as an 'important' event, but in relation to the fact that such events can be so readily appropriated as the basis for well-crafted, and if we apply Todorov's schema, prototypical stories. And this inevitably includes the ability to enact the moment of narrative closure. In what might be thought of as a concluding narrative move, community at risk stories start to fold back on themselves in order to return to the equilibrium that was initially disturbed and to re-establish the balance of the social organism. Confronting the dangerous double and subduing its destructive tendencies now becomes a narrational priority. The 'moment' of restoration can be broken down into a series of discrete phases which follow this type of pattern: deployment – delay (complications, doomsaying, suspense) – struggle – return. Not every story contains these phases, sometimes their presence is more implicit than actual, nor does the order of their appearance in a news item necessarily follow in this way; however, these phases might be viewed as that part of the news story's narrational structure which permits the re-establishment of a final equilibrium.

There are two other aspects of these types of stories which also might help to explain their persistence as news. On one level there is an ordering process at work – the movement from balance to imbalance and back again – which might be referred to as the story's syntagmatic organization. Whatever disturbance occurs, whatever vulnerabilities are produced, the community at risk in the narrative's terms is also the community which can overcome adversity, rallying spontaneously to save itself, expelling disorder and returning the world to its state of balance and equilibrium. At another level there is a more abstracted *conceptual* framework governing these stories which might be designated as the paradigmatic dimension at the centre of which stands a paradoxical relationship between two states of being: security and insecurity.

The very forces working to destroy the harmony of the community, creating insecurity, are paradoxically the forces that allow for a display of the community's restorative strength and the ability to re-establish security. These stories exploit the breakdown of order and causality but at the same time strongly invest in their maintenance. The moment of restoration is the pay-off of this investment.

This again brings into focus a question about 'positioning' with respect to involvement and identification in 'reading' these stories. Sociologist Emile Durkheim (1965) argued that what comes to be socially defined as religion and concomitant acts of worship are really no more than the veneration of society itself. An analogy can be drawn here in relation to community at risk stories. In such stories there is constructed what might be described as a kind of worshipful position for the viewer to 'occupy' which is given in relation to the social organism's ability – especially through its official representatives and agencies – to respond appropriately to the communal risk produced by unanticipated and perilous occurrences and 'put things right' again. From this story-type we learn repeatedly that on the one hand the world can be transfigured into potentially 'monstrous' forms but on the other that the forces of disorder are only ever temporarily out of control. In these reports our 'faith' in society may be constituted through a process of identification which comes with our inscription into the narrative particularly at the moment of restoration. In stories about victims, positionality is constructed in relation to individuals, psychologized and personalized; we are brought 'close' and given access to events through a discursive space which leaves open the option of involvement and the reflex of tears. In community at risk stories, we are positioned not strictly as individuals whose sympathy is being invoked but as members of a broader social grouping, members of the social organism itself. The narrative moment of restoration when all is accounted for and put back into place – like the buildings in the photographs of Darwin after the cyclone – is the moment when these stories reassure us that the social organism has an 'immune system' which can expel untoward and even astonishing interference. Risk to the community ultimately offers us 'faith' *in* the community.

Deployment

In narrative terms, the act of sending out 'counter-forces' or 'corrective' agencies is the first step towards the general process of re-establishing the harmony of the social organism. The deployment of specialist agencies acts something like the use of dramatic partners engaged in rescue attempts in victim stories. In the case of community at risk items, however, at least in this sample of news, rescuers are not given specific individuation as 'characters' or the chance to offer personal renditions of mishaps. Instead they are abstracted to represent broad aggregational categories – 'officials', 'authorities', 'repairmen', 'explosives experts', 'rescue workers'. In keeping with this process of abstraction these aggregates tend to be viewed at a distance at the visual level. The convention across these stories seems to be to keep the camera and microphone away in order to show rescuers at work collectively rather than striving for textual conditions which might allow for personal identification. When an exception to this practice was found in the sample, closer scrutiny revealed that the story's organization actually confirmed the rule. In the report of the train derailment in Florida on Channel 0 an interview occurs with a 'demolition expert' who 'uses his knowledge of explosives' to blow up the burning rail trucks. The story ran for two days and the interview appeared half-way through the second day's report. During the interview the expert offers an opinion on the method necessary to 'get rid of [the] dangerous problem', yet as we hear this, there is no accompanying image of the expert delivering his 'lines' in close-up, a device regularly used in victim stories. Instead, the spoken response of the expert is merely a disembodied voice-over, running alongside a sequence of images depicting the burning train cars. Rather than producing a 'character' to place at the centre of the tale, the expert is simply a representative functionary around which the deployment of community resources can be conveniently hung so that the narrative can progress towards a state of balance once more.[3]

Deployment of specialist agencies is often signalled in news talk with some measure of dramatic intensity which helps to 'set the scene' for the ensuing struggle between the forces unleashed by the monstrous double and the counter-forces sent to restore order and harmony. Deployment always seems to take place automatically, a reflex response which is built into the 'body' of the social organism. The language of deployment conveys both urgency and a sense of purpose. The story about the Canadian evacuation declares that 'one hundred and fifty firemen . . . *rushed to the scene* . . . '; the report on the overturned tanker states: 'rescue squad, police, ambulance and airport officials *rushed to the scene* . . . '; the story of the ship collision describes how 'teams of firemen . . . *rushed to* the Istanbul waterfront'. The sense of accelerated action and performance which news talk tries to cultivate when referencing the conditions of deployment would appear to be 'mirroring' the rapid on-set of disruption discussed earlier. It may be that a certain symmetrical tension and balance is achieved in the telling of the story through this pairing arrangement, precisely the sort of structuring dynamic that Todorov (1977) detects in the prototypical narrative.

Deployment also serves another function. Once specialists are sent out not only do they begin to gain ascendancy over the forces of disruption, but they also start to acquire control of the story's discourse. Specialists in these reports seem to function something like 'primary definers' (Hall *et al.* 1978: 57–9) setting the boundaries of explanation, ruling in and ruling out certain accounts of the event, commenting on the progress of restoration and even creating their own brand of suspense:

Officials say they're taking no chances with the escaped gas.

Scientists . . . say there is no danger from leaking gas.

According to fire brigade experts the explosion was probably caused by canisters of oxygen.

Authorities say that if it hadn't been for an off-shore wind the burning oil would have been carried right into the harbour.

Delay

Barthes (1974: 75) explains that the hermeneutic code operational in a narrative works by means of enigmas which set the story in motion and get solved by the closure of the tale. Along the way, however, there is a 'reticence' which prevents the story from progressing to its conclusion expressed as 'delays (obstacles, stoppages, deviations) in the flow of the discourse'. The moment of restoration in community at risk stories is governed by a similar kind of reticence. If news talk announces that 'about 250,000 people have been evacuated from their homes . . .', the story's hermeneutic trajectory encourages the reader to be asking: how, where, when, why and perhaps most importantly, will everything be alright in the end? Setting everything right, however, characteristically encounters obstacles and stoppages. So, although one hundred and fifty firemen have been promptly dispatched to the scene in Channel 0's coverage of the Canadian train derailment, it is also reported that 'five other tankers exploded, sending flames one hundred and fifty metres into the air', and worse still, 'fewer than half the residents had been moved to safety'. Continuing coverage the following day poses further complications when it is discovered that 'the deadly chlorine gas is the same type used in the trenches in World War I', and 'police, firemen and evacuees . . . complained of nausea, headaches and watery eyes'. A warehouse fire produces a litany of impediments:

> Fed by highly flammable materials . . . the fire [brought] the roof down into the centre of the building . . . making the firemen's task even more difficult. The flames swept on unchecked towards neighbouring buildings . . . residents were hastily evacuated . . . the danger was heightened by a number of drums of thinner stored inside the warehouse which could have exploded.

The narrative ploy of delay also widens the arena of danger, thus moving incidents through risk thresholds. Each obstacle encountered adds to the community's exposure to danger. In this sense the delay may have a similar function to doomsaying in victim stories, making the situation out to be worse than initially predicted. Delay also produces, in an abbreviated fashion, the suspense effect where specialists are not only confronted with the initial disruption but also have to handle the added burden of a continuously unfolding disturbance which seems to give no warning about its direction. We are left with a certain level of narrative suspense and the question of whether increasingly adverse circumstances can be overcome. The insertion of delay also functions to produce rescuers as heroes, subjected to a type of testing process reminiscent of the Russian folk tale (Propp 1968: 39–40). Confronted with additional complications, prevented from smoothly restoring order, placed in imminent danger, faced with an even greater task, the specialists are provided with the opportunity to demonstrate their real worth, to show their capacity to cope with the most difficult and unpredictable crisis. If injuries occur these are simply a sign of heroism not weakness ('one fireman had to be treated for cuts he received while fighting the blaze').

Struggle

In spite of delays, the deployed specialists eventually engage with the forces of disruption head on. In these moments, the language of news talk appears highly conventionalized across stories, especially when coverage is based on an occurrence which is still in progress. Although it might be argued that the imagery used to describe what the specialists do is merely a shorthand way to designate a complex series of actions, it seems significant that these actions are figured so regularly in terms which connote conditions of combat.

> Police, fire brigade units, ambulances and Sydney airport emergency services *battled* to prevent an explosion.

> Turkish naval vessels joined rescue boats *in the battle* against the flames.

> Rescuers *have been battling* through heavy rain and icy cold in their desperate search for survivors.

> (Emphasis added)

This 'battle' sometimes proves to be a long one:

> Tow truck drivers . . . took several hours to pull the semi back onto its wheels.

> Firemen are still fighting the fire that started twenty hours ago.

And filled with uncertainty about the possible outcome.

> Heavy machinery was brought in to lift the tanker upright so that the remaining methanol could be pumped into the waiting tanker. This was the most dangerous stage of the operation. One slight mistake could have spelt disaster.

But in the end there is a victory.

128

In Canada, fire fighters have contained a fire aboard a chemical loaded train.

Firemen in . . . Istanbul say they are now in control of the fire that threatened the city's waterfront areas.

Possibly the most dramatic action in community at risk stories is offered visually through images which seem to embody directly the struggle between the inanimate world in all its fitful turbulence and corrective agencies fighting to regain control of the forces of disorder. Perhaps the pictorial emblem most recognizably connected to this type of struggle is the filmed sequence where 'battling' fire fighters are shown confronting the monster which is metaphorically figured in the drama as 'the blaze'. Representations like these are entirely familiar, as much a visual cliché as the clichéd language of victim stories, so familiar in fact that they become illusive, appearing to simply 'speak for themselves', needing no further elaboration. How to approach such images? Compositional features may provide some indicators. Broadcast news reports about fires utilize multiple shots of the occurrence taken from a variety of angles and distances; but what might be particularly significant in this context is the graphic relation established between the specialists on the scene, dressed in the recognizable costumes of crisis, and the blaze itself. The relation is first one of proportion. Filmed from a certain distance, the fire can be made to appear disconcertingly large in relation to the battling 'fighters'. This compositional strategy, produced with wide-shots, including substantial sections of the burning object, establishes the physical dimensions of the struggle. Set up this way the forces of destruction can appear literally 'overwhelming'. Great size is also accentuated by the camera's angle as it 'looks up' at the smoke and flames rising skyward, from ground level. These relations of scale can now be codified within some notion of the monstrous, for what we seem to be witnessing is a battle between something grotesquely large and what we know to be our own community's representatives, who appear uncomfortably small. Yet the relation is also one of affirmation and strength, for despite the apparently overwhelming odds, the agencies that represent our well being are seen acting on our behalf. The relation of scale situates the struggle in terms of its potential for heroism: the greater the disproportions, the greater the potential for the battle to become heroic. The Canadian train derailment is exemplary in this regard. News film in the story begins with a shot from the air which looks down and locates the railway track, the train cars jaggedly twisted off the line, red fire trucks parked at a distance and the fire fighters in an uneven semi-circle spraying water onto the burning, smoking wreck. During the shot we see smoke billowing and churning upward, great black clouds in relation to which the firemen and their hoses appear small and ineffective. The discrepancy of scale is repeated in the next shot, this time from ground level where again the smoke is filmed so that it dominates the frame, looming ominously over the firemen working. Yet, despite the apparent discrepancies in connoted strengths, the 'fighters' struggle on, and importantly we see their efforts even while confronted by such a 'monstrous' adversary. This display of heroism does eventually win out as we are told at the end of the report: 'late today the fire was reported contained'.

RETURN TO NORMAL

The success of the struggle leads to the re-establishment of harmony and balance within the social organism. Disruption has ceased, the manifest-ations of the monstrous have been expelled or crushed, and everyday life can resume as before. Unlike the narratives discussed by Todorov (1970) where the final equilibrium is never the same as the one at the start, community at risk stories seem to imply a return to the way things were, more or less, exactly as before: 'harbour ferries were affected earlier, but were back in service after seven-thirty this morning'; 'traffic began to move normally again shortly after eleven'. Sometimes re-establishing equilibrium takes a little longer: 'damage in this winery alone has been estimated at somewhere between one and two million dollars, and it will take up to two years before everything is back to normal'. The severity of disruption may require a story to draw further attention to actions which directly convey to us the efforts being made in re-establishing equilibrium. News talk explains that:

> workmen were on the job at first light . . . repair[ing] splintered power poles and dangling high tension cables. Power saws and front end loaders were brought in to cut and remove huge tree trunks.

We can *see* the front end loaders doing their work and hear the drone of equipment. Filmed evidence is submitted which both displays the interfer-ence with the everyday world – 'splintered power poles', 'dangling high tension cables', 'huge tree trunks' – and the competence of specialists who engage in putting things right. An image of a white helmeted 'workman' starting a chain saw, its motor buzzing under the sound of the reporter's voice lends assurance that the community is coping and harmony will be restored once again.

Another part of this process of return is placing what was initially per-ceived as inexplicable and irrational – the monstrous double – into some context of commonly encountered frameworks of intelligibility.[4] This occurs by finding causes that are recognizable, discovering how one thing comes to effect another, and ultimately naming the 'real' source of disruption. Attribu-tions may not be found immediately or be immediately obvious, but the process of investigation itself is a reminder of rationality being applied.

> Technical supervisors . . . are examining the plant to *ascertain the reason* for the explosion.

This afternoon forensic experts and explosives specialists were going through the ruins . . . looking for . . . *what caused* the blaze.

According to fire brigade experts, the explosion was *caused* by canisters of oxygen.

(Emphasis added)

Setting the irrational into a rational context can also work through the emphasis placed on the estimated costs resulting from the destructive forces: the Sydney storms are responsible for at least 'two million dollars damage'; 'the damage figure may rise well past two million dollars' from the factory fire. On one level, these monetary estimates are simply a way of gauging the extent of destruction, providing another item in the inventory from which to ascertain the scope of impact. But, these figures may also serve another perhaps more crucial function, standing for more than a cash estimate of damage. Here, the irrationality of disruption is displaced by an 'explanation' grounded in one of the best known forms of taken-for-granted 'rationality' in everyday life: monetary value. Putting a price tag on the damage brings the inexplicable back into a symbolic universe which is already understood – a discursive move which further assists the return to normal.

TELLING COMMUNITY AT RISK STORIES

It may be appropriate at this point to offer some general observations about these kinds of news reports and the way that they are organized to produce meaning and adhere as a story-type. Underneath the various surface manifestations of such stories, there seems to reside a kind of preliminary structuration, something that might function like a 'model', upon which to build various story possibilities. Providing a basic set of 'logical tools' which give these stories shape, this model evinces a notable likeness to the syntactical architecture in Todorov's fundamental narrative: the world of accidents and emergencies as reported events appears to derive definition and substance through the workings of a form of proto-typical story construction. More abstractly, that 'primordial' structure might look like this:

balance > transition > imbalance > transition > balance

where each of these 'moments' incorporates statements, episodes or images explicated by the news story. Not all of these are necessarily included explicitly in every story, nor do they necessarily appear in this order, but there is enough regularity across stories to suggest a relatively stable logical framework. This is illustrated in Table 6.1.

In his study of Australian journalists Baker (1980) argues that despite their claims to be unaware about what it is or where it comes from, 'news sense' is located in the socialization process which operates when journalists learn the

Table 6.1   The Canadian train 'derailment' story (Channel 0)

Structure	Strategies	News talk
Balance >	Harmony, community	'taken from their homes' 'near Toronto Canada . . . residents'
Transition >	Disruption	
	the dangerous double	'a goods train carrying' 'the tanker jumped the rails'
	animation (speed of on-set, linked to deployment)	'poisonous chlorine gas . . . began spewing'
Imbalance >	Impact and Aftermath	
	the inventory	'a quarter of a million . . taken from their homes' 'train crew . . unhurt' 'one thousand hospital patients' 'no reports of injuries so far'
	images of discontinuity	[aerial shots of derailed train]
	scale	'sending flames 150 metres into the air'
Transition >	Restoration	
	deployment (speed of counter- forces, linked to animation)	'150 firemen . . . rushed to the scene'
	delay	'five other tankers exploded' 'choking fumes' 'fewer than half the residents . . . moved' 'the main concern was to stop the chlorine tanker exploding'
	struggle	'firemen are battling' 'threw up a wall of water' [images of firemen fighting 'the blaze']
Balance >	Return to normal	'Scientists are monitoring'

'priorities' of news organizations and the need to conform in order to 'get a run'. The point that needs to be made here is that news sense is not just a matter of organizational priorities, as expressed through work-based social practices, but also must include and take account of priorities that have to do with, and are aligned to, particular structures of story-telling – aesthetic practices – which can also be theorized as 'institutional'. News personnel not only learn to select and classify the news in organizational terms, but they also learn to situate those selections and classifications around institutionalized models of narrativity. These might even be called journalistic genres which use a recurring thematic focus and, importantly for the discussion here, recyclable and 'objectivated' patterns of structure and style. 'Getting a run' is not just a matter of focusing on certain occurrences to suit organizational preferences, but requires mobilizing preferential modes of news writing and in the case of television image-making as well. A closer examination of community at risk stories demonstrates that what journalists like to refer to as news sense has as much to do with the priorities of 'form' as it does with institutionally sanctioned content.

7

WILL THE CYCLE BE UNBROKEN?

Ritual, tradition and the past

This chapter is less like the previous ones and will be minimally involved in explaining the organization of preferred meanings in specific news items. Although examples will enter by way of illustration, the discussion of this particular story-type will have as its emphasis a gathering together and a putting in place of certain patterns and pre-occupations that seem to be emerging from our investigation so far. A preliminary overview of the 'other news' will be attempted, but in the specific context of a grouping of stories whose major thematic concern is ritual, tradition and the past.

To begin, a very general comment is offered about the kind of news reports which make up this story-type. I want to propose that the dominant form of thematization of this cluster of stories functions something like an *antidote* to what has previously been seen as the ways by which the 'other news' tends to fracture and subvert causality in the everyday world. In these terms, this grouping of stories can be apprehended as essentially restorative and regenerative, whereby the arrangements and exertions of causality are reasserted, and this operation is manifested especially in news items which have some notion of commemoration or cyclicality as a primary focus. The revitalization of causality begins in a process which might be described as the journalistic production and utilization of 'social memory' (Centre for Contemporary Cultural Studies Popular Memory Group 1982: 3). The field of reference for this social memory is a broad one, including not only the more obvious events offered by news makers as having significance in relation to the past and 'history', e.g. the fiftieth anniversary of the end of Second World War, but also those occurrences that rely on 'ritual action' (Bocock 1974: 39–41). These also depend, at least implicitly, on some memory of the past, even if this means simply performative repetitions – for example, the weekly news item which announces the winning lottery numbers every Monday. The formulation being proposed here is that beyond the immediate empirical cast of such stories – what they ostensibly declare themselves to be 'about' – the social memory utilized and serving as the basis for these reports is, on one level, a 'pre-text' for another discourse, one that has to do with what might be loosely described as a set of philosophical 'propositions' dealing with the nature of temporality and causality.

To situate this process initially and give the above ruminations some substance, it might be worth proceeding with a brief examination of three stories, each of which deals with a different 'historical' and commemorative occasion, but shares a common orientation – framing 'the past' in terms of contemporary events as constituted by means of specific, already well-known individuals.

> Members of the successful team which first conquered Mount Everest have held a reunion to mark the twenty-fifth anniversary of the ascent . . . Eleven of the original Everest party were [in Wales] to commemorate the time man first set foot on the summit of the world's highest mountain.

> Famous pioneer aviator Charles Kingsford Smith fifty years ago flew a light plane across the Pacific Ocean. Now Smith's son Charles Junior is re-creating that famous flight from the United States to Australia.

> It's fifty years since author A.A. Milne created the legend of Winnie the Pooh, the small bear who loved honey. And yesterday, the man who as a small boy inspired the book, was back on a bridge in East Sussex indulging in the pastime that has delighted generations of children.

Now it might be argued that given the classification system used to sort 'other news' items, these reports ought to be included as especially remarkable personal stories. This claim has some currency. The Everest reunion coverage, for instance, deals directly with the especially remarkable and even says so ('first set foot . . . '), however, the report's major form of thematization is its historical inflection which takes the focus away from a specific account of triumphant accomplishments and places it instead on the recollection of those deeds (' . . . it does bring back memories').

It is through this deliberation on the 'remembrance of things past' that these particular celebrity stories inscribe a type of 'philosophizing' about the fundamental operations of temporality and causality as these shape the world of our experience. What characterizes these three news items is a rhetoric of reiteration. In the case of the Everest reunion news talk explains that the team will spend their time 'climbing in Snowdonia where they prepared to conquer Everest'. The story of Kingsford Smith's son tells how he is timing his arrival for 9 June 'to make sure he gets to Brisbane's Eagle Farm on the same day as his father arrived, that half-century ago'. And the report on A.A. Milne's son describes how 'he is back on the little wooden bridge at Hartfield in East Sussex where he used to throw sticks to see which one floated downstream quickest'. To emphasize this point, accompanying news film reveals the now middle-aged son as he drops a 'Pooh stick' into the water below the bridge and peers over the railing to observe its progress, just the way it was, the story leads us to surmise, 'all those years ago'. The resurrection of the past through physical re-enactment is the locus of these stories' attention: the return, the recreation, the re-visitation. In the way that the memory of the event is filtered through individual achievement these stories do seem to fit the mould of especially remarkable person reports, but perhaps more indicative and central for our discussion is the perspective on temporality which emerges – a sense that although time passes, it has no effect on the world, that actions, especially if they are recognized as presage-ful ('first set foot . . . ', 'first ever flight . . . ') or mythically inclined ('created the legend . . . '), are etched and cast eternally, endlessly suspended and reproducible, resonating with the folk wisdom that claims the more things change the more they stay the same. Interestingly, apart from their names and their filial relation with their fathers, we find out nothing at all about Charles Kingsford Smith Junior or Robin Milne – their identities are simply certified in the terms which produce the social memory of their fathers' deeds.

From these observations a more general relation can now be specified between this type of news item and victim and community at risk stories, for in the latter two we find causality itself at risk – destroyed, deranged or subverted in a variety of inventive ways – whereas in the former fractured causality is reclaimed. The social memory produced reveals an immutable link of past to present, not just 'historical' but in the case of father and son even possibly genetic, a binding together of what has gone before and what is occurring contemporaneously. The past and present mirror and reproduce each other. The process at work here may in fact have a certain connection to Hobsbawm's notion (1983: 1) of the 'invention of tradition', which he explains as a set of practices governed by 'overtly or tacitly accepted rules of a ritual or symbolic nature' operating 'to inculcate certain values and norms of behaviour by repetition' and where possible attempting 'to establish con-tinuity with a suitable historic past'. When broadcast news offers accounts of the replication of such suitable historic pasts the affirmation of a causality is at work; and this affirmation is underwritten by what McArthur (1978: 28), in his analysis of the ways television presents history, calls 'the authority of the Real' – the past is constructed only in terms of tangible, visible evidence, the 'facts' of the phenomenal world. The *same* bridge, the *actual* training ground, the *exact* arrival time act to produce a 'common sense view of history' (Carr in McArthur 1978: 27), and at the same time, through the continuity bestowed on events by way of ritualized repetition (including crucial references to visible evidence), to prove that causality has not failed.

The link with victim and community at risk stories is made through the conditions of continuity and its demise. These story-types pose discontinuity as a constant – it occurs with alarming frequency, functions indiscriminately, arrives mostly without warning. In some cases a balance is restored but there is always the possibility that further disturbances are pending, not necessarily

136

here and now, but certainly sooner rather than later. Stories focusing on social memory, however, pose another set of circumstances, another level to life's trajectory, operating in what seems to be a more expansive horizon of events where an order of occurrence is invoked, which leaves that unremittingly precarious world of everyday life behind, or below. These stories suggest that woven through, or perhaps hovering around or above the vagaries and incessant fluctuations which characterize the universe of victims and communities at risk, a grander continuity can still be preserved, that causality *is* fixed and enduring, that the cycles of existence go on regardless and can be maintained in spite of it all.

The re-invigoration of causality through social memory continues through another cluster of stories thematically focused on the past. These are the news items which conjure up notions of cultural heritage and national identity: 'Melbourne stepped into the past ... with a parade of antique steam vehicles ... built in England and operated ... from 1918 to 1926'; a plaque is unveiled to commemorate the centenary of 'the wreck of the sailing ship Lochard ... the last ship to lose immigrant lives [coming] from Britain to Melbourne'; 'top sheep dogs ... [were] put through their paces' at the Victorian 'sheep dog trials'; the 'overseas market' for Australian Clydesdales, 'the horse that the pioneers used to open up the country', is growing; a bottle is discovered 'containing two handwritten notes ... thrown from a troop-ship sailing across the Great Australian Bite [by] ... seven Anzacs on their way to the Great War'; a 'team of scientists' solves 'one of Australia's intriguing geographical mysteries – the source of water for Lake George in Southern New South Wales'.

> Since the first stage coach plied this route between what's now Canberra and Goulburn, the secrets of Lake George have become legend. Where do the millions of litres of water come from and ... where do they disappear every few years?

These kinds of stories have been noted in other news research. Epstein (1973: 174), for example, has discussed the use of the 'nostalgia model' in American network news 'which in its most elemental form focuses on a traditional value threatened or replaced by a modern value'; while in their study of the British current affairs programme, *Nationwide*, Brunsdon and Morley (1978: 34–36) found that up to fifteen per cent of the programme's items were concerned with an 'image of England' founded on assumptions about 'traditional values' and a 'settled ... community'.

In his investigation of some of the foundational discourses of nation, White (1981) reminds us that:

> Most new nations go through the formality of inventing a national identity, but Australia has long supported a whole industry of image makers to tell us what we are. Throughout its white history there have

been countless attempts to get Australia down on paper [as well as on celluloid and videotape] and to catch its essence. Their aim is not merely to describe the continent, but to give it an individuality, a personality. This they call Australian . . . (my addition).

(White 1981: viii)

Drawing on the past as they do, these news stories operate like fragments inserted into the broadcast that, along with all the other 'countless attempts' to get the nation 'down on paper', contribute to the manufacture of an 'Australian' identity. Like the stories about historical celebrity, these reports constitute another domain of social memory which can be ritually mobilized for the invention of tradition and, in this sense, their placement in the news offers a type of journalistic rendering of and access to a number of often repeated, to use White's term, 'inventions' about Australia. The story of the Clydesdales acts as a way of both conjuring up an entire way of life – pre-industrial, rural, harsh – and producing a concrete symbol of the tough, self-sufficiency of the pioneering spirit needed to civilize the new frontier. Although it is a contemporary event the sheep dog trials provide yet another ritualized confirmation of the view that holds that the 'real' Australia is found not in those urban environments which cling to the coastline but with the inland countryside known as the bush. It is here, the claim is made, that Australia's national character was formed (Ward 1958). The story of the found bottle, with its handwritten message of resolve and camaraderie inside, once again invokes the imperatives of the 'digger legend' established around Australia's participation in the First World War: a testing time for the young nation, the strength of national character during crisis, the unique assets of Australian soldiers, the triumph of mateship (see White 1981; Encel 1970). Even the Lake George mystery echoes a special articulation of national identity which finds its lineage in the very earliest stages of colonization. As far back as the seventeenth century, according to White (1981) Australia was defined as the 'land of oddities'.

> Much play was made of the idea that in Australia there was an inversion of natural laws, an old idea but one that was popularized by Australia's zoological oddities. So Australia was the land which was upside-down, topsy-turvy, where it was day when it should have been night, summer when it should have been winter, where, it was said, grass grew on trees and rivers flowed uphill. It was an idea that continued to have a certain popular appeal long afterwards.

(White 1981: 9)

The central focus in the story of the antique steam vehicles is less directly oriented around the issue of national identity as such, yet its insistent desire to locate a representative 'materiality' from a national past also provides another illustration of how this story-type engages in the restoration of

138

causality. News film in this report relies on another version of the substantialization of the past through the authoritative presence of 'the real'. In this particular case it is the steam vehicles which concentrate the gaze of the camera: the visible phenomenal world concretizes history, giving it tangible form through the filmed image. The object is 'there', to be looked at and considered from a variety of angles and points of view, a process which in this story takes on a kind of photographic literalness. The steam vehicles get 'examined' in close-up, from a distance, assembled in a long line, and from the point of view of a driver in the cab. Each heritage story seems to rely on the convention of visual scrutinizing. The digger's letter, for example, is first displayed in full lying on a table, then it is peered at from above taking the point of view of an imaginary reader. There is a close up of the handwriting and special shot showing the date at the top of the page. In the Lake George mystery story the camera 'wanders around' the lake viewing it from a variety of heights, distances and angles. The very 'thereness' of all these objects, the tangibility evoked in the assemblage of these image sequences, invites perceptions of continuity, that what is examined in the present is inextricably connected with and validates a time past. These connections and validations mean that despite apparent fluctuations and uncertainties as evidenced by victim and community at risk stories, certain of life's rhythms still do have stability and are the product of what appears to be distinct and active causal connectedness. Time may be lost, but it is also found through these seemingly immutable objects on display, traces of the past that form our remembrances and our sense of what has gone before.

These objects also act as metonymic and metaphoric triggers. They have 'lived' in the past – as one old digger so succinctly put it in relation to the finding of the bottle: 'it's like discovering a little piece of history'. At the same time, through their recovery in the news story, such little pieces can put into play a number of themes and assumptions about that past and how it connects with qualities we recognize as 'our' identity as a nation. The finding of the bottle and note may be a chance event but it is not by chance that diggers are what they are. Their qualities are fixed somewhere in the past and the bottle finding is merely another occasion to reiterate what is already known i.e. their bravery, loyalty, egalitarianism, adaptability and so on. Although less specifically focused, the steam vehicles do their triggering work in the same fashion: signalling a 'bygone' era – this time it is the steam vehicles which provide the little piece of history discovered – but also standing for a way of life that is popularly conceived as slower, more deliberate, community-based, in short, the very antithesis of modern urban living ('lunchtime shoppers stopped and stared . . . '). These objects then, produce another form of causality at work – what Australia is, or what Australians are, is linked with the material residue and the concomitant discourses apparently located in the past: when the country was opened up, when the stage coaches travelled between towns, when our boys went to war. The objects testify to the causal linkages with the past which produce the social memory needed to invent Australia in the present.

One last observation about these stories can best be specified by reference to the opening statement of the steam vehicle story: 'Melbourne stepped into the past today'. As news talk, the assertion is unexceptional enough, but its implications are not because the sentence captures a particular order of modern experience, the ability to suspend the present and choose another temporal location, not in any literal sense of course, but in terms of a particular way of knowing and structure of apprehension. This fragment of news talk alludes to these possibilities and conceives of them as completely natural – the present can be momentarily ignored or simply bracketed out and contact with the past is as easy as 'stepping into' it. Or the procedure can work the other way around: the past catches up and makes a space in the present ('the procession [moved] through the heart of the city'). These transitions are produced in news talk as uncomplicated and taken-for-granted. The kind of temporal movement implied assures and affirms a sense of continuity, even perhaps of simultaneity, past and present co-mingling in these relics on parade. The result is a circuit of social memory that turns on itself, creating and re-creating forward and backward shifts leaving little opportunity for breaks or derangement. Through this news story a system of causality can be encountered again in a cultural moment which is both accessible and familiar: the spectacle of the object on display.

There is a further group of stories which can be examined in terms of reinvesting the world with causality. These are items which deal with what Bocock (1974: 39) describes as society's 'ritual occasions', social situations defined as separate, special, sometimes prescribing particular forms of behaviour and dress and set apart from the practices and concerns of everyday life: a celebration of Mother's Day by a 'group of Prahran's elderly citizens'; Remembrance Day in London 'sixty-one years after the Armistice that ended the First World War and forty years after the start of the Second'; the annual mass 'for the poor of the city [when] . . . food parcels are collected and blessed'; the street celebration for the 'local team Arsenal after their . . . win in this year's FA Cup Final'; 'the first snow of the season'; the 'winning entries [in] this week's Tattslotto draw'.

Some of the items listed here may seem inordinately prosaic, and one suspects that journalists as well as critics might wonder how precisely they could count as news. But in the context of our discussion, perhaps this is the point. Despite the diversity and range of occasions dealt with in these reports and regardless of news value one structure seems to bind them together: the events reported on the day are a singular instance in a series of scheduled, regularized, predictable instances. One background feature of such rituals is the condition which provides a sense of temporal continuity – these events are governed by calendrical regularity and recurrence, imbued with certainty in their coming and going. Reiteration becomes a feature of comprehensibility and social memory as the rhythms of life are synchronized through these seemingly inevitable cycles. Discussing the 'dramatic core' of ritual Chaney (1983: 120) explains that 'the meanings being enacted are those of a necessary structure and what is being celebrated is the ability to impose order'. Hence, the recurrence of the season's first snow becomes an antidote to the unpredictability of our weather taking a hand; the regularity of Mother's Day serves to counter the unanticipated villainy perpetrated in the name of love or family on hapless Mary Harrison and Annie McDonald. The rituals of conquest and defeat (the FA Cup Final, Remembrance Day) provide regularized, predictable affirmations of manhood, nation, and community. Even the lottery winner results, so much a part of the realm of chance, maintain an orderliness amidst uncertainty by appearing each week – same time, same channel. In stark contrast, then, to stories about victims and communities at risk these rituals, once absorbed by the 'other news', can produce a discourse which speaks of the world, despite evidence to the contrary, as suffused with an active causality thus implying that there are patterns and linkages, that events follow one another in smooth, seemingly even transitions, and the social memory which is produced and marked out by selecting such events as newsworthy becomes a way of establishing the presence of this causality.

Chaney (1983: 120) suggests that one of the most significant aspects of ritual is the way 'collectivity is shown to be possible . . . a collectivity is postulated or affirmed which might otherwise only have an ambiguous social existence'. To accomplish this in a 'mass society' however frequently requires the intervention of the mass media. For both Chaney and Bocock, civic rituals connected with the nation state are exemplary cases for demonstrating how the media and ritual occasion can merge. The news stories being dealt with here seem to indicate that the processes of ritualized social affirmation connected to media coverage may be at work for other types of collectivities as well. The ritual events being reported regularly in the early evening news may not be as unique, extensively orchestrated or panoramic as the Victory Parade and the Coronation in England discussed by Chaney, but their place-ment in the bulletin may serve a similar, albeit more regionalized symbolic 'communalization' function. Mothers, sports fans, old soldiers, gamblers and the poor all attain public acknowledgement of their pre-occupations and their social condition. But what also stands out with regard to the symbolic construction of collectivity in these news stories is that the communities constituted by ritual are accounted for in terms which suggest a durable continuity between present, past and future. The annual poor man's mass, the first snow of the season, this week's lottery draw and Mother's Day may not be the events which the lament or even working journalists want to see in the evening bulletin, but these are the stories which situate 'ritual occasions' and their respective constituencies in terms of remembered repetitions – a past affirmed by its recurrence, a future postulated by its inevitability, and a present which is linked to both. Like the stories which hold out the immutable object from the past, these stories designate a fixed invariant causal cycle that seems unshakeable, that cannot be deranged or fractured and has no room for deviations.

THE 'METAPHYSICAL' TERRAIN

Through their various encoding strategies and narrative arrangements those story-types focusing on especially remarkable people, victims, and communities at risk could be considered in one way or another, to be constructed on the basis of a causality which is unstable and in jeopardy. Stories about the especially remarkable utilize the twitch of mild surprise, victim stories pose the unexpected disruption to the normal course of events and community at risk stories rely on the fundamental astonishment provided by the dangerous double. In each story-type cause and effect are challenged and in some cases destroyed. Stories dealing with ritual, tradition and the past, on the other hand, seem to work towards reversing or inverting these tendencies, to re-invest the world with causality, to offer continuity and certainty, produced notably in forms of reiteration and social memory. When all these stories are assembled as a 'force field' of associative meaning, a kind of metaphysical configuration begins to take shape which 'postulates' questions to do with transformation and preservation, functioning essentially as a sub-system within the single news broadcast as well as across the flow of broadcasts and generating a 'commentary' on causality and its disintegration.

By narrowing the focus slightly, another emergent metaphysical configuration can be detected in the context of particular stories. It might be suggested that those stories which focus on the restoration of causality constitute a discourse on temporality, the specifics of which are manifested in a pre-occupation with the past, repetition and recurrence, while stories concerned principally with the breakdown of causality – like community at risk stories – offer a discourse on spatiality. A central precept which governs community at risk stories is some notion of 'territory' and how it is affected by a variety of disruptive forces. Destruction is always framed in spatial terms: How much of the factory burned down? How many buildings were threatened? How many homes had to be abandoned? How high the flames leap? How many sites of disruption can be tabulated? At the centre of stories about ritual, tradition and the past is the dominion of time: we are shown its cyclical passage (the *annual* mass), its startling recovery (shoppers *stared*) and its ritualized movement into the future (*this week's* winner means there is bound to be a next week's as well).

By shifting these 'co-ordinates' slightly so that spatiality refers not just to the realm of physical space, but to social space as well, another set of relations emerges. Now, especially remarkable people and victim stories can be included, and observed in their operations articulating a synthesis of time and space. For the especially remarkable, the movement in socio-spatial terms is down to up, low to high, while victims move in the opposite direction. For both, however, the moves up or down are processed temporally: a time 'when' to the present state of affairs.

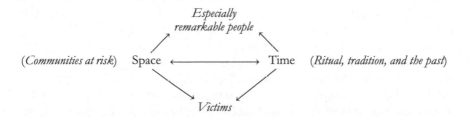

What is being suggested here then is that the 'totality' of these stories might be mapped as a metaphysical sub-system (or structure) of news with linkages and symmetries not readily apparent from the multiplicity of events which make up their regular inclusion in the news bulletin.

NEWS AND MYTH

A discussion of the relational aspects of these types of news stories leads back to a question posed earlier in the book: Why do stories like these have such a lengthy pedigree? How to account for their perennial appeal? During his exposition on the structure of myth, Lévi-Strauss asks a similar sort of question in the context of his own investigations:

> The question has often been raised why myths, and more generally oral literature, are so much addicted to duplication, triplication, or quadruplication of the same sequence. If our hypotheses are accepted, the answer is obvious: the function of repetition is to render the structure of the myth apparent.
>
> (1977: 229)

In the multiplication of 'other news' stories across bulletins every day, day after day, a structure of sorts, which might be called mythic, does begin to emerge. The structure which in its initial manifestation revolves around causality and its collapse might be re-posed in more general, abstracted terms – permanence and change. If the longevity and perennial journalistic production of the 'other news' can be situated in relation to these terms, and if this process can be understood, not by way of individual stories, but as part of an organized system whereby all stories are located in their relations with each other as specifiable types, a more fundamental structure, akin perhaps to myth, emerges which articulates a continuously 'spoken' discourse on patterns of permanence and change.

For Lévi-Strauss (1977: 229) the purpose of myth is to provide a model

143

capable of overcoming or mediating contradiction. In the terms to which these news stories refer, a formulation might be posed: How is it possible to conduct a life which is both permanent and changing, that has causal linkages and displays total randomness, that produces continuity yet is simultaneously discontinuous, that progresses with stability and is characterized by resounding instability? The contradiction is resolved by allowing for impermanence and change but within a 'bracketing' framework of broader cycles of causality where 'real' permanence resides. The deranged causality of the twitch of mild surprise is situated in the more enduring cycles of 'heroic' effort and triumphant accomplishment; the untoward disruption of everyday life for victims is framed by the permanent possibility of rescuer intervention; the reversals of the object world which puts collectivities at risk are countered by the regular remedial actions of communal agents. And punctuating these processes are the broad, seemingly immutable cycles of ritual, ceremony and social memory.

The resolution of the contradiction between permanence and change may operate at the formal level of the 'other news' as well. On the one hand there are the fluid variations, the continually changing parade of events, characters and occurrences; on the other hand there is the relatively permanent structure of 'other news' narratives and rhetorical procedures (recall Hughes on the 'good ones'), and beyond this, the stability of the news bulletin itself – newsreader, headlines, commercial break, weather – all seemingly resolute, perpetual, fixed. Form itself may constitute a negotiation of this contradiction. One can conduct a life in the face of uncertain change and instability if the knowledge is there that beyond these fluctuations reside the cycles of permanency inscribed in the ritual recurrence of the 'other news' itself, ceaselessly performed on time and in place. In its circulation and reception the ritual regularity of form can transcend the exigent instability of content, drawing into itself the confirmation of continuity.

It has been argued, more in popular than in scholarly terms, that news is, and must be, obsessively 'bad (negative) news'. This claim is reinforced by examples of 'good news' newspapers or television programmes failing miserably in the market-place. However, this argument is misplaced. On closer examination it can be seen that bad news may in fact be good news: the mediation of the contradiction between permanence and change in the 'other news' seems to provide an occasion to engage with a 'philosophical treatise' every night of the week. For those lamenting over television journalism having lost its way, these sorts of opportunities could hold out renewed hope, even if the news which does offer regular excursions into metaphysics is considered mostly 'bad' (negative and unworthy).

8

POLITICS, PLEASURES, 'SPIN-OFFS'

To address the question of the mass media's effects in terms of communicative power, the critical paradigm saw as necessary the foregrounding and analysis of the domain of ideology. In a liberal capitalist state, it was argued, the ideological is situated as the key arena around, and through which, the dominant groups or alliances of dominant 'fractions' are able to consolidate their influence through the social formation. This social power is exercised and accepted, not by way of the direct use of coercion, but by winning the consent especially of subordinate groups to particular ways of seeing the world which may systematically work against their interests in favour of the interests of the dominant groupings (Hall 1977: 332–3). By using what Hall (1982: 81–5) characterized as the 'enlarged concept of hegemony', the notion of 'dominance' was conceptualized not as the external imposition of, or total incorporation into, ruling ideas but a question of 'cultural leadership' which in the case of the media was manifested in 'the struggle over meaning' and public discourse. O'Sullivan *et al.* (1983: 103) point out that the concept of hegemony, as employed by the critical paradigm, was found most often in research which sought to demonstrate how everyday meanings, representations and activities were organized and used to understand the world in ways which presented the vested interests of the 'dominant bloc' as apparently natural and inevitable. It is through this process, as Hall (1977: 333) contends, that the 'subordinate classes "live" and make sense of their subordination'. For Goldman and Rajagopal (1991) hegemony has to refer not to 'a dominant ideology *per se*, but to practices and relations which predominate in structuring definitions of social reality'.

Studies examining the hegemonic aspects of culture tended particularly to 'focus on those forms and institutions which were usually taken to be impartial and neutral' (O'Sullivan *et al.* 1983: 103). The news, with its principles of objectivity, neutrality, impartiality and balance, was taken to be one such institution. But, as was consistently demonstrated, through processes of selection, classification and representation, the practices of journalism produced sense, meanings and interpretations of events which naturalized ways of looking at the world that were implicated in validating and reproducing the existing authoritative and distributive order. One key strength of the critical paradigm's examination of news, and the media more broadly, was that simple conspiracy theories and theories of class 'belonging-ness' could not be invoked in discussions of communicative power. News professionals' claims of independence had to be taken seriously. That journalism could both maintain its relative autonomy and reproduce the dominant ideological field was a paradox which had to be addressed.

Here, research primarily focused on the 'serious' news, which was also the news estimated to have the closest and most revealing links with political culture. The strategy was to take an event or issue, often one which was problematic for the holders of power – crime, deviance, race, industrial disputation, political dissent – and illustrate the ways that the dominant ideological fields penetrated the news, to become a primary source of explanation and intelligibility, in spite of journalism's professional practices and relative autonomy. The tendency, however, was to use these findings as the basis for generalizations about all news. The inclination, inadvertent perhaps, was to look at all news as more or less like the serious news, and to assume that the ideologies (re)produced and the structures of meaning gen-erated were uniformly activated within the same contexts of legitimacy, using the same kinds of representational strategies. A study of television's 'other news' suggests that this is not an entirely accurate appraisal. The ideological fields reproduced may be signified and inflected differently in different kinds of news stories. Moreover, particular story-types may be involved in the articulation of appreciably different ideological fields. If this is the case, it means that more account may have to be taken of the specificity of story-types: the 'good ones' which have persisted, and retained their form over time, may have a degree of relative autonomy within the totality of news. This also means that in discussions of news and ideology, it becomes less easy to slip into an analysis which only situates journalism in terms of the dominant ideology. A more comprehensive critical reading of news occurs when a plurality of story-types can be located in relation to a number of sometimes complementary, sometimes competing ideologies. Hence, 'the ideological' must be seen as a 'complex unity' which may retain differing emphases and enunciations, and refer to differing discourses encoded in specific story-domains.

Opening a space for difference also means opening a space for contradic-tion. Although the critical paradigm has recognized that securing consent is never automatic and that in the arena of the ideological there is always a 'struggle for the sign', these tendencies have not been particularly well appreciated in relation to news. A number of studies of various forms of popular culture have been ready to acknowledge that the textual operations connected to the workings of ideology are more porous and internally con-tradictory than might have been assumed at first (see White 1992). Given the critical paradigm's initial intellectual project to place the concept of communicative power onto the theoretical agenda of mass media research in the context of a 'minimal effects' tradition, this omission may be understandable. Now, however, it seems equally important to orient an investigation of news in terms that will take account of the uneven, incongruous and potentially contradictory tendencies within its ideological discourses. It will be suggested in these concluding remarks that because of a specific orientation unlike that of the serious news, the 'other news' may be a crucial region where some of the contradictory tendencies in television news surface and get played out.

THE IDEOLOGICAL SYSTEM

In his discussion of 'the framework of concepts and values' ideologically imbedded in news language Chibnall (1977: 12) cites such regularly used phrases as 'the national interest', 'the politically motivated strike', 'holding the country to ransom', 'extreme agitators', the 'silent majority' and 'wage inflation'. He explains that, with constant circulation, these phrases become 'ideological cues' which are legitimated and legitimating as common and immediately understood modes of expression, acting as a sedimented short hand for classifying, explaining and interpreting events. As such they fulfil an important political function in shaping the meaning of events and rendering them intelligible in terms of preferred readings within the repertoire of dominant ideologies. It might be argued that the story-types contained in the 'other news' exhibit a similar type of phraseological predisposition, operating as a network of descriptors which classify and shape the meaning of events and which ought to be seen in relation to the process of ideological cueing: 'with courage and determination', 'a great comeback', 'gaining his title', 'the dream of having a family', 'the world's fastest', 'the first ever', 'last chance to live a normal life', 'a close brush with death', 'lucky to be alive', 'the aftermath of tragedy', 'a sense of shock and disbelief', 'battling the flames', 'some of the most traumatic scenes ever witnessed', 'stepping into the past'. The particularity of this highly conventionalized vocabulary which inhabits the 'other news' is as immediately recognizable and conceptually evocative as those legitimating phrases which traverse the serious news.

The 'other news' also offers a set of relatively stable visual images which act to select, classify and assign meaning to events within preferred referential contexts. For example, the actuality of the 'trail of destruction' is succinctly represented by the splintered power pole; the 'aftermath of tragedy' by the smoking ruins of a domestic dwelling; a 'close brush with death' by the precariously dangling cab of the truck; the 'battle' by a fire fighter dwarfed by the undulating wall of smoke; 'a little bit of history' by sepia photographs of the troop ship. These images are coded within story-types with a regularity which suggests that they may have the characteristics of a visual iconography – a repertoire of image–signs which becomes well

147

rehearsed and continuous, so that past selections have a certain controlling influence over present moments of 'enunciation'. Sedimented with meaning, easily recognizable, this repertoire of images, combined with the language of news talk has the potential to produce as resonant and forceful a set of ideological inflections as any group of stories in the serious news.

The 'other news' does, of course, offer some of the same constituting ideological 'terms' as the serious news. The category of 'individual-persons' (Poulantzas in Hall 1977: 337) is central; but, there are other notions such as public/private, the community, the nation, consumers, ordinary Australians, public opinion which are common to both. The 'other news', however, also contains a distinctive representational orientation towards the construction of events and engages in the production of meaning after its own fashion. In this sense, those stories generally ignored by the critical paradigm and regarded by the lament as examples of how television trivializes news, are important, not only for demonstrating the way particular ideological discourses penetrates forms of broadcast news, but for uncovering ideological discourses not necessarily as fully constituted in the serious news.

The operation and unfolding of these discourses becomes most evident when the 'other news' is examined as a structured whole which might be understood in terms of a set of opposing but mutually referential conceptual categories. Specified as an active organization of meaning, ideological work is performed both in terms of individual stories and in the way that certain story-types are related 'in opposition' through a systematic structure. On the one hand, the 'other news' provides a selective inventory of occurrences, based on the activities and achievements of newsworthy 'personalities'. This is a domain of reportage centred on instant celebrities and 'élite persons' who by virtue of either doing-as-they-do in the way of unanticipated achievements or simply being-as-they-are come to dwell in the realm of the especially remarkable. This domain is constituted and signified by stories which focus on 'ordinary people' who breach expectations – an adult reads comics, a boy builds a hovercraft – and on extraordinary people doing ordinary things – visiting a foreign city, getting engaged. What is symbolically represented throughout the variations in surface content is not so much the 'personalities' and their actions – which would be too literal translation of the stories – but that individuals, through their already established credentials or through their own special efforts and actions, ought to be and indeed can be the principle instruments for making their own fate, creating their own destiny. The preferred reading of these stories is governed by a structure of meaning which situates mastery and control as an identifiable and valued 'lived reality'. Here is a world which endows both 'ordinary' and 'élite' persons with all the confidence, authority of conviction, command of resources, will to succeed, and self-motivating optimism to conduct their lives with a 'sense of potency': individuals in these stories are refracted through their own 'subjecthood' (Gouldner 1976: 67). These are subject–persons who demonstrate, in some cases through their determination and in others simply by their already established competence and ease in the world, the ability to perform in terms of their own expectations or those which are 'thrust upon them'. They can thus be seen as something like a pantheon of contemporary cultural heroes, both great and small, celebrated for performing masterful deeds which in turn transport them into the realms of the noteworthy and the exceptional.

On the other hand, framed in opposition to the imagery of mastery and control is another kind of 'lived reality'. This is constituted not by the actions and conquests of remarkable individuals but by the results – physical, psychological, personal, social, economic – of occurrences which have intervened in and transformed the on-going activities of everyday life, unpredictably and often inexplicably. This is the domain of events in which families get destroyed in house fires, children contract incurable diseases, truck drivers flirt with death, school teachers mysteriously disappear, hospitals explode, whole towns are abandoned, suburbs devastated, and historic moments put on hold. Out of these stories emerges a conceptualization of the world which stands dramatically opposed to notions of mastery and control. Rather than being makers of their fate, here individuals and indeed whole communities are made by fate, and become the unsuspecting and unprepared victims of capricious and unanticipated happenings. The resources, knowledge and confidence needed to act with a 'sense of potency' disappears. Even in those rare instances where victims are able to alter their circumstances, it is not a result of their own doing, but of the actions of others, who fortuitously appear (magically in Propp's terms) at the right moment to guide destiny. Mastery is negated and is replaced instead by malevolent external forces that strike indiscriminately, exposing people to the grossest changes of fortune and the most radical disruptions of everyday life (Gouldner 1976: 70). Rather than existing as acting subjects, individuals become objects acted upon by unpredictable, unaccountable occurrences which threaten everyday life and the security and trust invested in it. An undercurrent of fatalism seems to be a guiding principle in these stories. The external environment is an ominous place to venture, and danger and despair lurk at every turn. Even the most ordinary routines which make up the rituals of daily life – driving a car, going to work, sleeping in a bed – are precarious and potentially fraught.

Emerging from within these two expansive story 'constellations' we begin to detect a more central generative structure which works symbolically to locate events as news in terms of a paradigmatic system and to postulate the fluctuating conditions of mastery and control. This in turn, provides for the unfolding of a complex chain of associated meanings:

mastery and the possession of control/non-mastery and the loss of control

predictability/capriciousness
action/reaction
strength/vulnerability
safety/risk
knowledge/ignorance
heroes/victims
optimism/pessimism
secure/insecure
subject/object

The conceptual order which shapes the meaning of occurrences in the 'other news' thus brings it into the sphere of ideology. By situating the locus of conduct and control in terms of either the personal attributes and deeds of individual actors or the impersonal unaccountable interventions made by forces operating externally on individuals, the 'other news' offers modes of explanation and sense-making which displace and mask the social, political and historical context in which events occur and can be made to mean. The personal and the impersonal become 'naturalized' forms of expression and intelligibility within a news discourse which deflects attention from what is perhaps a more crucial factor in explaining the conditions of mastery and its nemesis – the structures of domination and subordination.

If the 'other news' constructs an ideological system which is specific to its types of stories, this system also has to be seen in the way it draws on and can be read in relation to already existing sets of social representations (Brunsdon and Morley 1978: 88). And it is here where the 'popularity' of these types of news stories and their persistence, even in the face of vigorous and sustained criticism, might be partially explained. Although class-based analysis has been pushed into the background on the stage of social theory, the work done by Parkin (1972) on the ways in which social inequality and the differential distribution of reward are interpreted by subordinate classes still offers a particularly useful illumination in trying to understand the operations of ideology in the instance of the 'other news'. Drawing on the tradition of class theory, and on Parkin's work in particular, is done for heuristic purposes – to demonstrate how the supposedly non-serious news needs to be taken very seriously in the way it places 'meaning in the service of power' – and is not an attempt to re-establish class as the pre-eminent social category around which all other lived realities depend. There is however a degree of 'political calculation' involved in utilizing this approach which has as its motivation a perceived need to refigure some of the key analytical tools used by the critical paradigm that, in more recent times, seem to have been lost, and to reprioritize the possibility of the media becoming once again a 'field of political inquiry' in a context especially directed 'to understand the dynamics of social and cultural inequality and the ways in which these are lived . . . ' (McRobbie 1991: 14).

How then might a class-inflected analysis assist in understanding broadcast television's disreputable news in terms of 'the dynamics of social and cultural inequality and the ways in which these are lived'? According to Parkin in class-based societies three major 'public meaning-systems' can be distinguished, each of which promotes a different interpretation of inequality. The dominant meaning-system, which essentially endorses the structure of the unequal distribution of reward as just and desirable, has its social source in those groups occupying positions of greatest power and privilege. It is this meaning-system which sets the parameters around which the others tend to be oriented, principally because it has been 'objectified and enshrined' in major institutional structures, providing a framework from which all competing meaning-systems must take their initial cues. The concept of the dominant meaning-system derives from Marx's proposition that 'the ideas of the ruling class are, in every age, the ruling ideas' (Parkin 1972: 82). The subordinate classes, in turn, can respond to the conditions of inequality and low status in several ways. One of these occurs through a deferential endorsement of the dominant meaning-system. This response sees inequality as inevitable but also just, whereby it is accepted that some people are inherently fit for positions of power. This interpretation relies on the view that the social order is an organic whole in which everyone, however humble, has a part to play, and all benefit from the 'stewardship' of the powerful. An aspirational response also sees inequality as inevitable, but emphasizes the possibilities for self advancement and social mobility i.e. certain individuals of talent and ability can, with effort and determination, rise above their circumstances.

Parkin further identifies what he calls a 'subordinate meaning-system', which has its origins in the lived experience of the subordinate classes. One of its key characteristics is a type of 'accommodative' orientation which recognizes inequality as unjust, but also sees the relative futility of trying to alter social arrangements on a large scale. The result is an emphasis on various 'modes of adaption' which allow people to have a 'liveable life' – trade unionism is one accommodative strategy, a tendency to define the social order in terms of 'us' and 'them' is another, and the mobilization of 'a kind of fatalistic pessimism' (Parkin 1972: 90) is a third. Lastly, Parkin (1972: 97) identifies a radical meaning-system capable of promoting an oppositional interpretation of class inequalities which is based on revealing the connection between 'personal fate and the wider political order'.

I want to posit that as a particular structuration – a journalistic 'formation' of meanings and narratives – the 'other news' may be in a position to offer what could be designated as 'discursive mobilizations' (Hartley 1992: 76) of these various subordinate meaning-system responses to and interpretations of class inequality and differential reward structures. The aspirational 'model', for example, has a correspondence with stories which promote the view that ordinary people can become especially remarkable by meeting challenges, overcoming obstacles, commanding resources, seemingly acting as the agents of their own fate. Class and status systems are inevitable but there is always a place for those who, through their own efforts, ability and determination can 'make something of themselves' – motorcycle stunt jumpers, iron lung mothers, hovercraft-building schoolboys, female competitors on the trotting track, record-setting barbers. The deferential model also has a correspondence with certain stories. Reports of the doings and sayings of those especially remarkable élites, who are newsworthy simply for their very-being-as-they-are, are implicated in assumptions about the inherent rightfulness of such individuals to occupy positions in the 'higher world'. Royalty and celebrity élites are offered as eminently suitable candidates for prestige and admiration. These stories actually incorporate a version of the deferential model into their construction by the insistent usage of subsidiary characters. Fans, on-lookers, crowds, and admirers are signs for proclaiming both élite suitability and deference due. In the case of show business celebrities the deferential response is produced in relation to our own position as viewers who are also potential consumers of celebrity entertainments. Their stardom, and all the 'powerless power' that attaches to it, is a particular form of stewardship from which every one of us can benefit – new television comedy shows to enjoy, new spectacular thought-provoking movies to ponder, new versions of Shakespeare to savour, new gossip to exchange. Although especially remarkable élites seem to be naturally endowed with the ability to inhabit the higher world, it does not follow that the 'ordinary person' is simply of no account. Even in its hierarchical organization, the social order needs everyone to play a part – the boy who builds a hovercraft, the adult who collects comic books, the cabinet maker who sits with snakes, even the man who talks to gnomes can take pride in their accomplishments and in 'making a contribution'. And of course, 'it takes all kinds to make a world'.

The accommodative response of the subordinate meaning-system attains discursive formulation in the 'other news' as well. Stories about victims and communities at risk in particular are imbued with a sense of the unexplained and the unexplainable which suggests that the world is organized around forces which are primarily outside of any real control. Communities may be able to deploy rescue operations to restore order, victims may have philanthropic helpers, but no sooner are these disasters discharged than other unplanned disruptions take their place: 'it's just one damned thing after another'. What is being premised in these stories is the feeling that there is not much that can actually be done about the world and its capricious ways; one then needs to 'grin and bear it', 'take life as it comes', 'make the best of a bad lot'.

In producing its 'sense' of the world the 'other news' appears to have appropriated and synthesized certain forms of popular wisdom, those 'orally transmitted tags enshrining generalizations, prejudices and half truths, elevated by epigrammatic phrasing to the status of maxims' (Hoggart 1957: 103), particularly as these have sedimented within the subordinate meaning-system. On the one hand the 'other news' reproduces the belief that 'there is always someone worse off than yourself', and 'there but for the grace of God/fortune go you or I'. If the world is such a dangerous and capricious place, it is best not to risk oneself in it. The rational response is to be satisfied with one's lot, to 'make the best of what you've got', to cultivate a kind of retreatism and isolationism ('don't stick your neck out'; 'you can't win so there's no use trying'). On the other hand, it is only 'right and just' that those few individuals who do take risks and are seemingly not afraid of coming in contact with this unpredictable world should be rewarded and celebrated for their mastery and subjecthood; after all, 'nothing ventured nothing gained', 'who dares wins'. These individuals are doubly remarkable: for the deeds they perform and the fact that these performances take place in spite of the hostile unpredictable world. And if, as it turns out, a handful of people are already situated in the 'higher world' they can be handled by other fragments of popular wisdom. In some cases, these individuals are brought down to our level: 'after everything is said and done', 'when it comes down to it', 'in the end, we're all just human, aren't we' (he may be a prince and she a princess, but when it comes to marriage he's still a father, she a daughter). In other cases they are made vulnerable: 'life's tough at the top' (he's a television star, but how does he like being the brunt of all those small man jokes?); 'the bigger they are, the harder they fall' (in their shining hour, our rock star heroes run foul of the law). This braiding together of a sense of pessimism, resignation and vulnerability with admiration for extraordinary individuals who manage to transcend the web of circumstance in which ordinary mortals are bound (but still retain their 'human' qualities) constitutes and is constituted by what Gramsci would call a 'spontaneous philosophy' (in Bennett et al. 1981: 231). And the modality of such a philosophy can be ominously conservative in its 'world view' and implications. The 'other news' plays out a common sense drama of fatalism. It substitutes any expressed potential to act in the world, or to act on that world in order to change it, with a fatalistic vision which holds that, however miserable or unrewarding one's life or circumstances might be, people should be satisfied and not complain, because 'things could get worse'. It follows then, that the world is better left untouched, or at least to only those remarkable few who are capable of dealing with it masterfully, but who still seem bound to us by their 'ordinary' sensibilities. In this way, through the generation of its conceptual structure, the 'other news' can, like the serious news, function so that existing arrangements and relations of power and privilege retain a resonant measure of legitimacy, making the 'thinkability' of alternative arrangements much harder to accomplish.

Ideology, it has been argued, works by way of interpellation, hailing subjects and presenting them with a 'place' from which they are invited to make sense of 'themselves' and the world in particular ways which tend to advantage the vested interests of dominant groups. In terms of the signifying practices of the media's output, ideology operates through complex codes and structures to 'position' the subject – places are inscribed in the text for reader 'occupancy' from which textual decipherment and then cognition ensue. However, according to this view, when readers adopt the subject position offered to make the text intelligible they also adopt a relation to preferred and dominant ideological meanings (Masterman 1985: 237). This way of looking at ideology seems to have a creditable presence in news studies attempting to uncover how the production of journalistic meaning is placed in the service of power (see Hartley 1982). The brief excursion into Parkin's analysis of the public meaning-systems, however demonstrates that the interpellation of subjects by news texts may take place in terms situated outside the realm of dominant ideology. The subject positions offered in the 'other news' actually seem to have a more decisive connection with subordinate rather than dominant meaning-systems – instead of endorsing the definitions of reality of the ruling groups, the 'other news' appears to be aligned with the lived experience of the subordinate groups. In this instance, perhaps television news cannot be so straightforwardly conceptualized as positioning subjects in relation to, and reproducing dominant ideology.

Paradoxically, it might be suggested that the communicative power of the 'other news' is all the more possible precisely because it does *not* do so. If, as Hall (1977: 333) argues, the ruling order rules, not by way of coercion, but by struggling for and winning the consent of the ruled, it also needs to be recognized that this is achieved not through manipulating the consciousness of the subordinate groups by pulling the ideological wool over their eyes. Rather, as Hartley (1982: 59) explains, 'it is won by taking the real conditions in which people live their daily lives and representing them in ways that *do* "make sense"'. The 'other news' might be seen to function in this way: it gives back to the subordinate groups their own 'conditions of existence' and endorses the lived experience of subordination, but does so, not in terms which locate such experience in specific social, economic or historical processes, but in relation to its drama of fatalism. Class inequality seen from this perspective then becomes just another lucky/unlucky break with seemingly no social causation or explanation: 'there's them that have and them that don't'.[1] Action for change is of little value, and even futile in this context. Combined with a metaphysical system which poses causal relations as fluctuating between grand cycles of external recurrence ('the more things change . . . ') the ideological system of the 'other news', despite its dependence on subordinate meanings and forms of popular wisdom, and the concomitant interpellation which this allows, is still able to maintain the interests of the dominant groups. Hartley (1982: 59) explains that 'to achieve hegemonic consent, not only must the real conditions of the subordinate . . . classes be taken into account, but they must be "represented" . . . on neutral terrain'.

With its claims to objectivity, impartiality, balance and transparency, and enduring audience perceptions about its trustworthiness and believability (Glasgow University Media Group 1976; Western and Hughes 1983; Tiffen 1989), television news, especially given its apparently unassailable propensity for the production of 'disreputable' reportage, seems an important site, in media terms, from which to perform ideological work.[2]

DESTABILIZING PLEASURES

The study of broadcast journalism and the issue of pleasure have very rarely met on the same investigative agenda.[3] For some time however, those lamenting the decline and fall of television news have been keenly aware of this connection:

> The biggest heist of the 1970s never made it onto the five o'clock news. The biggest heist of the 1970s *was* the five o'clock news. The salesmen took it. . . . By the 1970s, an extravagant proportion of television news answered less to the description of 'journalism' than to that of 'show business'.
>
> (Powers in Graber 1980: 57)

This particular reproach is foremost a reaction to the commodification of information; but it is also partially linked to the desire for an idealized 'information model' of news which, in order to exist in a 'pure' form, requires overlooking news as cultural discourse, already constituted as more than just information delivery. Unresolved tensions like these could have opened the way to ask some potentially interesting questions about television news-audience relations – show business is, after all, always more than just business, and to account for the 'show' inevitably means addressing issues connected to 'appeal' and 'pleasure' – but because of its prescriptive stance, the lament never seemed to follow through to the point where a more analytic approach might have examined some of these fundamental concerns in more depth. Ironically, it may be precisely around the 'show' and its pleasures where it can be demonstrated that ideology never works a 'perfect transmission', hesitating and faltering when 'speaking' to position its subject. As White (1992) explains, the operations of the ideological in television's texts always contain possibilities for instability and contradiction. If the process of winning consent is neither spontaneous nor a permanent state but has to be obtained in the struggle for the sign there will be ideological sites where consent can be acquired but equally where it can be forfeited. Importantly, in the light of this current inquiry into news and ideology it might be suggested that it is around the site of pleasure, as it is located in the 'other news', where some of these instabilities and contradictory tendencies get played out where paradoxically ideology can have both a uniquely forceful communicative power, because of an overwhelming commitment to a

155

mode of address and a discursive orientation shaped by the everyday and the mundane, and a kind of vulnerability which can destabilize this arrangement as a result of the 'show' which, as it were, 'choreographs' the performance of this communicative power. Television's least savoury news and the potential pleasures it can offer may in fact prove to be one important arena in the domain of broadcast journalism where counter-hegemonic tendencies within a broadly hegemonizing journalistic discourse are possible, and where the struggle over meaning is never a settled affair.

In her discussion of the imagination of disaster in 1950s science fiction films Sontag (1974) finds that what intrigues us about such films is the 'ingenuity' applied to create disorder and a dimension of 'artfulness' which allows for the possibility of letting go 'normal obligations' in order to gratify certain sadistic propensities in relation to the discomfort and suffering of others. Principally, this type of science fiction film for Sontag (1974: 425) 'is concerned with the aesthetics of destruction, with the peculiar beauties to be found in wreaking havoc, making a mess'. It might be posited that it is just such an aesthetics of destruction, the pleasure that comes from making a mess, which informs so much of the 'other news' – the physical mess made when the materiality of our world is literally turned upside down, and the social and psychological mess when the orderly arrangements of everyday life inexplicably collapse in various ways.

Journalists sometimes use a derogatory term for the kind of television news selection process which has visual impact as the only criteria of newsworthiness – the falling chimney syndrome. Fortuitously, during the four-week sample, a literal manifestation of the falling chimney syndrome appeared: a 'report' on the removal of a chimney of gigantic proportions being knocked down in a brickworks to make way for new technology. In the context of this study, the irony of this accident of sampling was not lost. On one level here was an exact expression of the 'syndrome', a television news item which was really nothing more than an opportunity to convey a spectacle of destruction purely for its own sake. However, at another level this was a report, included in the bulletin, which captured in its most elemental form the journalistic prototype of a news story which could illustrate in a completely unencumbered way how the apparently solid, fixed materiality of the world can be suddenly bent and toppled out of shape. The response to the most riveting image of the story – a single wide-shot held long enough so that the huge chimney is viewed, first in a normal upright condition and then after the dynamite charge does its work, in slow collapse, snaking downward into a massive pile of rubble – was clearly meant to be framed in terms of amazement and wonder. Sontag (1974: 428) contends that the 1950s science fiction film was, at the time, one of popular culture's purest forms of spectacle. Perhaps the chimney destruction story, after a fashion, demonstrates the way television news could be operating out of a similar cultural tradition. The 'other news' is a litany of these 'peculiar beauties'. Each day is filled with unsuspected and ingenious ways in which havoc can occur. Nothing it seems is spared, nothing is out of range of potential chaos. Our position as spectator is constructed as both one of empathy and identification but also one of distance and detachment. We alternate between going close and remaining apart, an arrangement which has a certain formal correspondence with the switching between reporter on the spot and newsreader in the studio – the former involved in the 'dirty business' first hand, the latter 'clean', merely watching (glancing down at a hidden screen as the story moves by way of news film from studio to the scene). Simply looking on as spectators means we can potentially be released from our normal obligations, including perhaps requisite empathetic responses, and even surreptitiously take a degree of perverse enjoyment from the suffering of others. So, although the generative structure of the 'other news' produces a sense of fatalism and retreat, which proclaims that we ought to stay put, and make the best of what is ours because things could get worse, there is another position constructed, which might be seen to work against this structure and instead proclaims: the worse it gets, the better I like it. This position is organized around the complementarity of the ludic and the luddite. In the 'other news', the world that we know is played with, toyed with, tossed around, tickled, stretched and pulled out of shape, and in the end gleefully destroyed. But only momentarily, because it always seems to spring back into shape, like the characters in an animated cartoon (or as in the classic cinema trick, having the fallen chimney reassemble in reverse motion) in time for the next day when further disorder can be invoked. Both of these domains add up to a celebration of the ludicrous the world in its social and physical arrangements, is inherently absurd and ridiculous, floating and slipping, where 'all that is solid melts into air'. In this sense, the ideology of fatalism and retreat seems to bump up against a kind of anarchic existentialism.

What could be called the pleasure of uncertainty can be situated as an extension of the aesthetics of destruction. Implied in the ideological system of the 'other news' is a sense that if there is a possible counter move that could be made against the loss of mastery and control it would be found in the search for orderliness. One way that this orderliness can be secured is by retaining the existing regimes of stability unaltered, investing in 'the way things are'. This solution assumes that the comfort one takes in resignation and acceptance has order as a natural self-evident state of being. Philosopher and physicist Alfred Bork (1980) speculates that, in fact, premises about order may be misplaced, and that historically the twentieth century can be distinguished from the nineteenth by its fascination with and reliance on what he calls 'randomness'. Whereas the nineteenth century could be characterized by the search for a rationalistic, ordered predictable universe, the twentieth has, in a number of intellectual fields, including physics, the visual arts, literature and philosophy, been much more prepared to entertain and utilize the random as an 'organizing principle'. Interest in cause and effect is supplemented and sometimes superseded by a consideration of chance and accident. Randomness, contends Bork, has a 'validity of [its] own' which can ultimately be connected with what he terms 'joy'. The seemingly haphazard occurrences which crowd the 'other news', situated in this context, are not necessarily circumstances to be troubled by, but ones that may be capable of generating just such 'joy'. A capricious world as the focus of news produces both an ideologically inflected sense of resignation and restraint, and a type of modernist pleasure in random unrestraint. Bork (1980: 73) quotes artist Ben Shahn who explains the pleasure and the politics of randomness: 'I love chaos. It is a mysterious unknown road with unexpected turnings. It is the way out. It is freedom, man's best hope'. The daily encounter with uncertainty may add another layer of pleasure to the 'other news'.[4]

There is also 'the pleasure of the text', the grip of the narrative, the savouring of the story regardless of the fact that it is news; and it may be the narrative's status as news, as 'the real', that actually enhances pleasure. For George Herbert Mead (1926) there were two modes of reportage in journalism.[5] One he called the information model which was primarily oriented to convey factual material such as election results, or financial news, the emphasis on 'the truth value of news'. The other model emphasized the 'enjoyability' and 'consummatory value' of news, functioning to provide satisfying 'aesthetic' experiences which helped people interpret their own lives. The latter Mead referred to as the story model of journalism, observing that 'the reporter is generally sent out to get a story not the facts'. Broadcast journalism in particular has been keenly aware of the relationship between narrative and the processing of news, and influential news producers like Reuven Frank have made this relationship a core broadcasting principle (Epstein 1973). If pleasure can be derived from television news, it may well be for the reason that this type of journalism is always premised on the assumption that it needs to offer 'good stories, well told'. Stam (1983: 31) explains that 'in this sense all [television] news is good news . . . because [it] entail[s] the pleasurability of fiction itself'.

All television news may be narrative, but the 'other news' is of a special kind, often succinct, self-contained, referring to nothing outside itself and usually beginning and ending in a single report. These qualities, it might be suggested, inflect the 'other news' towards what could be characterized as a more forthright declaration of 'story-ness'. Whereas the serious news is also based around a story model, it pretends that it is not – it asserts that its major concern is with imparting the important information of the day. The 'other news' in its conciseness and 'immanence' (Barthes 1977a: 187) can more readily signal a story-like constructedness, positioning its reader/viewer into a kind of mutually confirming declaration with the response: that was a good one! By drawing attention to its story-ness the 'other news' may start to 'blow the cover' of all the news. What is exposed is that the world of fact and the world of fiction are bound more closely together than broadcasters are prepared to have us believe. In this context the lament's objections to the disreputable news may be seen to involve not just the content or subject matter of such stories, but their form as well, since what the 'other news' is declaring and the serious news is duplicitously denying is that this is a story – no more, no less (Tuchman 1976: 93). One might speculate then that at the ideological level, the recognition of the story-ness of the 'other news' may act, not to engage the viewer/reader in its premises and potential outcomes, but to produce distantiation: these are real people, here is misadventure, but after all, it's only a story.[6]

This discussion of pleasure has been undertaken to demonstrate, albeit briefly, that the hegemonic trajectory of the 'other news' is not automatically set into place, that ideological effectivity may be worked against by shifting emphases internal to the text and in the text's relations with its readers. However, even though these operations are taking place, the offer of such pleasures may also be crucial for winning consent, for extending and securing the ideological reach of the 'other news'. Because such pleasures attract and hold our attention by giving voice to such utopian possibilities (Dyer 1981) – the *beauties* in making a mess, the *joy* of uncertainty, the *pleasure* of the text – they act as a mode of address, a 'hailing' mechanism which encourages entry into the fabric of the 'other news' and organizes the conditions around which a connection with ideologically preferred readings of events can be made. Analytically, what has to be faced is the contradictory and sometimes ambiguous relations that are being played out between audience and the 'other news' story-texts, where positions are given 'as a continuous process of formation and superseding of unstable equilibria' (Gramsci in Hall 1977: 334), both winning and losing consent on the terrain of the ideological.

What this study has called the lament over the 'other news' on television has a great deal of affinity with the lament over mass culture in general. Like mass culture, the 'other news' has been accused of triviality, leading people away from more important concerns, being perpetrated solely for motives of profit, slowly eating away at the distinctions between good culture and bad, cashing in on audiences' baser desires and instincts, having a pernicious influence on its producers, being symptomatic of some grander and more profound cultural failing. The work done here has attempted to attend seriously to that television news declared by the lament to have least claim to seriousness, to be least worthy of the journalistic enterprise. It has tried to establish some of the ways in which this disreputable, non-serious news is patterned as particular story forms which produce meaning by using a variety of textual and narrative strategies. It has also attempted to situate the politics of this apparently non-political news, demonstrating that when the news is examined in relation to communicative power, the specificity of story-types and their interrelations needs to be taken into account. As well, there has been an effort made to explain how such news can be crucial within the totality of television news both for winning consent, and for offering pleasures which might work against the production of such consent. In retrospect, it might be suggested that claims for the specificity of the 'other news', in its form and ideological function, have to be approached cautiously. All news on television probably contains elements of the 'other news'. What distinguishes the 'other news', however, is its excesses, its flamboyant gestures. It takes the codes and conventions of the news in general and inflates, exaggerates and displays them more openly for what they are. The 'other news' is disreputable possibly because it is disrespectful, more forthrightly acknowledging and flaunting the devices and constructions which the serious news suppresses and hides. Perhaps, in the end, this is why the liberal lament is so harsh on this kind of news, because it is what news is, only more so.

RECENT ARTICULATIONS

The recent proliferation in what broadcasters sometimes like to refer to as 'reality programming' and others are prone to label 'tabloid tv' has already been the object of controversy and deliberation (Rowe 1993). Once again the lament arrived early on the scene, assessing these developments and certainly not holding back in aiming its critical barbs at a whole new range of targets (see Glynn 1990; Lumby and O'Neill 1994). To leave this study of the 'other news' before offering at least a few observations which take account of these emergent trends in television journalism does not feel like the appropriate moment for 'closure'. From the preceding discussion the connections between the two, on one level, are all too obvious. What follows then is a series of tentative, and necessarily brief rounding out speculations which attempt to examine what might be termed, using a rather clumsy but, as we shall see, appropriate neologism, the 'other-news-ization' of broadcast journalism.

Programmes like *Hard Copy, A Current Affair, Cops, Rescue 911, Emergency 000, Police, Camera, Action, Inside America's Courts, Australia's Funniest Home Videos, Before They Were Stars, Lifestyles of the Rich and Famous* can be loosely grouped together as examples of what Fiske (1992b: 48) has called 'tabloid journalism' – a type of reportage where the emphasis is on topics 'produced at the intersection between public and private, [a] style [which] is sensational, sometimes sceptical, sometimes moralistically earnest; [a] tone which is populist and [a] modality fluidly deny[ing] any stylistic difference between fiction and documentary, between news and entertainment'. One common explanation for the form that this type of journalism on television takes rests on an assumption that the tabloid press exists as a direct and directing antecedent, that broadcast journalism simply picked up and mirrored the presentational codes and pre-occupations of print tabloid formats (Knight 1989; Lumby and O'Neill 1994). However, as this study indicates, it also might be shown that the lines of descent have already been figured and embedded in the routine discourses of television journalism. The impulse towards tabloidism, as we have seen, resides very firmly in 'other news' story-types regularly utilized by one of broadcast journalism's premier productions, the early evening news. The drift to tabloid, it could be argued, may owe as much to a current recirculation and proliferation of those story forms as it does to an appropriation of the conventions of the tabloid press. In his discussion of Hollywood prime-time television Gitlin (1985: 78) explains that the creation and production of programmes is resolutely governed by a 'recombinant style' which makes itself felt in programme lineage and conception. Recent developments in television programming stylistically and thematically, tend to come through a line of descent connected to what is already deemed successful. Like sitcom characters, whose popularity is such that they eventually 'get their own show', tabloid tv may be broadcast journalism's attempt at the 'spin-off'. In this context, most revealing perhaps is the way in which many of the thematic and narrative pre-occupations of this type of television journalism seem to re-iterate and embellish what is already an established focus of this 'other news'. The world of celebrity, ordinary people doing extraordinary and remarkable things, the plight of the victim and communities at risk all have a major part in the repertoire of tabloid reportage (see Rowe 1993). In programming terms, it appears as if television producers decided to take a particular fragment of an already workable popular genre and expand it to fill an entire programming 'slot', in order to address a wider and potentially more profitable viewership. This is not to discount or diminish the influence of the press version of tabloid journalism in providing models to emulate, but we might have to be careful in assuming, as Knight (1989) does, that the features of the tabloid print media are merely 'carried over' intact to television. For example, unlike its press counterpart the television tabloidesque seems less inclined towards the 'wild stories' (Peterson 1991) characteristic of so much of the print media form. Although, to some extent, retaining a propensity for excess, hyperbole and intensification, television's version of tabloid does not seem to focus to quite the same degree on sensational subject matter. The alien visitation or the wife meeting her dead husband in the Devil's Triangle (Fiske 1992b: 50–2) may not be outside the realm of story possibility for broadcast tabloid, but the inclusion of such items is likely to be on a less than regular basis. The television variant of tabloid may be noted for its moralism and its 'general offensive vulgarity' (Fiske 1992b: 48), but it still seems to operate with reportorial practices which rely in some part on those conventional broadcast news values such as credibility, authority and trustworthiness. A programme like *Hard Copy*, for instance, may have all the right credentials for qualifying as tabloid television, but it still sees itself maintaining some kinship with the protocols of the documentary tradition and 'current affairs' journalism; the official label

161

favoured by broadcasters to describe what they do is 'reality programming' and not tabloid television.

'Hailing' new audiences

In recent years there has been an on-going discussion about the historical importance and social location of what is periodically referred to as the 'new middle class' or more expansively, the new professional and managerial middle class (Ehrenreich 1989; Wright 1989; Baxter, Emmison and Western 1991; Frankel 1992). Although acknowledged as a notoriously slippery social grouping to pin down with the kind of precision some social scientists would prefer, several features seem to keep reappearing when the social and experiential constituents of this class are posited. 'Intellectually trained', the professional middle class tends to spend long periods of time attaining certain occupational and status-related credentials. Some, like physicians, lawyers, therapists, public relations personnel and so on are self-employed, but the pattern over the years has been for the new middle class to work as salaried wage earners absorbed into large bureaucratic or corporate organizations including instrumentalities developed out of the post-war expansion of state activities. Perhaps most spectacularly, the new middle class, or at least parts of it, has been frequently recognized in popular as well as more specialist scholarly discourse by its very visible patterns of consumption/ 'overconsumptionism' (Ehrenreich 1989; Frankel 1992).[7] With the expansion of professional and managerial jobs accompanying the growth of public and private sector corporate bodies, including the rapidly expanding service and financial sectors, the 1950s and 1960s saw the emergence of the new middle class as a substantial and growing social entity. However, by the late 1980s its ascent was faltering. For example, Connell and Irving (1992: 239) specifically point to the collapse of full employment as 'one of the most dramatic and far-reaching reversal of the trends which had been taken ... to characterize the administered economy of advanced capitalism'. Although this experience was unevenly spread across social groups with unemployment in the first instance concentrated among the more marginalized and less powerful, by the end of the 1970s in Australia as in other comparably wealthy countries more broadly based unemployment began a substantial upward turn. In particular, the new middle class which had initially benefited from post-war expansion increasingly began to feel the effects of economic restructuring during the 1980s. The shrinkage of the public sector meant the once large and growing army of salaried and professional administrators, social workers, teachers, researchers, technicians and others making up the ranks of one 'fraction' of the new middle class became increasingly vulnerable. Meanwhile, those members of the new middle class directly employed and connected to the private sector, dependent on their employers' business success also became increasingly insecure.

When describing the changed fortunes of this class in Australia Frankel (1992) caustically explains:

> Thousands of members of the 'new middle class' regularly become members of the 'welfare class' when their employers 'rationalize' their jobs away and they have to go on the dole after their private savings run out. High-flying middle and senior executives are not immune to recessions just because they are called 'new middle class'.
>
> (Frankel 1992: 118)

Ehrenreich (1989), on a slightly different tack, observed that the continued existence of the 'professional middle class' as a class, even without accounting for the ravages of restructuring, was by the mid-1980s already in doubt as a 'frantic repositioning' began to take place.

> One chunk is moving up, perhaps to join *en masse* the corporate élite from whose hand it now securely feeds. The lawyer specializing in mergers and acquisitions, the professor with his own bioengineering firm, the celebrity commentator – these mingle now with the heads of companies, even heads of state. Meanwhile, another layer – less plucky or perhaps more stubbornly independent – sediments towards the white-collar end of the working class.
>
> (Ehrenreich 1989: 246)

Now, if we can talk about the dissolution and social relocation of the position of the new middle class, or at least a substantial 'fraction' of it, as a shift downwards towards something that might look like a relation of subordination, then perhaps there is also an accompanying shift in the kind of meaning system in Parkin's sense that this downwardly realigned group needs to use to make sense of its lived experience. New social positionalities may require new ways to make the world intelligible. The 'other-newsization' of aspects of broadcast journalism, intensifying as it does more or less during the same historical moment as one 'layer' of the new middle class 'sediments' downwards, may be one of the available discursive options that has the potential to contribute to this sense making process. This, however, is not a case of 'necessary belongingness'. That is, it is not being suggested that the forms of intelligibility offered by tabloid journalism 'belong' in any strict sense to a reconstituted subordinate consciousness of a particular class or class fraction. Rather this connection, if it can be postulated, might be best appreciated in terms of what Hall (1986: 53) calls a theory of 'articulation', which offers 'a way of understanding how ideological elements come, under certain conditions, to cohere together within a discourse, and a way of asking how they do or do not become articulated, at specific conjunctures, to certain political subjects ... the theory of articulation asks how an ideology discovers its subject ... '. If there is substance in the argument that reality programming is in some measure a 'recombinant' journalistic discourse of the 'other news, it might also be argued that the 'spontaneous philosophy', so much imbedded in the ideological field of such news, is also taken up and 'recombined' by this recently expanded genre and as a result can now be given a more pervasive reach as it becomes increasingly widespread and free floating through a whole range of new programme possibilities. Unhitched from the early evening news, the spontaneous philosophy inscribed in the 'other news' and now 'spun off' into 'reality' formats is a way by which ideology can discover its subject. For the new middle class, the lived reality of sedimentation and dislocation is given the opportunity to find its circumstantial and conjunctural moment 'articulated' to the kinds of vicissitudes which reach across the narratives assembled by reality programming, where like the 'other news', the available maps of meaning are predominantly framed by categories which almost always privilege the personal and the impersonal, rarely the social, the historical or the political. The powerlessness and contingency inscribed in the drama of fatalism which pervades the 'other news' can now be 'given back' on a broader television programming front to an increasingly subordinated fragment of the new middle class. It might be said that their realigned positionality is interpellated by the preoccupations and associated structures of meaning of a tabloidism journalistically descended from the 'other news'.

But do they watch 'reality programming', this destabilized, educated layer of the new middle class? If what has been written about the possible relations between tabloid journalism as popular culture and 'the people' is taken as an initial indicator (see Fiske 1992b), the most likely conclusion would be, they do not. Of course, a detailed and accurate assessment is not possible until further work is undertaken, but in the meantime, there are several pointers which suggest that for the new middle class tabloid television may not be the culturally 'bad object' one might initially suppose it to be. If we listen to Gordon Elliot (in Rowe 1993: 38), the weekly presenter of *Hard Copy* in Australia, this programme's mode of address is clearly meant to be as socially and culturally inclusive as possible.

> I believe the same people can read the Melbourne *Age* [a quality daily], watch *Hard Copy*, go to the opera, enjoy a stag night, pick up a copy of *Truth* [a weekly tabloid] and then go home and read a novel written by Gabriel Garcia Marquez and enjoy the subtext. I don't think the audience can be defined as simply as some people would like.

The cultural legitimacy of such tabloid television may also be enhanced by its gesture towards the protocols of the 'respectable' current affairs format and its careful negotiation around the 'wild stories' more typical of the tabloid press. *Hard Copy*, for example, always finds its presenter located in a setting very reminiscent of what we have come to understand as a 'news room', which implies, at least to some degree, a position and attitude aligned to the kind of journalism associated with a more conventional current affairs broadcast. While the tabloid press may have too many cultural demerits to warrant sustained attention, especially for the 'intellectually trained', tabloid television through a diplomatic mediation of excess by way of format and content may just qualify with enough legitimacy to attract a more socially diverse audience. Finally it needs to be added that what sometimes gets referred to as the 'quality' media – and this would include the quality press which, if taste cultures can be assumed to be at work in class terms, would most likely be the press of choice of the new middle class – has itself gone through a period of 'tabloidization', to the point where one now finds, with some degree of consistency, regular and extended reportage on celebrities, victims, personal tragedies, the plight of communities and so on (see Langer 1994). If the new middle class are among the regular reading constituency of a tabloidizing quality press, the cultural credentials of tabloid television may currently not be as distant as they, at one time, might have been (see Sparks 1991).

To leave these speculations about the ideological reverberations between tabloid television and the 'other news' at this point would create the more than somewhat erroneous impression that this recent form of broadcast journalism had an exclusive linkage with the sedimenting layers of the new middle class. The pervasiveness and popularity of reality programming clearly suggests otherwise. And here I want to posit that tabloid television, following closely the 'other news' emphasis on fatefulness and contingency is discursively in a good position to interpellate another beleaguered and sedimenting 'layer' of another social grouping. If it can be acknowledged that economic restructuring, deindustrialization, new technologies, the reorganization of work, the globalization of production and the recession have together created the conditions for large scale and long term social and economic dislocation in what would have once been called the working class, then it might also be argued that this social grouping – whose lived experience is already one of relative powerlessness and subordination, and whose 'belief system' probably comes closest to the fatalistic pessimism described by Parkin – has in recent times encountered such major structural changes to its conditions of existence that its currently constituted lived experience produces an even more profound and debilitating sense of subordination and accompanying fatalism. Precisely against this backdrop of social and economic realignment, television tabloidism begins to make its mark and flourish.

Now to make a connection between tabloid television and the restructuring of labour and capital is no simple matter. Complexities abound and I am fully aware of the potential accusation of reductionism and essentialisation. The point however is this: if we follow through with Hall's notion of articulation – whereby certain ideological elements 'cohere' (get articulated together) as a discourse and then at specific conjunctures get 'articulated' (linked) to specific political subjects – it might be suggested that tabloid television with some of its ideological roots in the 'other news' is capable of articulating ('language-ing') and being articulated (hooked on) not just to the recent lived experience of subordination in the new middle class, but contemporaneously to the recent manifestations of powerlessness, marginalization and subordination now encountered by a substantial 'layer' of the already subordinated. With the proliferation of tabloidism in television the common sense drama of fatalism can now be played out journalistically right across the programming schedule, no longer confined to the early evening news. At the historical moment when the fragility and instability of traditionally subordinate groups has been substantially escalated and become more widespread, the spontaneous philosophy 'spun off' from the 'other news' becomes more free floating and more broadly accessible through a type of recombinant programming which proliferates across the broadcast schedules of major television channels. The fatalistic pessimism which according to Parkin characterizes the subordinate accommodative response to the conditions of inequality can now be registered and given back from any number of television sites: in terms of a theory of articulation, ideology has expanded possibilities for discovering its political subject. If life is increasingly prone to dealing out nasty destabilizing blows, if the lived experience of subordination is now spreading into social regions previously relatively removed from this experience and if social regions already familiar with the lived experience of subordination have been placed in an even more precarious kind of subordination as capital rearranges itself on a global scale, tabloid television can help in the search for causes. Not in historical or social conditions but instead by mobilizing and endorsing (articulating) fate and contingency as the 'logical' way of making sense of the world – things are bad now but it could easily get much worse (look at them); at least we've got our health (look at them); there but for fortune go we (just look at them).

The logic of this kind of sense-making might be traced further, into an even broader hegemonic moment which negotiates to win consent and secure the ideological conditions of domination by underwriting some of the recently emergent yet fundamental routines and practices which frame everyday life. At this level the ideological possibilities of tabloidism can be viewed not only in terms of sedimenting class fractions but in relation to a more broadly based consideration of lived experience. It is something of a theoretical commonplace today to offer the observation that the structural engine of contemporary capitalism has been reassembled and reassigned from the sphere of production to that of consumption, and that one of the pressing issues for contemporary cultural criticism is to provide adequate accounts of how consumption works, particularly through the texture of everyday life (McRobbie 1991). What is less agreed upon are the accounts themselves, where to begin the investigation of processes and consciousness which enhance and contribute to 'popular consumerism' as a structural imperative in the organization of the social formation. In the context of discussion here perhaps it could be suggested that tabloid television, with its investment in the fatefulness of the world, begins to play at least some small part. For if the world is such an unpredictable place, and if there is the sense that intervention of whatever kind has attached to it an ultimate futility – like the 'other news' the structure of tabloid television relies on creating the impression that it is 'just-one-damned-thing-after-another' – and that the problems confronting and devastating the world are intractable, 'logically' it pays only to look after yourself.

In its current profusion, with its appropriation and elaboration of the codes and frames of reference of the 'other news', in its own small way through its own version of the drama of fatalism, tabloid television produces the conditions for a retreatism which can be 'turned' and then 'articulated' to the structural needs of a consumption-based capitalism. If control 'out there' is not possible, as tabloid television reiterates on a daily basis, perhaps it can be attained in the realms of the private and the personal, an increasingly large part of which, as it turns out, has now been incorporated into the processes of commodification and consumption. Fatalism does not lead to popular consumerism – such a grand claim would surely be inadequate and naïve – but it may provide at least one of the ideological pre-conditions which 'prompts' consumerism into becoming naturalized as part of everyday consciousness and practice, in this context a reasonable, even 'rational' response.

About us

Near the start of this study, it was suggested that what distinguished the 'other news' from the serious news was the former's emphasis on and investment in the domain of the ordinary: if serious news was about society's power brokers and influentials, the 'other news' always began or ended with a focus on the identifiably ordinary and the everyday. And if élites did appear, in the form of stars or celebrities, their placement was characteristically tempered by a narrative 'twitch' that provided the option of seeing them, finally, as quite like you or I – he may be a prince, but he certainly acts like a regular dad. The massive investment in the everyday, as it is constituted in television's 'other news', it was argued, was one way that broadcast journalism could 'hail' viewers, giving them leverage into a place 'inside' the news text itself – a kind of 'para-social' dimension (Horton and Wohl 1956) created through projection or identification. A further observation that could be made about 'reality programming' concerns its ability to offer an expanded and more widely dispersed version of this interpellation. Tabloid journalism is also acutely aware of the ordinary and the everyday: even though its propensities swerve towards sensation, spectacle and the exotic, these are typically registered in terms of ordinariness as 'background expectancy'. Susan Sontag's parodic 1950s sci-fi dialogue again comes to mind: come quickly, there's a monster in my bathtub! In tabloid the bizarre and the startling are routinely colliding with the recognizable solidities of everyday life. The scattering of tabloidism across the television programming schedule means that even as sensationalism and prurience spread, a special structure of 'hailing' is able to spread as well. At a time when traditional institutional arrangements are perceived as routinely unresponsive and often downright hostile to the concerns of ordinary people (see Marshall *et al.* 1988), through the process of reality programming and 'other-news-ization' television is able to declare that it has more 'capacity', more inclination than almost all established institutions to be for, and about 'us'. To be the focus of some rarely given institutional attention, especially from a central cultural apparatus like television, may be one of the first steps in the process of winning consent to a 'way of seeing' the world which assists in reproducing the ideological conditions of domination.

'Being' on television

Candid Camera is celebrating its fortieth year on American television with a one-hour special which looks back on some of its 'best moments'. Mid-way through the programme we encounter a sequence which omits the usual set-up and gag, but instead shows us their aftermath. It is a wide-shot of a room – presumably where the stunt was conducted – and a man is facing the camera. He seems rapturous with an as yet explained excitement, gesturing, grinning, laughing. And he begins to shout something like this: I've waited all my life to be on your show. I've dreamed about it. And now its happened! I can't believe it!

Trying to specify some of the operations and consequences which occur when a culture progressively becomes a landscape of unending images, Kroker and Cook (1986) explain that what does not pass under the sign of television, what is not 'videated as its identity–principle' is increasingly registered as culturally insignificant, possibly non-existent altogether. This stands, of course, as a rather large assertion, yet if Kroker and Cook are even partly right the *Candid Camera* incident can be taken as more than simply a nostalgic fragment from the television comedy archives.

Cultures like ours still make claims about the openness of society, that mobility, the good life, status and prestige can be acquired or be delivered through various social and institutional mechanisms: hard work, money, education, occupation, entrepreneurial endeavour, technological know-how and so on. Yet increasingly members of the culture feel, at the level of lived experience that these kinds of arrangements do not work, are deeply flawed or are not within reach and never will be. At a time when the traditional social methodologies for the confirming of identity and prestige are perceived to no longer work or to remain inaccessible, other sites of social validation and identity affirmation may come into play. I want to suggest that the possibility of an appearance on television may be one of these newly constituted sites, that the 'other news' and now more expansively reality television offer 'videated' spaces where these appearances can regularly occur, and that, in a culture where an 'identity–principle' is increasingly 'ratified by publicity', these sites become significantly more important for identity validation and the confirmation of prestige when the more traditional and conventional mechanisms are perceived to have broken down or failed completely. This is especially relevant when looked at in the context of reality programming where apparently 'being on television' frequently does not require people to be anyone in particular. Routinely individuals who become the subjects of this type of broadcast journalism seem to be just plain folks – ordinary people without undue status or power in the public world. In fact the very ordinariness of their lives and their preoccupations actually provides the 'reality' premise and the initial excuse for television's attention in the first place: so, if it can happen to them, in all their ordinariness, it can also happen to me.

Perhaps in this regard Andy Warhol's assessment about a future where everyone would be famous for fifteen minutes should be revised slightly. In the future, it would not be just a matter of everyone getting the chance to be famous for the requisite fifteen minutes, rather that everyone would *have* to be, not only for the fulfilment of dreams of the good life and self-worth but for a certain kind of ontological endorsement, and if Kroker and Cook are right the terms of reference would have to be 'videational'. Sociologist John O'Neill (1983) puts it this way: 'televideo ergo sum'. Given the proliferation of tabloid journalism and the move to reality programming, along with a number of other sites where subjects can be *on* television – game shows, talent quests, vox pops, live studio audiences, opinion panels, and of course the 'other news' – this may not be such a wild-eyed conjecture. Now we come to understand the implications of the excitement displayed by the contestant from *Candid Camera*: not only has his dream as a television viewer come true – being on the programme – but his 'being' attains a type of truth value as well. In a cultural 'scene' where existence increasingly depends on being seen, his ontological status is confirmed: videated, now he knows he *is*.

APPENDIX

Table 1 Average total 'other-news' time as a percentage of total news time, by channel

Channel	Average total
2	16.2
7	30.5
9	42.8
0	32.8

Table 2 Time taken by 'other-news' as a percentage of total news time per week, by channel

Channel	Week I	Week II	Week III	Week IV
2	17.6	21.1	12.2	14.2
7	31.3	31.9	20.3	38.5
9	52.5	47.6	33.9	37.5
0	26.7	35.5	34.6	34.3

Table 3 Time taken by 'other-news' as a percentage of total news time each day of sample weeks

Week I	Day 1	Day 2	Day 3	Day 4	Day 5
2	13.3	24.3	8.8	26.0	17.6
7	44.0	42.3	10.8	24.8	36.2
9	59.0	52.2	–	39.0	61.1
0	14.7	42.4	10.8	41.8	26.3

Table 3   continued

Week II	Day 1	Day 2	Day 3	Day 4	Day 5
2	21.0	5.5	30.7	25.7	22.9
7	27.6	28.2	54.5	19.8	30.2
9	40.7	32.8	61.1	40.0	·63.6
0	43.4	27.8	–	22.4	48.2

Week III	Day 1	Day 2	Day 3	Day 4	Day 5
2	5.6	8.4	–	15.6	19.5
7	8.9	13.6	33.0	–	33.0
9	26.6	22.4	37.1	–	51.0
0	24.1	12.9	42.9	44.1	42.5

Week IV	Day 1	Day 2	Day 3	Day 4	Day 5
2	22.2	10.2	10.2	–	–
7	40.8	35.8	38.4	39.1	–
9	53.4	40.2	35.9	20.7	–
0	36.9	18.8	32.8	48.7	–

NOTES

1 THE LAMENT, THE CRITICAL PROJECT AND THE 'BAD' NEWS ON TELEVISION

1 A wide range of studies could be included to illustrate this tradition. For just a few of the more interesting and formative examples, see Halloran, Elliot and Murdock (1970) on the reportage of mass demonstrations; Cohen (1973) on the media and moral panics; the Glasgow University Media Group (1976, 1980) on industrial disputes and the economy; Chibnall (1977) on the press reporting of crime; Hall, *et al.* (1978) on crime waves and law and order; Gitlin (1980) on the media and the New Left; Bell, Boehringer and Crofts (1982) on television politics.
2 For a relatively recent example, see Dahlgren and Sparks (1992).

2 OF PARADIGMS, PENDULUMS AND MEDIA POWER

1 Morley's work was followed by a number of further studies which attempted to explore the commensurability of textual operations as signifying practices with 'real' readers. See Moores (1993) for a summary of some of the recent work on audiences.
2 Questions too have been raised about the 'ethnographic' method favoured in the new reception studies, the interpretation of findings, the claims about textual 'openness' and the explanatory adequacy of concepts like reader resistance. See, for example, Nightingale 1989; Condit 1989; Curran and Sparks 1991.

3 SITUATING THE 'OTHER NEWS'

1 Criticism of this aspect of the Althusserian notion of ideology argues that too much acquiescence is assumed on the part of the subject 'positioned' by the interpellation of the text: the 'Hey, you', critics say, may be met with 'Huh? You got the wrong person'. But it is more likely that a 'Hey, you' will get a positive response if the 'waving hand' is recognizably like our own.
2 It was not possible to obtain more extended periods of off-air material due to limited resources but given that the focus of the analysis was not based on any notion of comprehensive sampling or statistical distribution, the amount of material collected was already felt to be extensive. There should have been a total of eighty broadcasts making up the sample over the four time periods, but ten bulletins were missed due to technical failures and unforeseen complications leaving a pool of seventy.

3 See, for example, Cohen and Young 1973; Chibnall 1977; Fishman 1980; Hall *et al.* 1978; Ericson, Baranek and Chan 1991.

4 The insistent call to insert 'real' audiences who consume media texts into research and de-emphasize textual analysis does not seem to have plagued the fields of literary studies or film studies to the same degree as it has in an analysis of the media. These discipline areas seem to go on analyzing texts, whatever theoretical discussion emerges about 'centring' the audience. Perhaps this is a result of social and institutional definitions which lend legitimacy to the objects studied in these fields, regarding them as 'art' or 'culture' which has the 'right' to a certain cultural autonomy, whereas the cultural status of television or journalism as 'media' has always been bound up with questions about popular consumption and social impact.

5 Along similar lines Hall (1975: 13) talks about 'a long preliminary soak, a submission by the analyst to the mass of . . . material'.

4 THE ESPECIALLY REMARKABLE

1 The point here is not to suggest that news stories about élites never contain incidents where fluctuations of control are a focus of concern. Journalism invests considerable resources and energy into producing just such narratives. Members of the higher world do lose control, and the 'exposé' which ensues and the 'juicy scandal' which follows are well-known forms of public drama. However, normally, there are not enough of these to satisfy television journalism's requirement for stories about the higher world on a day-to-day basis (Bell, Boehringer and Crofts 1982). If this sample of broadcasts can be taken as at least partially representative of the contents of television news, in between 'big' exposé and scandal coverage, the tactic seems to be to simply repeat the emphasis on control, in order to reiterate especially remarkable qualities with the result that when the loss of control does occur, its 'intensity' can register as all the more profound merely because of its unusualness. Another point worth making in this context concerns the 'recovery rate' as this might apply to élites; that is the scandal might indicate a type of lost control but sometimes its restoration seems as effortless as the control exercised in the first place prior to its loss. For example, within months of the 'shattering break-up' of her marriage, photographs appeared in Australian women's magazines showing Princess Diana romping in the surf, looking tanned, relaxed and singularly untroubled, given what we had been led to believe had gone on previously. One conclusion from such reporting could be that only the especially remarkable have the ability to recover from 'personal devastation' with this seeming degree of ease.

2 Here, I am simply taking Barthes's usage and inserting examples relevant to this study.

5 VICTIMS

1 It is possible to group all stories about animals together (Bell, Boehringer and Crofts 1982; Hughes 1968) but this would not account for the different thematic inflections or narrative differences within a variety of animal stories. In Chapter 7 we see, for example, how animals can be used in news stories for the production of social memory and the past.

2 News items such as these could potentially be categorized differently. In the context of Bell, Boehringer and Crofts' Australian news content profile (1982) the story about the handicapped girl could be situated as a 'social welfare' item, and the female trainee pilot coverage might qualify as an 'industrial affairs' report, but

because the dominant emphasis is on the protagonist as victim they were considered appropriately included as part of this story-type.

3 Some stories in the sample contained all of these techniques while others included only a few but cumulatively as they appear across a range of stories over time, such techniques do seem to provide a set of general structuring principles which inform and allow the possibility of the news discourse on victims.

6 COMMUNITIES AT RISK

1 A process similar to this has been detected in the 'signification spirals' (Hall *et al*. 1978: 223–7) used by the press in reporting 'social problems', making them seem more threatening than they might otherwise be by pushing them through a tolerance threshold. For example, the 'permissiveness' of the hippie subculture can be made more menacing when 'long hair' and 'free sex' are signified as inevitable forerunners of drug taking, or when marijuana smoking is defined as a natural prelude to heroin use.

2 Occasionally, as with some victim stories, the normal course of events is much more explicitly marked, providing reference to the very moment when routines are shattered by the circumstances of disruption: 'a fifteen strong team of surgeons and nurses had just completed an operation . . . ' when the hospital explodes; a truck driver 'had just taken the right hand bend from Robie Street into Qantas Drive at Mascot [Airport] when his tanker carrying 28,700 litres of methanol slipped into the guard rail, punctured and tipped on its side'.

3 A case is not being made that community at risk stories never produce reading positions which encourage involvement and sympathy through the psychologization and individuation of 'character' – this was clearly not so, for example, in the actual coverage of Darwin's Cyclone Tracy which produced many 'local heroes' (Goldie 1984). However, given that this category of mishap, which in Britton's terminology would qualify as a 'disaster', is rare, it is important to determine the *routine* ways of constructing communities at risk in television news. In their very regularity, the signifying practices used to construct accidents and emergencies may, in the end, prove to be important for understanding much larger scale disaster coverage.

4 This is also a strategy sometimes employed in horror/suspense films. I'm thinking here, for example, of the ending of *Psycho*, where the killer's irrational behaviour is 'explained' within the framework of psychiatry.

8 POLITICS, PLEASURES, 'SPIN-OFFS'

1 Aubert (1980: 93) in his essay 'Chance in Social Affairs' explains it this way:

> There is one, and only one area of life into which all men [sic] are born equal, and also remain equal throughout their lives, independent of physical, pecuniary, intellectual or moral achievements: the pure game of chance. Small wonder then many people . . . have sought refuge from the inequalities and injustices of real life in this model of an egalitarian society. Interpreted as divination . . . it creates an egalitarian distribution of God's grace.

2 These observations might be usefully connected with audience demographics for television. In Australia, for example, Windschuttle (1984: 61–2) found that: 'People whose education ended at primary school or the early years of secondary school [had] three times the propensity to be heavy viewers than those with tertiary education. At the other end of the scale those with tertiary education and/or incomes of $20,000 per year had double the proportion of light viewers as those on low

incomes or with little schooling' and of those who were light viewers the largest proportion tended to watch the state run channel (the ABC). In the sample broadcasts collected for this study the ABC had the least number of 'other-news' stories.

3 More recently, attempts have been made to assess tabloid journalism as a form of popular culture (see Dahlgren and Sparks 1992; Glynn 1990) as well as to re-theorize the popular press as a discourse governed as much by entertainment as news values (Curran and Sparks 1991). Still, despite this newly found interest in 'the pleasure of the (news) text' regular news bulletins on television have not been particularly central in the discussion. In this context, Stam's work (1983) on the pleasures offered by television news, stands out as a useful exception, one which helped, if not the substance at least the orientation of these concluding comments.

4 The love of chaos has also been noted by Barthes (1977a: 191) in connection with the *fait-divers*, as it randomly unhitches the sign from its referent creating a 'panic sentiment'. According to Barthes, chaos such as this is the essential ingredient for giving the *fait-divers* its artfulness.

5 See Schudson (1978) for a discussion of how these two models developed in the American press during the 1890s.

6 There are numerous other pleasures which might be alluded to, perhaps less destabilizing and contradictory in their tendencies: the pleasure of repetition, where the stories that made 'good ones' in the past are recycled to make good ones again and again (see Kawin 1972); the pleasure of 'being-on-television', or more accurately, seeing others like ourselves on television, the highly prized moment of media glory increasingly desirable in our culture (this issue will be further elaborated, but see also Schickel 1986); the pleasure of confirmation, receiving back the common-sensical assumptions with which we are already familiar, giving the world and our place in it coherence and unity.

7 These are the derisively labelled 'yuppies' we used to hear and read so much about in the media during the mid 1980s – the young upwardly-mobile professional.

BIBLIOGRAPHY

Alberoni, Francesco (1972) 'The powerless élite: theory and sociological research on the phenomenon of the stars', in D. McQuail (ed.) *Sociology of Mass Communications: Selected Readings*, Harmondsworth: Penguin.

Alloway, Lawrence (1971) *Violent America: The Movies 1946–1964*, New York: Museum of Modern Art.

Altheide, David and Snow, Robert (1991) *Media Worlds in the Postjournalism Era*, New York: Aldine de Grutyer.

Althusser, Louis (1971) 'Ideology and ideological state apparatuses', in *Lenin and Philosophy and Other Essays*, London: Monthly Review Press.

Aubert, V. (1980) 'Chance in social affairs', in J. Dowie and P. Lefrere (eds) *Risk and Chance, Selected Readings*, Milton Keynes: Open University Press.

Baker, Ian (1980) 'The gatekeeper chain: a two step analysis of how journalists acquire and apply organization news priorities', in P. Edgar (ed.) *News in Focus*, Melbourne: Macmillan.

Barthes, Roland (1974) *S/Z*, New York: Hill and Wang.

—— (1977a) 'Structure of the *fait-divers*', in R. Barthes, *Critical Essays*, Evanston: Northwestern University Press.

—— (1977b) 'The photographic message', in R. Barthes, *Image – Music – Text*, Glasgow: Fontana.

—— (1977c) 'Rhetoric of the image', in R. Barthes, *Image – Music – Text*, Glasgow: Fontana.

—— (1977d) *Elements of Semiology*, New York: Hill and Wang.

Baxter, J.; Emmison, M. and Western, J. (eds) (1991) *Class Analysis and Contemporary Australia*, Melbourne: Macmillan.

Bazalgette, C. and Paterson, R. (1980/81) 'Real entertainment: the Iranian embassy seige', *Screen Education* 37.

Becker, H. (1967) 'Whose side are we on?' *Social Problems*, 14: 239–47.

Bell, Phillip, Boehringer, Kathe and Crofts, Stephen (1982) *Programmed Politics: A Study of Australian Television*, Sydney: Sable.

Belsey, Catherine (1980) *Critical Practice*, London: Methuen.

Bennett, Tony, Martin, Graham, Mercer, Colin and Woollacott, Janet (eds) (1981) *Culture, Ideology and Social Process: A Reader*, London: Batsford.

Bennett, W. L. (1988) *News: The Politics of Illusion*, 2nd edn New York: Longman.

Berger, Arthur Asa (1991) *Media Research Techniques*, Newbury Park: Sage.

Bird, Elizabeth and Dardenne, Robert (1988) 'Myth, chronicle and story: exploring the narrative qualities of news', in J. W. Carey (ed.) *Media, Myths and Narratives*, London: Sage.

176

Bocock, R. (1974) *Ritual in Industrial Society*, London: George Allen and Unwin.

Bonney, Bill and Wilson, Helen (1983) *Australia's Commercial Media*, Melbourne: Macmillan.

Boorstin, Daniel (1963) *The Image*, Harmondsworth: Penguin.

Bordwell, David and Thompson, Kristin (1979) *Film Art: An Introduction*, Reading, MA: Addison-Wesley.

Bork, Alfred (1980) 'Randomness and the twentieth century', in J. Dowie and P. Lefrere (eds) *Risk and Chance, Selected Readings*, Milton Keynes: Open University Press.

Bourne, Geoffrey (1981) 'Meaning, image, ideology', Unit 14, in *Open University Course on Popular Culture: Form and Meaning*, Milton Keynes: Open University Press.

Bramson, Leon (1961) *The Political Context of Sociology*, Princeton, NJ: Princeton University Press.

Britton, Neil, R. (1986) 'Developing an understanding of disaster', *Australian and New Zealand Journal of Sociology* 22(1).

Brunsdon, Charlotte (1989) 'Text and audience', in E. Seiter *et al.* (eds) *Remote Control: Television, Audiences and Cultural Power*, London: Routledge.

Brunsdon, Charlotte and Morley, David (1978) *Everyday Television: 'Nationwide'*, London: British Film Institute.

Burgelin, Olivier (1972) 'Structural analysis and mass communication', in D. McQuail (ed.) *Sociology of Mass Communications*, Harmondsworth: Penguin.

Centre for Contemporary Cultural Studies Popular Memory Group (1982) 'What do we mean by popular memory?', *Stencilled Occasional Paper 67*.

Chancy, David (1983) 'A symbolic mirror of ourselves: civic ritual in mass society', *Media, Culture and Society* 5(1).

Chibnall, Steve (1977) *Law and Order News: An Analysis of Crime Reporting in the British Press*, London: Tavistock.

Clements, Ian (1986) 'The ravenous half shut eye manufacturing bad news from nowhere', *Media Information Australia* 39.

Cohen, Stanley (1973) *Folk Devils and Moral Panics: The Creation of the Mods and Rockers*, London: Paladin.

Cohen, Stanley and Young, Jock (eds) (1973) *The Manufacture of News: Deviance, Social Problems and the Mass Media*, London: Constable.

Condit, Celeste (1989) 'The rhetorical limits of polysemy', *Critical Studies in Mass Communication* 6(2).

Connell, Ian (1978) 'Monopoly capitalism and the media', in S. Hibbin (ed.) *Politics, Ideology and the State*, London: Lawrence & Wishart.

—— (1979) 'Television, news and the social contract', *Screen* 20.

Connell, R. W. and Irving, T. H. (1992) *Class Structure in Australian History: Poverty and Progress*, 2nd edn, Melbourne: Longman Cheshire.

Conrad, Peter (1982) *Television: The Medium and Its Manners*, London: Routledge & Kegan Paul.

Corner, John (1991) 'Meaning, genre and context: the problematics of "public knowledge" in the new audience studies', in J. Curran and M. Gurevitch (eds) *Mass Media and Society*, London: Edward Arnold.

Curran, James (1990) 'The new revisionism in mass communication research: a reappraisal', *European Journal of Communications* 5 (2–3).

Curran, James, Douglas, Angus and Whannel, Garry (1980) 'The political economy of the human-interest story', in A. Smith (ed.) *Newspapers and Democracy: International Essays on a Changing Medium*, Cambridge, MA: MIT Press.

Curran, James, Gurevitch, Michael and Woollacott, Janet (eds) (1977) *Mass Communication and Society*, London: Edward Arnold.

—— (1982) 'The study of the media: theoretical approaches', in M. Gurevitch *et al.* (eds) *Culture, Society and the Media*, London: Methuen.

Curran, James and Sparks, Colin (1991) 'Press and popular culture', *Media, Culture and Society* 13.

Dahlgren, Peter (1988) 'What's the meaning of this? Viewers' plural sense-making of TV news', *Media, Culture and Society* 10.

Dahlgren, Peter and Sparks, Colin (1992) *Journalism and Popular Culture*, London: Sage.

Darnton, Robert (1975) 'Writing news and telling stories', *Daedalus* 104.

De Fleur, Melvin (1970) *Theories of Mass Communication*, 2nd edn, New York: David McKay.

Diamond, Edwin (1975) *The Tin Kazoo: Television, Politics and the News*, Cambridge, MA: MIT Press.

—— (1982) *Sign Off: The Last Days of Television*, Cambridge, MA: MIT Press.

Dimock, Wai Chee and Gilmore, Michael (eds) (1994) *Rethinking Class: Literary Studies and Social Formations*, New York: Columbia University Press.

Dubord, Guy (1983) *Society of the Spectacle*, Detroit: Red and Black.

Durkheim, Emile (1965) *The Elementary Forms of the Religious Life*, New York: Free Press.

Dyer, Richard (1979) *Stars*, London: British Film Institute.

—— (1981) 'Entertainment and utopia', in R. Altman (ed.) *Genre: The Musical*, London: Routledge & Kegan Paul.

—— (1987) *Heavenly Bodies: Film Stars and Society*, London: Macmillan.

Eagleton, Terry (1983) *Literary Theory, An Introduction*, Oxford: Basil Blackwell.

Eco, Umberto (1979) *The Role of the Reader: Explorations in the Semiotics of Texts*, Bloomington: Indiana University Press.

Edelman, Murray (1964) *The Symbolic Use of Politics*, Chicago: University of Illinois Press.

Ehrenreich, Barbara (1989) *Fear of Falling: The Inner Life of the Middle Class*, New York: Harper Collins.

Emmison, Michael and Western, J. (1991) 'The structure of social identities', in J. Baxter, M. Emmison, and J. Western (eds) *Class Analysis and Contemporary Australia*, Melbourne: Macmillan.

Encel, Sol (1970) *Equality and Authority: A Study of Class, Status and Power in Australia*, Melbourne: Cheshire.

Epstein, Edward Jay (1973) *News From Nowhere: Television and the News*, New York: Vintage Books.

Ericson, Richard, Baranek, Patricia and Chan, Janet (1991) *Representing Order: Crime, Law and Justice in the News Media*, Toronto: University of Toronto Press.

Esslin, Martin (1982) *The Age of Television*, San Francisco: W.H. Freeman.

Fishman, Mark (1980) *Manufacturing the News*, Austin: University of Texas Press.

Fiske, John (1982) *Introduction to Communication Studies*, London: Methuen.

—— (1987) *Television Culture*, London: Methuen.

—— (1992a) 'British cultural studies and television', in R. C. Allen (ed.) *Channels of Discourse, Reassembled*, London: Routledge.

—— (1992b) 'Popularity and the politics of information', in P. Dahlgren amd C. Sparks (eds) *Journalism and Popular Culture*, London: Sage.

Fiske, John and Hartley, John (1978) *Reading Television*, London: Methuen.

Frankel, Boris (1992) *From the Prophets Deserts Come: The Struggle to Reshape Australian Political Culture*, Melbourne: Arena Publishing.

Freud, Sigmund (1965) 'Jokes and the comic', in R.W. Corrigan (ed.) *Comedy: Meaning and Form*, Scranton, PN: Chandler.

Frye, Northrop (1957) *Anatomy of Criticism: Four Essays*, Princeton, NJ: Princeton University Press.

Galtung, J. and Ruge, M. (1973) 'Structuring and selecting news', in S. Cohen and J. Young (eds) *The Manufacture of News*, London: Constable.

Gans, Herbert J. (1977) 'The disaster films', in J. Tulloch (ed.) *Conflict and Control in the Cinema*, Melbourne: Macmillan.

Gerdes, Peter (1980) *TV News in Brief: A Research Report*, Kensington: University of New South Wales.

Gerdes, Peter and Charlier, Paul (1985) *TV News – That's The Way It Was: A Comparative Analysis of Sydney's Television News*, North Ryde: Australian Film and Television School.

Gitlin, Todd (1980) *The Whole World is Watching – Mass Media in the Making and Unmaking of the New Left*, Berkeley, CA: University of California Press.

—— (1985) *Inside Prime Time*, New York: Pantheon.

Glasgow University Media Group (1976) *Bad News*, London: Routledge & Kegan Paul.

—— (1980) *More Bad News*, London: Routledge & Kegan Paul.

—— (1982) *Really Bad News*, London: Readers and Writers.

Glynn, K. (1990) 'Tabloid television's transgressive aesthetic: *A Current Affair* and the "shows that taste forgot"', *Wide Angle* 12(2).

Goffman, Erving (1974) *Frame Analysis: An Essay on the Organization of Experience*, New York: Harper and Row.

Goldie, Jan (1984) 'Darwin – a decade after Tracy's fury', *The Australian Women's Weekly*, December.

Golding, Peter and Murdock, Graham (1979) 'Ideology and the mass media: the question of determination', in M. Barrett *et al.* (eds) *Ideology and Cultural Production*, London: Croom Helm.

Goldman, R. and Rajagopal, A. (1991) *Mapping Hegemony: Television News Coverage of Industrial Conflict*, Norwood: Ablex.

Goodwin, Andrew and Whannel, Garry (eds) (1990) *Understanding Television*, London: Routledge.

Gouldner, Alvin W. (1976) *The Dialectic of Ideology and Technology*, London: Macmillan.

Graber, Doris A. (1976) *Verbal Behavior and Politics*, Urbana: University of Illinois Press.

—— (1980) *Mass Media and American Politics*, Washington: Congressional Quarterly.

Grossberg, Lawrence (1992) *We Gotta Get Out of This Place: Popular Conservatism and Postmodern Culture*, New York: Routledge.

Gurevitch, Michael and Blumler, Jay G. (1977) 'Linkages between the mass media and politics: a model for the analysis of political communications systems', in J. Curran, M. Gurevitch and J. Woollacott (eds) *Mass Communication and Society*, London: Edward Arnold.

Gurevitch, Michael, Bennett, Tony, Curran, James and Woollacott, Janet (eds) (1982) *Culture, Society and the Media*, London: Methuen.

Hall, Stuart (1973a) 'The structured communication of events', *Stencilled Occasional Paper 5*, Centre for Contemporary Cultural Studies, University of Birmingham.

—— (1973b) 'The determinations of news photographs', in S. Cohen and J. Young (eds) *The Manufacture of News*, London: Constable.

—— (1973c) 'A world at one with itself', in S. Cohen and J. Young (eds) *The Manufacture of News*, London: Constable.

—— (1975) 'Introduction', in A.C.H. Smith (ed.) *Paper Voices: The Popular Press and Social Change, 1935–1965*, London: Chatto & Windus.

—— (1976) 'Television and culture', *Sight and Sound* 45.

—— (1977) 'Culture, the media and the "ideological effect"', in J. Curran,

M. Gurevitch and J. Woollacott (eds) *Mass Communication and Society*, London: Edward Arnold.

—— (1980) 'Encoding/decoding in television discourse', in S. Hall *et al.* (eds) *Culture, Media, Language*, London: Hutchinson.

—— (1982) 'The rediscovery of "ideology": return of the repressed in media studies', in M. Gurevitch *et al.* (eds) *Culture, Society and the Media*, London: Methuen.

—— (1986) 'On postmodernism and articulation: an interview with Stuart Hall (edited by Lawrence Grossberg), *Journal of Communication Inquiry* 10(2).

—— (1989) 'Ideology and communication theory', in B. Dervin *et al.* (eds) *Rethinking Communication, Volume 1: Paradigm Issues*, London: Sage.

Hall, Stuart, Critcher, Chas, Jefferson, Tony, Clarke, John and Roberts, Brian (1978) *Policing the Crisis: Mugging, The State, and Law and Order*, London: Macmillan.

Halloran, J., Elliot, P. and Murdock, G. (1970) *Demonstrations and Communication*, Harmondsworth: Penguin.

Hartley, John (1982) *Understanding News*, London: Methuen.

—— (1992) *Tele-ology: Studies in Television*, London: Routledge.

Hawkes, Terence (1977) *Structuralism and Semiotics*, London: Methuen.

Heath, Stephen (1990) 'Representing television,' in P. Mellencamp (ed.) *Logics of Television: Essays in Cultural Criticism*, Bloomington: Indiana University Press.

Hebdige, Dick (1979) *Subculture: The Meaning of Style*, London: Methuen.

Hobsbawm, Eric (1983) 'Introduction: inventing traditions', in E. Hobsbawm and T. Ranger (eds) *The Invention of Tradition*, Cambridge: Cambridge University Press.

Hoggart, Richard (1957) *The Uses of Literacy*, London: Pelican.

—— (1979) 'Forward' in E. Goffman, *Gender Advertisements*, London: Macmillan.

Horton, D. and Wohl, R. (1956) 'Mass communications and para-social interaction', *Psychiatry* 19.

Hughes, Helen MacGill (1968) *News and the Human Interest Story*, New York: Greenwood Press.

Jensen, Klaus Bruhn and Jankowski, Nicholas (eds) (1991) *A Handbook of Qualitative Methodologies for Mass Communication Research*, London: Routledge.

Kartman, Ben and Brown, Leonard (eds) (1971) *Disaster!*, Freeport New York: Books for Libraries Press.

Kawin, Bruce F. (1972) *Telling It Again and Again: Repetition in Literature and Film*, Ithaca: Cornell University Press.

Klapp, Orin E. (1964) *Symbolic Leaders, Public Dramas and Public Men*, London: Minerva Press.

Knight, Graham (1989) 'The reality effects of tabloid television news', in N. Raboy and P. Bruck (eds) *Communication For and Against Democracy*, Montreal: Black Rose.

Kress, G. and Hodge, R. (1979) *Language as Ideology*, London: Routledge & Kegan Paul.

Kroker, Arthur and Cook, David (1986) *The Postmodern Scene: Excremental Culture and Hyper-Aesthetics*, Montreal: New World Perspectives.

Kumar, Krishan (1977) 'Holding the middle ground: the BBC, the public and the professional broadcaster', in J. Curran, M. Gurevitch and J. Woollacott (eds) *Mass Communication and Society*, London: Edward Arnold.

Langer, John (1983) 'Broadcast forecast: whither weather', *Media Information Australia* 30.

—— (1994) 'A calculus of celebrityhood: where would news fit into the equation?', *Australian Journalism Review* 16(1).

Lasch, Christopher (1979) *The Culture of Narcissism*, New York: Warners Books.

Lévi-Strauss, Claude (1977) 'The structural study of myth', in *Structural Anthropology*. Harmondsworth: Penguin.

Littlejohn, David (1975) 'Communicating ideas by television', in D. Cater and R. Adler (eds) *Television as a Social Force: New Approaches to TV Criticism*, New York: Praeger.

Lowenthal, Leo (1961) 'The triumph of mass idols', in *Literature, Popular Culture and Society*, Palo Alto, CA: Pacific Books.

Lumby, Catherine and O'Neill, John (1994) 'Tabloid television', in J. Schultz (ed.) *Not Just Another Business: Journalists, Citizens and the Media*, Leichard: Pluto.

McArthur, Colin (1978) *Television and History*, London: British Film Institute.

McQuail, Denis (1969) *Towards a Sociology of Mass Communications*, London: Collier-Macmillan.

—— (ed.) (1972) *Sociology of Mass Communications: Selected Readings*, Harmondsworth: Penguin.

—— (1977) 'The influence and effects of mass media', in J. Curran, M. Gurevitch and J. Woollacott (eds) *Mass Communication and Society*, London: Edward Arnold.

—— (1983) *Mass Communication Theory, An Introduction*, London: Sage.

McRobbie, Angela (1991) 'New times in cultural studies', *New Formations* 13.

Mackay, Ian (1982) *Great Australian Disasters*, Sydney: Rigby.

Malik, L.P. (1970) *Sociology of Accidents*, Pennsylvania: Villanova University Press.

Marshall, Gordon *et al.* (1988) *Social Class in Modern Britain*, London: Hutchinson.

Mast, Gerald (1974) 'Comic structures', in G. Mast and M. Cohen (eds) *Film Theory and Criticism, Introductory Readings*, New York: Oxford University Press.

Masterman, Len (1985) *Teaching the Media*, London: Comedia.

Mead, George Herbert (1926) 'The nature of aesthetic experience', *International Journal of Ethics* 36.

Mellencamp, Patricia (1992) 'TV time and catastrophe, or *Beyond the Pleasure Principle* of television', in P. Mellencamp (ed.) *Logics of Television: Essays in Cultural Criticism*, Bloomington: Indiana University Press.

Mendelsohn, Harold (1964) 'Listening to radio', in L. A. Dexter and D. M. White (eds) *People, Society and Mass Communications*, New York: Free Press.

Metz, Christian (1974) *Film Language: A Semiotics of Cinema*, New York: Oxford University Press.

Miliband, Ralph (1991) *Divided Societies: Class Struggle in Contemporary Capitalism*, Oxford: Oxford University Press.

Mills, C. Wright (1956) *The Power Elite*, New York: Oxford University Press.

Modleski, Tania (1979) 'The search for tomorrow in today's soap operas', *Film Quarterly* 13.

Monaco, James (1977) *How to Read a Film: The Art, Technology, Language, History and Theory of Film and Media*, New York: Oxford University Press.

—— (1978) *Celebrity: The Media as Image Makers*, New York: Delta.

Moores Shaun (1993) *Interpreting Audiences: The Ethnography of Media Consumption*, London: Sage.

Morley, David (1980) *The 'Nationwide' Audience: Structure and Decoding*, London: British Film Institute.

—— (1992) *Television, Audiences and Cultural Studies*, London: Routledge.

Murdock, Graham (1973) 'Political deviance: the press presentation of a militant mass demonstration', in S. Cohen and J. Young (eds) *The Manufacture of News*, London: Constable.

—— (1989) 'Cultural studies at the crossroads'. *Australian Journal of Communication* 16.

Murdock, Graham and Golding, Peter (1977) 'Capitalism, communication and class relations', in J. Curran, M. Gurevitch and J. Woollacott (eds) *Mass Communication and Society*, London: Edward Arnold.

Nightingale, Virginia (1989) 'What's "ethnographic" about ethnographic audience research?', *Australian Journal of Communication* 16.

Nordenstreng, Kaarle (1972) 'Policy for news transmission', in D. McQuail (ed.) *Sociology of Mass Communications: Selected Readings*, Harmondsworth: Penguin.

Nowell-Smith, Geoffrey (1977) 'Minnelli and melodrama', *Screen* 18.

O'Neill, John (1983) 'Televideo ergo sum: some hypotheses on the specular functions of the media', *Communication* 7.

O'Sullivan, Tim, Hartley, John, Sanders, Danny and Fiske, John, (1983) *Key Concepts in Communications*, London: Methuen.

Parkin, Frank (1972) *Class Inequality and Political Order*, St Albans: Paladin.

Pearson, Roberta (1992) 'The San Francisco earthquake and the 1989 World Series', in P. Dahlgren and C. Sparks (eds) *Journalism and Popular Culture*, London: Sage.

Peterson, Mark Allen (1991) 'Aliens, ape men and whacky savages: the anthropologist in the tabloids', *Anthropology Today* 7(5).

Philo, Greg (1990) *Seeing and Believing*, London: Routledge.

Postman, Neil (1985) *Amusing Ourselves to Death: Public Discourse in the Age of Show Business*, London: Methuen.

Postman, Neil and Powers, Steve (1992) *How to Watch TV News*, New York: Penguin Books.

Propp, Vladamir (1968) *Morphology of the Folktale* 2nd edn, Austin: University of Texas Press.

Rachlin, Allan (1988) *News as Hegemonic Reality: American Political Culture and the Framing of News Accounts*, New York: Praeger.

Rock, Paul (1973) 'News as eternal recurrence', in S. Cohen and J. Young (eds) *The Manufacture of News*, London: Constable.

Rowe, David (1993) '*Hard Copy*, soft porn: tabloid TV and the sexualization of violence', *Metro, The Media Magazine* 93.

Rutherford-Smith, R. (1979) 'Mythic elements in television news', *Journal of Communication* 29.

Ryall, Tom (1975) 'Teaching through genre', *Screen Education* 17.

Schickel, R. (1986) *Intimate Strangers: The Culture of Celebrity*, New York: Fromm International.

Schlesinger, Philip (1978) *Putting 'Reality' Together: BBC News*, London: Constable.

Schudson, Michael (1978) *Discovering the News: A Social History of American Newspapers*, New York: Basic Books.

Schwichtenberg, C. (ed.) (1993) *The Madonna Connection: Representational Politics, and Cultural Theory*, St Leonards: Allen & Unwin.

Seaman, William (1992) 'Active audience theory: pointless populism', *Media, Culture and Society* 14.

Shulman, M. (1973) *The Least Worst Television in the World*, London: Barrie & Jenkins.

Smith, A.C.H. (1975) *Paper Voices: The Popular Press and Social Change, 1935–1968*, London: Chatto & Windus.

Sontag, Susan (1974) 'The imagination of disaster', in G. Mast and M. Cohen (eds) *Film Theory and Criticism, Introductory Readings*, New York: Oxford University Press.

Sparks, Colin (1991) 'Goodbye, Hildy Johnson: the vanishing "serious press"', in P. Dahlgren and C. Sparks (eds) *Communication and Citizenship: Journalism and the Public Sphere in the New Media Age*, London: Routledge.

Sperry, Sharon Lynn (1976) 'Television news as narrative', in R. Adler and D. Cater (eds) *Television as a Cultural Force*, New York: Praeger.

Stam, Robert (1983) 'Television news and its spectator', in E. Ann Kaplan (ed.) *Regarding Television*, Los Angeles: University Publications.

Sternberg, Jason (1995) 'Sign of *The Times*: television current affairs as "meaning and pleasure"', *Metro: Film, Television, Video, Multi-Media* 101.

Thompson, John B. (1990) *Ideology and Modern Culture: Critical Social Theory in the Era of Mass Communication*, Stanford: Stanford University Press.

Tiffen, Rodney (1989) *News and Power*, Sydney: Allen & Unwin.

Todorov, Tzvetan (1970) 'The fantastic in fiction', *Twentieth Century Studies* 3.

—— (1977) *The Poetics of Prose*, Ithaca: Cornell University Press.

Tuchman, Gaye (1973) 'Making news by doing work: routinizing the unexpected', *American Journal of Sociology* 79.

—— (1976) 'Telling stories', *Journal of Communication* 26.

—— (1978) *Making News: A Study in the Construction of Reality*, New York: Free Press.

Turner, Barry (1978) *Man-Made Disasters*, London: Wykeham.

Ward, Russel (1958) *The Australian Legend*, Melbourne: Oxford University Press.

Westergaard, John (1977) 'Power, class and the media', in J. Curran, M. Gurevitch and J. Woollacott (eds) *Mass Communication and Society*, London: Edward Arnold.

Western, J.S. and Hughes, C.A. (1983) *The Mass Media in Australia*, 2nd edn, St Lucia: University of Queensland Press.

White, D.L. (1977) 'The poetics of horror: more than meets the eye', in B.K. Grant (ed.) *Film Genre: Theory and Criticism*, Metuchen, NJ: Scarecrow Press.

White, Mimi (1992) 'Ideological analysis and television', in R.C. Allen (ed.) *Channels of Discourse, Reassembled: Television and Contemporary Criticism*, 2nd edn, London: Routledge.

White, Richard (1981) *Inventing Australia: Images and Identity 1688–1980*, Sydney: George Allen & Unwin.

Windschuttle, Keith (1984) *The Media: A New Analysis of the Press, Television, Radio and Advertising in Australia*, Harmondsworth: Penguin.

Wood, Robin (1985) 'An introduction to the American horror film', in B. Nichols (ed.) *Movies and Methods: An Anthology, Volume 2*, Berkeley: University of California Press.

Wright, Eric Olin (1989) *The Debate on Classes*, London: Verso.

INDEX